# Exploring Media Discourse

# Exploring
# Media Discourse

Myra Macdonald

ARNOLD

Orders: please contact Bookpoint Ltd, 130 Milton Park, Abingdon, Oxon OX14 4SB.
Telephone: (44) 01235 827720. Fax: (44) 01235 400454. Lines are open from 9.00–6.00,
Monday to Saturday, with a 24-hour message answering service. You can also order through our website
www.hodderheadline.co.uk

*British Library Cataloguing in Publication Data*
A catalogue record for this title is available from the British Library

ISBN 0 340 71989 3 (PB)
ISBN 0 340 71988 5 (HB)

First Published 2003
Impression number    10  9  8  7  6  5  4  3  2  1
Year                 2007  2006  2005  2004  2003

Typeset by Phoenix Photosetting, Chatham, Kent
Printed in Great Britain for Hodder & Stoughton Educational, a division of Hodder Headline plc,
338 Euston Road, London NW1 3BH by MPG Books Ltd., Bodmin, Cornwall.

# Contents

# Acknowledgements

This project has had a long gestation and would not have been completed without the support of a number of people. I would like to thank Lesley Riddle of Arnold Publishers for providing constant encouragement and showing considerable forbearance in the face of a number of delays. I am very grateful, too, to students at Glasgow Caledonian University and the University of Sunderland whose feedback helped in the development of this book's ideas. The support of my colleagues and the School of Arts, Design and Media at the University of Sunderland in enabling periods of research leave was invaluable, and allowed me to develop the chapter dealing with the aftermath of September 11th. My colleague, Dr Amir Saeed, offered helpful suggestions on the two chapters on discourses of Islam. All errors or omissions remain, as always, my own. Alexia Chan, Tessa Heath and Colin Goodlad of Arnold have seen this book through its final stages of preparation smoothly and efficiently. My thanks are also due to my friends and members of my family who have had much less of my attention than deserved over the past few years.

Craig Oliphant, Peter Burt and Phil Biggs, University of Sunderland, provided much appreciated assistance in the production of illustrations. I also acknowledge the help of a number of individuals and organizations in the granting of permissions to reproduce cartoons, newspaper material and television stills: PA Photos and the *Guardian* for the photograph of the Lawrences; Popperfoto for the photograph of the five youths alleged to be the killers of Stephen Lawrence; Mirror Syndication for the Bill Clinton front page from the *Daily Record*; the *Sun* and © News International Newspapers Limited for the page on BSE; Kipper Williams and the *Guardian* for the GM cartoon; BBC News and BBC Worldwide for permission to reproduce the two stills from *Correspondent*; Nik Kowsar and the Cartoonists & Writers Syndicate/cartoonweb.com for permission to reproduce the Bush cartoon; and Atlantic Syndication for the Marshall Ramsey 'Iwo Jima' cartoon. Every effort has been made to contact copyright holders. The author and publisher would be pleased to hear from any copyright holders they have not been able to contact and to print due acknowledgement in any subsequent edition.

# INTRODUCTION ☐

The start of the twenty-first century has been marked by an intensifying sense of social, political and economic uncertainty, most specifically in the western world. This shift in the mood of the times has been dubbed 'postmodern', as if this label could, paradoxically, define the emerging scepticism about all forms of knowledge or 'grand narratives' that previously enabled shared ways of understanding the world. The media, viewed through a postmodern prism, appear as intertextual pedlars in image, sound and word, concerned less with making meaning than with producing stunning effects. Yet in everyday conversations, and in the thinking of politicians and other opinion-formers, the media still figure strongly as narrative-makers, capable of influencing public perceptions of a 'reality' beyond their borders. By exploring media discourse, this book examines changing modes of configuring the relationship between media texts and the social world. Rejecting the postmodern thesis that differing versions of 'reality' no longer vie for power, but merely co-exist, it argues that 'discourse' allows flexibility in exploring the ongoing contest between differing ways of configuring 'reality'.

My use of discourse is based on the writings of the French historian and philosopher Michel Foucault (1926–84), but takes a number of liberties with his thinking that will be explored further in the initial chapters. Although, as Chapter 1 will clarify, Foucault proposes that discourse should replace the material world as a valid object of analysis, one of my key claims for the concept is that it obliges us to reinstate the relationship between the operation of the text and the world beyond the text. In recent years this has been most actively pursued through discussions of media policy and through a shift of emphasis from texts to audiences. A critical concept of discourse puts media communication back into its social and political place. Although discourse can be a complex and often confusing concept, it will be used throughout this book to refer to *a system of communicative practices that are integrally related to wider social and cultural practices, and that help to construct specific frameworks of thinking.* These 'specific frameworks of thinking' are themselves provisional, open to contest and debate, making discourse more understandable as a *process* of making meaning, rather than a fixed position.

A number of challenges confront anyone writing a book with the words 'media discourse' in the title. Because of its fuzzy edges, the concept of 'discourse' is often accused of replacing familiar concepts such as 'language' or 'representation' with unhelpful academic jargon. Where 'language' and, more especially, 'representation' urge us to examine communicative strategies, discourse can appear to be an abstract concept, ill-suited to the analysis of media texts. Its stress on systematic patterns emerging across and within texts seems additionally to defy the passion for creativity, imaginative difference and innovation that motivates most students and practitioners of the media. This book aims to dispel these anxieties and to argue that a concept of discourse offers a variety of insights into the media's current strategies for communicating with their publics. Discourse acknowledges more readily than other analytical concepts that the media are now at best partial originators of ideas and values. The demands of accountants and advertisers, spin doctors and other lobby groups, together with audience tastes that require careful and sometimes subtle massaging, ensure that the creativity of the media professional lies more in manoeuvring a way through pre-existing and competing discourses than in inventing anything from scratch. Discourse reminds us that the media's forms of talking and thinking interact with those of the wider society – sometimes setting an agenda, but frequently reacting to perceived public desires or concerns.

Analysing the media through the lens of discourse also emphasizes the relations between and across different media forms. While much critical anxiety has been invested in drawing boundaries between the media, and supporting these through the application of distinctive theoretical paradigms, contemporary developments in technology and viewing practices question the long-term viability of this approach. The growing technological proximity between film and television in terms, for example, of aspect ratio and sound quality, and the expansion of 'new media', throw into disarray the arduous struggle to distinguish between television and film in theory and analytical method. The media also interrelate through their expanding zeal for talking about each other's practices in a process of mutual surveillance inspired partly by commercial competition. By accentuating public worries about each other's harmful effects, they suggest how thin a dividing line often separates allegedly 'public' concerns from their construction or amplification by the media. Discourse provides a sensitive probe for exploring how far categories of recent public concern about the media (such as 'infotainment' or 'fakery') have been nurtured into maturity by the media themselves. Category concerns of this kind frequently proceed to shape media policy and then loop back into media practices.

A focus on media discourse avoids both the narrowness of semiotic analysis, with its tendency to focus solely on the text, and the broad generalizations that often characterize ideological analysis of media representations. Although Barthes evolved a semiotics that was sensitive to the embedding of sign systems in cultural systems of thinking, through his analysis of myth and the 'second order' of signification (1973: 119–26), his method has been applied principally to still images such as advertisements. Where ideological analysis begins with a specific issue (such as race, or gender, or sexuality) and works back through the evidence of media texts, an analysis of discourse starts its enquiry with an ear to the texts themselves, and in a spirit of openness to the patterns that may emerge. It also avoids the pitfalls of an ontological/epistemological split between an objective 'reality' out there in the 'real world' (ontological 'state of being') and an interpretative form of knowing (epistemology) achieved through the media. Instead, it acknowledges the role of the media in constituting the very realities that are referenced in media texts (the 'public outpouring of grief' attending the death of Diana, Princess of Wales, in 1997 or the perception of 'public risk' from food are cases in point which will be explored further in later chapters).

The move from a representational model to a constructionist one may initially appear to be a pedantic distinction, but its importance will become clear as the book progresses. It clarifies a shift in philosophical thinking about media texts that has already been widely recognized, at least by inference, in critical writing. At the same time this book will argue against a determinist model of discourse. Between the extremes of behaviourist accounts of media impact and John Fiske's utopian vision of active readers producing their own scripts from media texts (1987: 95–9), critical thinking about audience/text relations has tended to settle around the notion of 'negotiation' between text and reader advanced by Christine Gledhill (1988). The analysis of discourse provides a framework for detailing how such negotiation operates. Audience responses to storylines about teenage pregnancy in soap opera, for example, will vary, amongst other discursive criteria, according to how individual viewers think about 'sexual morality', the 'nuclear family' or 'abortion'. By focusing on discourse, cruder attempts to relate textual codification to social groupings (such as class, age, gender) can be replaced by a finer attention to the interplay between these types of social indicator and more modulated frameworks of thinking.

Although this book proceeds by analysing discourse, its approach diverges from the methodology known as 'discourse analysis'. Developed primarily by linguists and, to a lesser extent, by social psychologists (e.g. Potter and Wetherell, 1987), discourse analysis concentrates on verbal texts and on forms of social interaction such as the interview or the talk show. While 'discourse analysis' details the intricacies of communicative practice for their own sake, the methodology that has become known as 'critical discourse analysis' (or CDA) explores what these reveal about power relations. Although my approach in this book shares the critical discourse analysts' aims of relating discourse to power, it differs in method in a number of ways.

First, instead of focusing on the detailed structuring of individual texts, my central attention will be on the evolving patterns of discourse traceable across the contemporary media. In addition, my approach to discourse includes consideration of visual as well as verbal signification. Discourse, historically, refers to verbal communicative strategies. Within media studies, work identified as being about discourse has tended to replicate this emphasis. Norman Fairclough's *Media Discourse* (1995) is written by a linguist and almost entirely focuses on questions of language use, 'voice' and patterns of interaction, even though Fairclough clearly acknowledges the visual aspect of television (see, for example, 1995: 17, 54). Related works, such as Paddy Scannell's edited collection, *Broadcast Talk* (1991), Roger Fowler's *Language in the News* (1991), Teun A. van Dijk's work (1988; 1991; 1997), and Allan Bell and Peter Garrett's *Approaches to Media Discourse* (1998) have all repeated this emphasis. The journals *Discourse and Society* and *Discourse Studies* have similarly engaged with media texts primarily through a detailed analysis of linguistic features. Valuable though these approaches are, they are becoming increasingly artificial as interaction between visual and verbal signifiers becomes a condition of all media apart from radio (even here, the growing use of sound effects in talk programmes complicates forms of analysis that isolate linguistic elements).

Some linguists are increasingly recognizing, at least in principle, the need for what Theo van Leeuwen has called a 'pan-semiotics' (1996: 34), capable of being sensitive to interactions between different modalities of signification. In 1997, he (together with others) argued for a 'discourse semiotics' capable of analysing multi-modal structures (Kress, Leite-García and van Leeuwen) while respecting the specificity of individual semiotic modes. More recently, the stress on specificity has given way to a new recognition that in an era of multi-modality in media production, 'common semiotic principles operate in and across different modes' (Kress and van Leeuwen, 2001: 2). In their emphasis on the multi-modal quality of contemporary media discourse, these critics' approach has kinship with mine (although my analysis here is restricted to word and image, whereas theirs explores a wider range of possible modalities). Their focus on the micro-analysis of texts differs, on the other hand, from my attempt to map broader trends and changes over time and across genres. Although their earlier work lays stress on the ideological operation of sign systems, seeing these as 'set in the field of politics; in structures of power' (1997: 259), this emphasis is much less pronounced in their later work. In their close attention in *Multimodal Discourse* (2001) to *how* meaning is constructed, Kress and van Leeuwen consider only sketchily *in whose interests* this occurs, whereas this question forms a central preoccupation of my approach.

Visual signification, even in its routine manifestations, can illuminate the interests at play. Routine images of defendants being hustled, their heads bowed and hooded, from police van to court building signal culpability and shame, however clichéd the representation and however pragmatic the reasons for this mode of appearance. Visual signification of this kind forms part of the *system of communicative practices* intrinsic to discursive formation. Images also have the symbolic capacity to epitomize key historical moments in potent discursive form. Widely disseminated images of 'Wang Weilin', the lone individual who stepped out in front of the tanks advancing on Tiananmen Square in Beijing at the time of the massacre in 1989, mythologized, in Barthian terms, the confrontation between individual rights and the power of an autocratic Chinese state. Etching themselves into popular memory, images reproduce discourse long after words have faded. Earl Spencer's eulogy at the funeral of his sister, Diana, attracted widespread comment at the time for its construction of a repressed and repressive British monarchy, but his words are probably less remembered now than either Elton John's rendering of 'Candle in the Wind' or the haunting image of a card bearing the single word 'Mummy' attached to Diana's sons' floral tribute. Sound reconstructs mood and atmosphere; image anchors the discursive memory of the event.

The discussion that follows is divided into three sections. The first highlights conceptual issues, locating 'discourse' in relation to more familiar analytical concepts, and demonstrating its usefulness through case studies. Chapter 1 outlines the background to some of the confusions that have dogged the concept of 'discourse' and reviews its relationship to 'representation', while Chapter 2 reconsiders both its kinship to, and difference from, 'ideology'. The second section of the book examines some of the internal shifts taking place in 'systematic communicative practices' within the media. It questions the binary framework that has discursively inclined us to perceive these shifts in oppositional terms, such as 'information' versus 'entertainment', 'public' versus 'private'. These provoke anxieties while obscuring other potential definitions of change.

The third section explores how the media, within and through these changing discursive patterns, also construct identifiable hegemonic discourses that both find resonance in and borrow frames of thinking from the wider society. In order to give this discussion a manageable focus, the media's contribution to definitions of 'risk' will be examined. The contemporary era manifests a heightened awareness of risk from a diverse range of sources. Chapters in this section will consider media constructions of risks to children (especially from child abuse and 'paedophiles'), risks perceived to arise from 'unsafe' food, and the globalized risk thought to be emanating from 'Islamic fundamentalism' (including preliminary consideration of how this has been inflected by the events of September 11th 2001). The implications of conceptualizing such diverse phenomena within a singular framework of 'risk' will be considered, especially in terms of its tendency to replace analysis of power relations with a fascinated absorption in an amorphous 'condition of the age' that appears beyond control and responsibility. In taking us into territory apparently beyond ideology, 'risk' is also a useful means of interrogating discourse's relationship to that older, and often prematurely discarded, concept.

Section

# Mapping key terms

# Chapter One

# DISCOURSE AND ☐ REPRESENTATION

The old adage that 'sticks and stones may break your bones, but words will never hurt you' encapsulates a common belief that language has little power relative to physical actions. Representation, in whatever form or medium, appears insubstantial alongside the materiality of real occurrences. Yet words and images, by defining and labelling phenomena, frame the terms in which we think about these and may, in turn, influence policy-making. Journalism's tendency to elide distinctions between rape by an acquaintance and rape by a potential partner by including both under the single term of 'date rape' may, for example, make jurors or judges reluctant to convict, because 'date rape' hints at a degree of voluntary (and potentially sexual) involvement (for a fuller discussion of this see Lees, 1997). Similarly, perceiving or presenting 'domestic violence' or 'child sexual abuse' as always perpetrated by men against women (again a regular pattern in journalism and elsewhere) erodes the rights and dignities of male survivors of both female and male abuse, and also of female survivors of female abuse, and inhibits provision of relevant resources and support services. Word choices frequently operate by stealth: images have a more forceful presence. When photographs of the Taliban and Al-Qaeda suspects being held at the Guantanamo Bay prison camp in Cuba were released to the media by the US government in January 2002, they produced widespread anxiety (outside the USA) that the prisoners were not being treated in accordance with the civilized and humane principles proclaimed as justifying the 'war on terrorism'. The images of hooded, dazed and shackled men, shorn of their customary beards, evoked connotations of slavery and cast doubt on America's claim to be waging a war for civilization against barbarity.

The meanings we attribute to words and images depend on cultural assumptions, and help, in turn, to perpetuate these. Habitual ways of thinking about femininity intersect with traditional thinking about domesticity and the family in blaming women for rape, while exonerating them from domestic violence and child abuse. Single women are routinely seen as fickle, vengeful and wily manipulators of men (plausibly, therefore, 'crying rape' for their own ends), while women operating within a domestic or caring role are seen as nurturing, gentle, non-aggressive, and incapable of violence or abuse, especially that directed against children. Civilized societies, adhering to the rule of law, retain a belief in treating prisoners with respect and dignity, even if both fictional and non-fictional representations query the degree to which this typifies actual practice. Verbal labels and visual signifiers cannot avoid carrying social and cultural baggage.

What I have been describing is the operation of 'discourse'. This is language or image with its socio-cultural roots exposed and its socio-cultural effects revealed. Single terms or images do not, of course, achieve this by themselves, as the working definition I outlined in the Introduction emphasizes: *a system of communicative practices that are integrally related to wider social and cultural practices, and that help to construct specific frameworks of thinking.* Just as our choices of what clothes to put on in the morning may appear to be purely whimsical and idiosyncratic, but in reality either fit into or adapt specific paradigms within current cultural practices of dress and self-presentation, so our selection of forms of language or image is both bounded by unacknowledged conventions and yet allows for variation. 'Date rape' and 'domestic abuse' acquire discursive status through being networked into wider-ranging cultural and social assumptions about male and female sexuality, and about the home and the body as privately controlled spaces. Collective images of prisoners, herded together in confined spaces, and bowed into submissive pose, cannot be abstracted from a history of imagery stretching from slavery to the concentration camp. Far from being mere abstractions, these networks of ideas relate integrally to patterns of individual behaviour, and to social and institutional practice.

It is tempting to isolate and exaggerate the role of the media as the key institutions that originate and then sustain prevailing discourses. A number of considerations challenge this claim. First, in complex, multi-cultural democracies, it is difficult in many contexts to identify with any certainty what are the 'prevailing' or 'dominant' discourses; and this difficulty is compounded by the rapid expansion in media outlets and distribution channels. In both Britain and in Australia, for example, in recent times, although for different reasons, there has been considerable debate about the future role of the British monarchy. Yet in neither country would it be easy to identify the dominant discourse on this issue, because of the degree of regional, class and ethnic variation in attitudes, and the potential lack of congruence between the views of the majority of particular publics and the opinion-formers in the media. Even within a western context, it would be equally difficult to establish a dominant discourse on environmentalism or on genetic engineering (and the very terms in which we refer to these require, themselves, to be unpacked as forms of discourse).

Second, in contemporary society, the activity of publicity machines in influencing and popularizing discourses muddies any account of media institutions as authoritative originators of discourse. Groups as diverse as politicians, corporate spokespeople and non-governmental organizations (NGOs) plan their own utterances and releases of information to ensure that they are not only media-friendly, but play to public desires whilst allaying public concerns. A model of the media as merely transmitting raw information becomes untenable in these circumstances, and a model of the media as acting essentially as 'gatekeepers', allowing some information through but not all, appears unduly simplified. We need to re-examine connections between media discourses and a varied set of public discourses, some clearly generated institutionally, but not necessarily originating in any pure or simple sense within that institution. If the 'information society' allows greater than ever access to a diversity of sources of ideas and information, all institutional communicators increasingly operate within an awareness of their audiences' preconceptions and their competitors' alternative perspectives. Instead of a transmission model of communication, we need to redefine the relationship between media and public discourses as one of constant interaction.

Even in less information-rich times, the media have had to bear in mind the likely reception of their output by audiences and readers. Commercial success has depended on innovating within the framework of already established and workable categories ('genre' fulfils this function, after all, across a variety of media), and on treading a fine line between stale repetition and causing undue offence and shock. The market testing of new films, television shows or magazines is only the most concrete evidence of this ongoing process. The media can also operate at a meta-discursive level, helping to set the terms in which we think about the media themselves. As later chapters will demonstrate, many of the issues that we think of as public concerns about the media, ranging from invasions of privacy to anxieties about children's exposure to violence, are themselves orchestrated in terms the media help to shape. The boundaries around 'public discourse' and 'media discourse' are, then, much less secure than we like to think when we identify the media as the essential scapegoat for society's problems.

Key questions about discourse as a means of analysing the media will be raised in the remainder of this chapter and in the next. All relate to a concept of discourse based on the work of the French philosopher and historian, Michel Foucault. Foucault did not, however, write specifically about the media, and his ideas need to be evaluated in this context. This chapter will consider the significance for media analysis of two issues:

- how a concept of discourse differs from a concept of representation
- what role remains for human agency and decision-making if we accept a concept of discourse.

Chapter 2 will consider how Foucault's notion of discourse relates to the older Marxist-inspired concept of ideology, and whether discourse is now the more appropriate analytical tool. As we will see, these questions are not self-contained or mutually exclusive, but in the interests of clarity they will be separated out initially.

## DISCOURSE, REPRESENTATION AND 'THE REAL WORLD'

Foucault's concept of discourse suggests that our forms of communication can never capture reality in its natural or essential form, however that might be construed. Instead, all forms of knowing and talking about reality require position-taking, and consequently help to construct the very phenomena of which they speak. Foucault allows that reality may exist independently of discourse, but argues that it is only through discourse that we can exchange ideas about it. Critics of media and cultural representation have reached similar conclusions. As Stuart Hall comments:

> My own view is that events, relations, structures do have conditions of existence and real effects outside the sphere of the discursive; but only within the discursive, and subject to its specific conditions, limits, and modalities, do they have or can they be constructed within meaning. Thus, while not wanting to expand the territorial claims of the discursive infinitely, how things are represented and the 'machineries' and regimes of representation in a culture do play a *constitutive*, and not merely a reflexive, after-the-event, role.
>
> (Hall, 1996: 165)

Yet this attribution of a constitutive role for media representations has acquired support only from the late 1980s, and even since that time postmodern thinkers have subjected it to dispute. At least four different formulations of the media's role in talking to us about our world have been variously advanced within popular discourse and critical thinking:

- the media reflect reality
- the media represent reality
- the media operate discursively
- the media offer simulations.

Each of these propositions, except the first, enjoys continuing support from media critics. Although my discussion favours the third of these formulations, this needs to be set within an understanding of the other contentions.

## A LITTLE HISTORY

A notion of the media reflecting reality, especially in their informational genres, is regularly perpetuated in popular discourse. Even where such a direct connection to the real is discounted, claims about media developments reflecting social changes (as, for example, in advertising's representations of women, or in the growing attention to celebrities) continue to be voiced. One of the founding premises of critical study of the media, on the other hand, is that the media cannot and do not offer a simple reflection of the real world. Instead, media analysts have favoured the concept of representation, with metaphors of distorting lenses or selective filters replacing those of reflection's clear mirrors or translucent windows. 'Representation' recognizes the media's dependence on sign systems that operate symbolically and connotatively. Yet this term has also resonated with demands for enhanced political representation by groups such as women, minority ethnic communities, and gay men and lesbians. In the first flush of media studies in the 1970s, analysis of media representations often implied that victims of stereotyping could be more satisfactorily presented in media terms. Positive images or representations often seemed the answer both to exclusion from the mainstream media and to forms of representation disdainful of the rights of the relevant group.

Initially, the ample supply of examples of 'bias' or 'misrepresentation' masked trickier questions about the media's desired relation to 'reality', but debates about realism, already mapped out philosophically, were reinvigorated in discussions about the visual media. Colin MacCabe, Colin McArthur and others engaged in a lively discussion in the journal *Screen* in the latter half of the 1970s over the difficulties of presenting historical realities satisfactorily through the media of film and television (an edited version of this debate is available in Bennett *et al.*, 1981: 285–352). The form of the 'classic realist text', with its privileging of a particular discourse, its narrative closure and its masking of its own processes of production, was accused by MacCabe of failing to deal with reality in its intrinsic contradictoriness. Despite sharing some sympathy with his basic premise, MacCabe's critics contended that his thesis was unduly negative, ignoring the capacity of individual realist texts to raise political consciousness in a way that would still be accessible to the majority of the population. This was very much a debate of its time, dependent on Marxist theories of revolution and a belief that an unmasking of the hidden contradictoriness of existing social and political structures was a precondition for change.

Although the terms of this debate may seem dated now, it marked a more general widening of concerns about representation and reality. At its most basic this revolved around two issues: that of the fundamentally conservative nature of the form of realism, outlined by MacCabe; and the problem of deciding, even if reality were desirable, *whose* reality was going to be represented, and from whose point of view? Critics of the representation of women, minority ethnic groups, and gay men and lesbians, were quick to raise the second issue in the 1980s. Black women (e.g. hooks, 1984; Walker, 1984), lesbian women (e.g. Rich, 1979; Lorde, 1984) and working-class women (e.g. Steedman, 1986; Walkerdine, 1986) pointed out that white, heterosexual, middle-class feminist critiques of the family, for instance, ignored their perspectives and experiences. While the notion of 'positive representation' for these and other groups appeared laudable in principle, debates about what this might mean in practice suggested that 'reality' was always bound to be contested territory. At the same time, a growing attention to audience responses to texts uncovered surprising pleasures gained from apparently conservative gender representations in romantic fiction (Radway, 1987) or soap opera (Ang, 1985; Modleski, 1982). Feminist criticism of these genres was torn between celebrating the enjoyment women derived from them and decrying their tendency to reproduce, textually, some of the limited discourses of femininity that feminism aimed to contest.

Representation was also a troublesome concept in its suggestion that the world of external reality and the world of textual representation were separate or at least separable entities, and that the real world always existed in material form prior to its representation. Critics of what became known as the 'images of women' approach to analysis of women's representation in the media and culture (Griselda Pollock set this discussion in motion as early as 1977) pointed out that the media and cultural output also manifestly have a hand in *constructing* ideas of femininity in the public mind that make an input to the 'reality' of gendered behaviour and attitudes. This idea that the media do more than represent, that they help to construct our ideas about the real world, is especially pertinent in thinking about a topic such as 'race', which defies attempts to define what it 'really' is. 'Race', as a number of commentators have pointed out (see, for example, Miles, 1989; Young, 1996), is an ideological construct with no basis in scientific reality, yet we discuss racial stereotypes as if these masked some (discoverable) 'real' racial categorization. Stuart Hall exemplifies the move beyond a concept of representation to that of construction in discussing this subject:

> What [the media] 'produce' is, precisely *representations* [my italics] of the social world, images, descriptions, explanations and frames for understanding how the world is and why it works as it is said and shown to work. And, amongst other kinds of ideological labour, the media *construct* [my italics] for us a definition of what *race* is, what meaning the imagery of race carries, and what 'the problem of race' is understood to be.
>
> (Bridges and Brunt, 1981: 35)

The construction of what 'race', or 'femininity', or 'Islam', or 'media violence' might mean becomes an important feature of the media's productive work. The notion of construction implies neither an intention to deceive, nor an ability on the part of the media to determine our thinking. Instead, it suggests a vital interaction between the media's role in forming the 'frames for understanding' we construct in our heads about the material world, and the actuality of our behaviour and attitudes. How this works will be considered in more detail later.

To avoid exaggerating the uniqueness of the media's role, it is useful to refer to the media as *helping to construct* versions of reality. The move from a concept of representation to one of construction is not a seismic shift (indeed, the two terms often appear side by side in the critical literature, as the quote from Hall indicates), but the notion of construction aptly captures the shaping and structuring role of media codes. While on occasion the media do appear to be striving (merely) to re-present material or physical reality (especially within 'fly-on-the-wall' documentaries or in natural history programmes), they still cannot avoid providing an interpretation. In fictional genres, of course, versions of contemporary or historical realities place a primary value on particular ways of thinking about these, rather than on the events themselves (Mel Gibson's reworking of Scottish history in *Braveheart* (1995) or Michael Mann's reinterpretation of the life of Muhammad Ali in *Ali*, (2001) would be cases in point). Where representation tends to idealize the possibility of attaining proximity to 'the real', concepts of construction and discourse emphasize the provisional and contested nature of forms of knowing. Postmodern thinking, on the other hand, denies the point of positing any link whatsoever between media or cultural texts and reality. What these present is neither a representation nor a construction, but a mere simulation: 'simulation envelops the whole edifice of representation as itself a simulacrum'

(Poster, 1988: 170). Baudrillard's concept of the 'simulacrum' removes the possibility of sign systems referring to anything other than further sign systems.

Semiotics (the science of signs) placed emphasis on the relationship between the material embodiment of the sign, the idea it formed in our heads, and (at least amongst the followers of the American semiotician C.S. Peirce) the object to which it referred. Even in the Saussurean model of semiotics, revealing the internal structures of signification was intended to enhance our understanding of meaning constructions about the world we live in. As adapted and developed by Roland Barthes (1973), the link between the minutiae of textual structuring and the value-systems of specific societies was well established through the concept of 'myth' and what he called the 'second order' of signification. Postmodern thinkers deride, by contrast, any search for meaningfulness beyond the sign. While semioticians might have been fascinated by the intertextuality of contemporary signification, intertextual play becomes the essential condition of sign systems in the postmodern universe. Signs refer us to other signs, until the relation of these to the world beyond diminishes to vanishing point.

Many of the most extravagant-sounding claims within postmodernism have come from French thinkers used to a tradition of provocative debate. While the orthodox French approach to presenting an argument has been to work from a thesis through an antithesis to a synthesis, many of these thinkers focus primarily on the second stage, developing the antithesis to conventional complacency and received wisdom. This produces apparently extravagant and implausible claims that nevertheless shock us into a re-inspection of our common-sense assumptions. Jean Baudrillard, for example, startled the world with his assertion that the Gulf War had not really taken place, printed in *Libération* (29 March 1991). However manifestly absurd this claim was, it also contained enough acuity about the video game simulation of the war's nightly presentation on western television screens to contain a nugget of plausibility. What we were being offered, it could be alleged, was not a representation of the reality of the Gulf War, nor even an approximate construction of its characteristics, but a set of signs that bore no relation whatsoever to the reality of the war.

What masks the extravagance of this claim is the precision with which it taps into an aspect of our contemporary textual and cultural experience. Baudrillardian antitheses have a knack of hitting evocative targets. This should not, however, disguise the sophistry of any attempt to seal off the world of signification from social realities. Hi-tech wizardry and precision bombing did not, as later revelations made clear, define the essence of the events that became known as the Gulf War, but to claim the impossibility of evaluating the validity of specific media constructions depoliticizes the processes of signification. It removes the decision-making responsibilities of information providers and inhibits investigation of competing constructions. It also fails to recognize that signs establish their own materiality by forming templates for planning further forms of action. Belief in the possibility of 'clinical warfare' may not have emerged out of any material reality, but it speedily acquired the power to influence defence spending policy and military decision-making. Conceptualizing signification as free-floating in its own universe implicitly denies any social or political motivation for changes in that sphere, and any social or political consequences. One of the key attractions of the concept of discourse as I have outlined it is that it refuses this kind of autonomy to sign systems, and conceptualizes them, instead, as essential constituents in our social and political operation.

To sum up the discussion so far, the concept of discourse is sympathetic to the notion that the media help to construct versions of reality, and that these constructions are always open to contest. It refuses a sharp dividing line between 'reality' and its 'representation', especially since apparent realities are often discursively shaped. Even statistical accounts of social phenomena will be strongly influenced by the terms in which we talk about these, or, indeed, by our reluctance to discuss them. Incidents of the abuse of men by women, or of Muslims by Sikhs will be difficult to establish if victims feel that existing discourses of 'domestic violence' or 'racism' exclude their experiences. Where the concept of discourse sits in relation to the postmodern concept of simulation is a trickier issue, especially since Michel Foucault subscribes to the perspective that reality is, in practice, unknowable. He does, however, regard discourse as intertwined with evolving social practices and much of his writing is preoccupied with tracing discourses' historical transformations. This weaves discourse into the fabric of our efforts to come to terms with an understanding of the world in which we live. Postmodern thinking, on the other hand, in stressing the surface intertextuality and self-referentiality of sign systems, abandons this as a futile project.

## AND SO TO FOUCAULT

Since Foucault's ideas are wide-ranging and often hard to summarize, this section explores their relevance to media analysis in terms of the questions indicated earlier: how, if at all, does Foucault establish a relationship between discourse and the social and material world in which we live; and to whom or what does he attribute the origins of discourse? The first question is important in establishing the relationship that Foucault envisages between the worlds of representation and reality; the second has significant implications for how change might be achieved. The media coverage of the sudden death of Princess Diana on 31 August 1997 provides a useful focus for investigating these questions.

Although Foucault is sometimes referred to as a theorist of discourse, his approach consistently avoids advancing general theories. He insists instead on investigating the operation of discourse in specific times and situations, adopting a methodology that is essentially historical. Initially he describes his approach as akin to that of the archaeologist, but in subsequent writing he prefers the Nietzschean concept of genealogy. The latter term marks Foucault's commitment, in his later work, to revealing the interaction between discursive change and the operation of knowledge and power. Throughout, however, Foucault sought to do justice to the specific twists and turns of historical development, and refused to subscribe to notions of history as continuous progress. Although Foucault consistently avoids the articulation of a grand theory of discourse, his writing is highly theoretical in nature, and driven by a desire to pinpoint the rules that govern discourse's operation in practice. The lack of straightforward definitions makes him a challenging writer but it is, nevertheless, possible to isolate essential elements in his approach that have a bearing on the issues of representation, material reality and the media text.

Foucault does not deny the existence of material reality, nor does he categorically deny the possibility, in principle, of gaining access to this. In a discussion of 'madness' in his early work, *The Archaeology of Knowledge*, he writes:

> We are not trying to reconstitute what madness itself might be, in the form in which it first presented itself to some primitive, fundamental, deaf, scarcely articulated experience, and in the form in which it was later organized (translated, deformed, travestied, perhaps even repressed) by discourses, and the oblique, often twisted play of their operations. *Such a history of the referent is no doubt possible* [my italics]; and I have no wish at the outset to exclude any effort to uncover and free these 'prediscursive' experiences from the tyranny of the text.
>
> (1972: 47)

This acknowledges the ontological existence of a reality beyond discourse, but Foucault is also asserting the futility of trying to discover this. Reality remains profoundly unknowable since our only access to it is through the constructionist prism of discourse. It therefore becomes pointless, in the Foucauldian view, to argue about the accuracy of any representation of the real world. If all we can ever compare are two or more constructed *versions* of reality, then how can we know which one is more truthful or less blinkered than the other? To establish that, he implies, we would need to have access to 'the truth' that is being evaded or distorted, and since this is impossible, attempting judgement is pointless. Foucault's emphasis, in his later work, on the provisional nature of discourse and knowledge brings him into sympathy with poststructuralist thinking, although he himself rejected the poststructuralist label.

Although Foucault did not write specifically about the media, his approach to discourse suggests that attempts to investigate the truthfulness of media representations can produce only a wild goose chase. Accordingly, asking whether the media accounts of the 'nation in mourning' that followed Diana's death offered a true account of what was actually happening in Britain during September 1997 would be unproductive because we have no way of stepping outside the bounds of discourse to establish this definitively. Yet avoidance of this question is particularly difficult when evaluating media discourses because the media themselves make claims for truthfulness and accuracy in relation to their coverage of real events and, despite the turn to the postmodern in academic criticism, much of the lay public's discussion of news and current affairs programmes centres on the credibility of what is seen and heard. Refusing any attempt to assess the validity and veracity of an account because it is philosophically impossible to set an absolute criterion of truthfulness is, I will argue, too rigid and extreme a position. Foucault's emphasis on our lack of access to ultimate truth should not prevent a comparative assessment of discourses along a sliding scale of viability.

To make such an evaluation, we need to weigh up the contested evidence, in the manner of contemporary historians, taking as wide a sample as possible. The search is less for a singular 'truth' than for the distilled wisdom achievable through an examination of multiple and contrasting discourses. The availability of cross-cultural comparisons and conflicting discourses through the Internet makes this a more feasible task than it once was. In the First World War it would have been impossible for any but those with experience of life on the front to challenge the British press's account of what was happening in the battlefield, but in the coverage of more recent wars (despite the much greater sophistication of government public relations machines), television pictures from unfriendly countries, interviews with opponents, and the diversity of opinions available via the Internet, all enable journalists and the wired-up section of the public to test discourses against each other. This comparative process is how judgements have always been made about the validity of accounts of actuality, and to introduce a criterion of absolute truthfulness or the uncovering of the naked referent is in many ways a distraction. It would patently be absurd to claim that there is no way of knowing whether Diana *really* died in a car crash in Paris, or whether this was merely a malign discursive construction. Although Mohammed Al Fayed's contention of a conspiracy by the British security services to kill Diana may have internal plausibility, it is still possible to evaluate the likely veracity of such a thesis through careful analysis of alternative constructions. The difficulty of reaching definitive conclusions is testimony to the provisional nature of knowledge, but this does not, it seems to me, invalidate the evaluative search.

Foucault, of course, is not advocating relativism: merely producing this effect by refusing to regard the relationship between discourse and material reality as a central concern. Instead, he focuses on the construction of discourses in themselves:

> . . . what we are concerned with here is not to neutralize discourse, to make it the sign of something else, and to pierce through its density in order to reach what remains silently anterior to it, but on the contrary to maintain it in its consistency, to make it emerge in its own complexity.

> (1972: 47)

In a later interview, Foucault embellishes this argument by proposing that the question is not whether discourse is truthful but 'how effects of truth are produced within discourses which in themselves are neither true nor false' (Gordon, 1980: 118). Discourses are to be explored for what he calls their 'tactical productivity' (what they achieve in terms of power and knowledge) and for their 'strategical integration' (what circumstances and rules give rise to their use in particular circumstances) (Foucault, 1981: 101–2). Discourses' 'tactical productivity', the mechanics through which they achieve power, will be explored further in the next chapter, but their 'strategical integration' involves taking account of their interaction with material realities. By considering discourse as a social practice rather than as a self-enclosed or free-floating symbolic system, the Foucauldian approach differs radically from Baudrillard's emphasis on the simulated nature of contemporary signification.

Discourse, Foucault tells us, is more than language, and it is this 'something more' that binds it particularly strongly into social and cultural processes. Foucault claims that the development of medical science in the West, for example, cannot be understood merely as 'a series of descriptive statements' but needs to take account of how linguistic formulations intersect with 'a group of hypotheses about life and death, of ethical choices, of therapeutic decisions, of institutional regulations, of teaching models' (1972: 33). Elsewhere, he talks about the need to relate the discursive to the 'non-discursive domains', which he defines as 'institutions, political events, economic practices and processes' (1972: 162). This rare acknowledgement that a 'non-discursive' realm does indeed exist confirms that Foucault accepts the material reality of a world beyond discourse, even if its mode of operation remains indistinct in much of his work. One of the challenges of applying a Foucauldian methodology in media analysis is that Foucault offers no template for understanding the mechanisms through which the discursive and non-discursive intersect. Each instance, in his view, has to be examined in its particularities. One of the most vivid instances of this in his own work is his discussion of the Benthamite 'panopticon', a method of constructing institutional buildings (such as prisons, and schools) in the nineteenth century that was the material embodiment of discourses of surveillance and regimentation of the time (Foucault, 1979). In general, however, Foucault puts more effort into investigating the historical development of discourse than into tracing the nature of the relation between discourses about the world, and its material and physical constitution.

## THE CASE OF DIANA'S DEATH

How, then, might these ideas be applied to the aftermath of the death of Princess Diana in 1997? During that period, questions quickly arose about the relationship between the physical manifestations of the apparently mourning crowds on the streets of London and the media representations or constructions of that phenomenon broadcast nightly on British television screens. The construction that rapidly began to dominate was that of a 'nation in mourning' as public reaction unfolded on a scale that took the public authorities, the House of Windsor and the media themselves by surprise. Critics debated whether this was a relatively faithful re-presentation of a tangible reality, or a discursive construction reducing a complex phenomenon to a singular interpretation, or, in Baudrillardian terminology, a 'pure simulacrum' with no relation to reality whatsoever (see, for example, Silverstone, 1999: 72–7). At one level, media discourses could be seen to be following and representing the public mood in a way that captured its essence. Even the sceptical Channel 4 newsreader and commentator, Jon Snow, who attracted considerable criticism for reporting a rift within the royal family on appropriate responses to Diana's death (Channel 4 News, 8 September 1997), wondered (in an article published on the same day) if he had been unduly cynical when he went with his family to visit Kensington Palace:

> . . . every single day last week I found myself asking, 'Have we got this right? Are we exaggerating, leading, massaging the national mood?' This, in the end, was what defined the uniqueness in the British end of this news story. The gathered masses waiting to pay their respects spontaneously offered their views – they did not have to be looked for, invented or requested.
>
> (*Guardian*, 8 September 1997)

Yet, if the crowds were real, their motivation for being there was likely to be much more diverse than the 'outpouring of national grief' discourse allowed. Comments from some of the *vox pop* interviews on the day of the funeral suggested that participating in a moment of history-in-the-making was a stronger motivation than any personal sense of loss or mourning. The constant clicking of cameras confirmed the desire to possess a personal record of a public event that in more private forms is rarely photographed. If the media were not 'massaging the national mood' they had created a powerful sense that a unique moment of popular memory was in the making.

The overwhelming uniformity of media discourses around this event also involved ignoring contrary evidence. Few commentators asked how many of the 'nation in mourning' were spectating tourists rather than native Britons. On the day of the funeral, television footage from around the country persisted in universally depicting streets devoid of traffic or people, even if later reports from several parts of Britain reported ordinary life being minimally disrupted. On the Sunday that broke news of Diana's death to the world, the BBC, responding to what it perceived to be the mood of the nation, took the decision to cancel its regular schedule on both channels and broadcast reports and analysis of the day's events instead. The volume of complaints from the viewing public forced a rethink as the day proceeded, with BBC2 deciding to resume its regular programmes from midway through the afternoon. ITV, the BBC's commercial competitor, also reported higher than normal audience figures for its regular Sunday evening programming (Mark Lawson, writing in the *Guardian*, 4 September 1997). People's reactions, then, were more varied than the media suggested, but also subject to influence by the media. Because it was a Sunday, more people were available for watching or listening to the unfolding events than would have been the case on a weekday. Alternative views that queried the sufficiency of the 'nation in mourning' thesis were slow in being aired on British television, and then appeared most vocally on the minority Channel 4 network.

The Foucauldian approach is helpful, then, in highlighting how the discourse of 'a nation in mourning', despite being apparently verified by witnesses on the streets of London, remained an overpowering construction privileged over a number of other possibilities. Different and more varied interpretations would have been at least equally plausible. Yet this construction also resisted the Baudrillardian thesis that it had no basis in material reality. The crowds lining the streets were real enough and their tributes often written with evident personal feeling, but it is equally hard to believe that public reaction would have taken the form it did without the persistently elegiac and canonizing tone of the intensive media coverage. Foucault's perception of the difficulty, and indeed sometimes the impossibility, of disentangling the precise origins of a discourse is apt in this context. The interaction between media and public behaviour was patently neither one-way nor simple. Media discourses were forged out of an interactive dynamism between (at least) natural feelings of shock, growing doubts about the role of the monarchy in late twentieth-century Britain, Diana's iconic status as the world's most glamorous 'wronged woman', and the surprise effect of an unanticipated moment of public occasion and national history. Most such occasions in post-war Britain have been pre-planned or at least foreseen; the frequently invoked parallel between the shock effect of Diana's death and the assassination of President Kennedy was telling about the scarcity of such events.

Foucauldian thinking offers no ready reckoners for evaluating the adequacy of media discourses. If the purpose is to consider the 'effects of truth' rather than the truthfulness of media constructions, we enter difficult terrain where it is hard to see how judgements can be securely offered and relativism ultimately avoided. Tracing how media discourses emerge is a fascinating exercise comparable to the uncovering of one's own family tree, but, as will become clearer in the next chapter, a sharper set of criteria seems necessary to enable us to evaluate discourses, without lapsing into oversimplified thinking about the ease with which such judgements can be made. Within a Foucauldian model, discourse also appears peculiarly disembodied and abstracted from those whom media biographers especially delight in presenting as the key movers and shakers: whether media moguls, like Rupert Murdoch; decision-makers such as editors and programme controllers; or those who, day to day, produce words, sound effects and images for the increasing number of media outlets. Foucault does ask 'how is it that one particular statement appeared rather than another?' (1972: 27) but this indicates a quest for the implicit rules governing a statement's production, not a search for an originating source.

Agency, the making of things happen, is of less significance to Foucault than the issue of how discourses evolve through time. Although his aim is to avoid a simplistic attribution of responsibility or blame, his imprecision in this area thwarts the media analyst's natural impulse to seek out the source of a way of talking and representing in order to highlight the possibility of change. It may make sense in tracking the long history of ways of thinking about psychiatry, madness or sexuality to characterize the changing pattern of thinking as a slowly evolving process, but media producers appear to take more instantaneous and identifiable decisions. The merit of the Foucauldian approach lies in underlining how many of these decisions rest on routine responses that are informed by culturally and socially acceptable ways of thinking. Vagueness about agency does, however, prevent clarity about responsibility and about how change can be effected.

## DISCOURSE AND AGENCY

In common with other poststructuralists, Foucault denies human subjectivity the controlling status it has been granted since the time of the Enlightenment in the eighteenth century. This move, often referred to as a 'decentring of the subject', does not deny human cognition and creativity, but disputes individual ability to direct social action and exercise independent free will. It shifts attention away from human consciousness: 'the analysis of statements', Foucault writes, 'operates . . . without reference to a cogito. It does not pose the question of the speaking subject, who reveals or who conceals himself in what he says, who, in speaking, exercises his sovereign freedom' (1972: 122). Although critics of Foucault have often alleged that he gives no place whatsoever to human individuality and agency, Foucault addresses this issue directly at several points in his work. At the end of *The Archaeology of Knowledge*, he even recognizes how difficult it is for people, used to thinking about their own ability to influence events, to cede authority to less clearly defined forces (1972: 210–1). Foucault is at his most abstract in explaining where responsibility for the constantly dynamic pattern of discursive interactions lies, and it is this that makes poststructuralist thinking appear devoid of political purpose. The 'enunciative domain' of discourse is, in his words, 'described as an anonymous field whose configuration defines the possible position of speaking subjects' (1972: 122). This both fails to specify where originating power lies and reverses the pattern of western assumptions that it is human beings who determine discourse, not the other way round.

In media studies, two forms of agency have been extensively explored. From a political economy perspective, the power of owners and producers of texts to determine their form and content has been long debated, while from a cultural studies perspective, especially from the 1980s onwards, the role of the reader in the active interpretation of a text's meaning has been a major strand of critical investigation. Neither of these approaches would be satisfied with the view that discourse is autonomously driven by its own histories and rules of formation, however integrated these may be within wider cultural practices. In newspapers, in particular, owners' political objectives are regarded as influencing discourses on a variety of topics, beyond party politics itself. The Murdoch papers in Britain have been accused, for example, of skewing their reporting on the future of television, on sport and on international affairs (especially in relation to China) in line with their proprietor's commercial and expansionist interests. Even without this form of pressure, standard accounts of print or broadcast news production emphasize the role of editorial selection, journalistic deployment and routine professional practices. What we see and read, it is argued, is the result of human choices and decisions, not a production of anonymously generated discourses. If this is true of genres constrained by the demands of actuality, it will apply even more emphatically to fictional genres where creativity has an apparently free hand (within the bounds of censorship constraints, at least). The analysis of discourse pays little attention to these questions of authorial influence, choosing instead to examine *what* is being communicated, and *in whose interests*.

More than other methods, however, the analysis of discourse is philosophically sceptical about the independence of creativity and decision-making, since the basic materials that production teams work with – words, sound and image – are already organized discursively and come bearing their cultural imprint. Discourse-based analysis might, for example, argue that perceiving the Murdoch papers' reluctance to be critical of human rights abuses in China as a special case ignores the wider discursive hesitancy in the British media about criticizing repressive regimes with whom Britain has lucrative trading contracts. Personalizing an issue, according to this way of thinking, merely enables a ready stalking horse to distract attention away from a more pervasively operating discourse. However pertinent such observations may be, they do appear to distance those who engage in the act of producing or reproducing specific discourses from assuming responsibility for their actions. Even if we accept that the formation of discourse is often beyond individual control, the role of individuals in perpetuating or challenging already existing discourses, and in shaping those of the future, needs to be acknowledged more strongly than Foucauldian approaches allow. Terry Eagleton, amongst other critics, has drawn attention to the illogicality of theorists claiming that subjects are situated by discourse while they themselves are apparently able to escape out of that bubble to offer criticism. If 'regimes of power constitute us to our very roots, producing just those forms of subjectivity on which they can most efficiently go to work . . . what is there "left over", so to speak, to find this situation so appalling?' (1991: 47).

In relation to the consumption of media texts, current thinking within media studies is highly resistant to any idea of audiences, spectators or readers being positioned by textual discourses. Theories, heavily influenced by psychoanalysis, and first outlined in the journal *Screen* in the 1970s, depicted the cinematic text as having extensive unconscious powers over the spectator's reactions and the evocation of desire. These ideas were strongly criticized by, amongst others, members of the Birmingham Centre for Contemporary Cultural Studies (BCCCS), who argued that '*Screen* theory' privileged a purely textual subject, ignoring the influences on spectators arising from their class, ethnicity, gender or other social factors. The reaction against this theoretical approach helped to prompt qualitative methods of audience and readership analysis such as ethnography, associated especially in the 1980s and early 1990s with David Morley (1986) in Britain, and Janice Radway (1987) and James Lull (1990) in the United States. Since that time, the focus on audience studies has become so insistent in media studies that some academics have made a plea for a return to serious analysis of textual determinants (see, for example, Brunsdon 1989; Corner 1991). These critics argue that surveys of audience reactions are guilty of overemphasizing the power of the audience (as in the wilder claims of John Fiske), and tend to deliver more sociological information about audiences' leisure pastimes and lifestyles than about their interpretations of media texts. Despite these worries, most academic writers are now united in agreeing that any study of meaning in the media will be handicapped if it ignores audience or reader responses.

Discussions of media texts in terms of discourse may appear to make this a problematic undertaking. If the media help to construct versions of reality for us, then how do we, as subjects of discourse, arrive at differing responses to them, as research findings and anecdotal evidence confirm? Despite Foucault's skirting around the question of subjectivity, there is less incompatibility between his approach to discourse and variability of responses than has often been alleged. We are never, after all, for long the subjects of a single discourse, even if we accept a strong version of individual subjection. Choices have constantly to be made between competing versions of reality. This is especially likely to be true in a media- and information-rich age, where access to the Internet adds considerably to the diversity of accessible perspectives. Within such a mêlée, confusion or apathy may be predictable responses, but a different possibility is that our inherent need to make sense of our experiences drives us to negotiate a way through often incompatible discourses, aligning ourselves with some, rejecting or exhibiting indifference to others. If 'in-betweenness' typifies the contemporary experience of identity for many of us living in a mobile, globalized and fast-changing world, it is not surprising that we are faced daily with a tangled mix of often competing and contradictory systems of thinking and talking. The choices that we make may well involve weighing up the competing (and incomplete) versions of reality on offer within our cultures, but the act of doing this is a matter of individual agency. There is considerable evidence that people can and do resist media discourses, especially when they feel their own values are threatened. Liverpool readers of the *Sun* reacted angrily when that paper ran a front-page splash blaming drunken Liverpool fans for helping to produce the disaster at the Hillsborough football stadium in Sheffield in 1989, in which 96 fans lost their lives. Sales of the paper fell sharply on Merseyside and copies were reputedly burned in the street. During the European football championships in 1996 the *Sun*'s main rival, the *Daily Mirror*, ran a notoriously jingoistic front-page assault on the German opposition, headed 'Achtung! Surrender' (24 June 1996). So many readers objected vociferously that the paper was forced to apologize and the incident has gone down in British newspaper history as a classic misjudgement of British popular taste.

Discourse can, then, be conceptually helpful in understanding the processes through which we react differently to media texts. Initially, audience studies, such as David Morley's *The 'Nationwide' Audience* (1980) attempted to correlate varying responses to the same text with social differentials such as gender, class or ethnicity, but empirical evidence suggested that this model was too crude. As Shaun Moores comments 'probably the most significant conclusion to be drawn from the research is that viewers' decodings of a TV current affairs text cannot be reduced in any simple way to their socioeconomic location' (1993: 21). John Fiske, in the less fanciful aspects of his theorization of an 'active' or 'producerly' reader, suggests instead that the decoding of 'open' or 'polysemic' popular texts (open to multiple possible readings) will occur in line with personal interests and tastes (1987: 65–72). Popular hospital dramas, for example, are likely to be read differently by those who work in the health service and those who do not, and differently again by those workers who regard the health service as a successfully functioning organization and those who are cynical about its resourcing and mode of operation. In everyday language, this might seem equivalent to arguing that reading is influenced by our attitudes and beliefs, but attitudes and beliefs involve stances taken in relation to a pre-existing object (in this instance 'the health service'), whereas discourse insists that the very formation of that object in cultural thinking contributes to our understanding of it. Since we all identify with different mixes of discourses (or discursive repertoires), and will often continually change our minds about these in the course of our lives, variability in our responses to media discourses is bound to ensue.

In addition, few texts offer a single, unified discursive position; and few of us as readers have synthesized our own exposure to a variety of discourses into a totally harmonious blend that elides contradictoriness and some degree of fluidity from one moment to the next (indeed, it might be argued that bigotry would result if we did). Fervour about nationalist discourses, for example, varies dramatically according to circumstance. Some people will be passionate nationalists on every occasion, but for many others self-expression through nationalist discourses will be limited to major international sporting fixtures or to other occasions when their national identity is under threat of attack, neglect or ridicule. Women, too, can have differing forms of relationship to feminist discourses, according to circumstance, point in life cycle and experience. Feminists who are also Roman Catholics may have to juggle their own reactions to abortion against a mix of competing discourses. This confirms that, while we are subject to discourse, we are not its victims. For these reasons, Christine Gledhill's (1988) notion of a continual 'negotiation' between text and reader still seems the most apposite model of this transaction, as long as we do not regard this as a negotiation between equals. The next chapter will consider in more detail how discourse relates to power and to the concept of ideology.

## CONCLUSION

My outline of Foucault's thinking has suggested a number of problems with a Foucauldian approach to media analysis. Yet there are several advantages to be gained from Foucault's ideas. Some of these will become clearer in the next chapter, but to sum up what can be established so far, Foucault makes a potentially positive contribution to our understanding of media operation through his attention to:

- the historical evolution of discourses
- shifting discursive constellations, and the relation between these and socio-cultural change
- the relation between media discourses and wider public discourses.

The historical emphasis of Foucault's work is especially fundamental to this book's focus on the changing pattern of media discourse. Many of the terms in which these changes have been discussed suggest a binary framework of thinking: entertainment as against information, for example, or public as against private. This prejudices thinking about the nature of change and forecloses a number of alternative perspectives. The ratings popularity of the *Big Brother* TV programmes might, for example, be attributed to a global shift from public to private values, as the audience's attention in a number of countries becomes increasingly absorbed by the minutiae of other people's daily living habits and interactions. But this formulation would miss a number of at least equally interesting considerations, such as the influence of the performative aspects of participation on the pleasures on offer to audiences, or the increasing focus on losers rather than winners that is visible also across a number of other genres, including quiz shows and talk shows.

Foucault's approach is also valuable in suggesting that a concern with themes may be less rewarding in media analysis than a focus on the frameworks within which we think about topics and issues. Instead, for example, of defining crime as an apparently stable and fixed phenomenon of contemporary society, Foucault asks 'how criminality could become an object of medical expertise' (1972: 48) or how it has been variously constituted at particular points in time. In considering crime as a topic favoured by the media, both in its factual and fictional modes, his method invites us to explore how criminality is perceived and talked about (for example, as a threat to social stability, or as a disease, or as a source of exciting narrative); how it is defined (in relation to offences against the person, or against individual or corporate property); and how these forms of thinking and talking have changed through time. This pulls into the frame of comparative analysis genres that are normally discussed in isolation from each other (such as, in this case, news, crime dramas, aspects of 'reality TV' and money programmes), and highlights interconnections between how we think about crime and how we think more generally about social responsibility, or property, or individual rights in the face of an increasingly surveillance-driven economy. Instead of looking at themes as self-evident, bounded phenomena, an analysis of discourse emphasizes interconnections in modes of perception between topics that on the surface appear detached from each other.

Discursive kinships that may have been curious and unexpected at their point of formation do, of course, quickly become incorporated into the naturalized landscape of cultural expectations. As such they are often accorded familiarizing labels that delimit rather than open up their discursive complexities. To return to the media and public responses to Princess Diana's death, discourses of a movement in British national mood, defined as a process of modernization or feminization, were frequently invoked in commentaries in the immediate aftermath, and became a benchmark for thinking about public responses to another type and scale of death in the wake of September 11th 2001. But the form of this new emotionality, and the beatification and sanctification of a cultural icon, whose death ironically eclipsed even that of Mother Teresa of Calcutta less than a week later, were less rigorously explored. While discourse is analytically helpful in exploring connections and relationships, and opening up discussion of what events tell us about ourselves and our own moulds of thinking, the search for familiar frames of reference can at the same time foreclose the opportunities this offers. The notion of an ongoing contest between competing discourses also leaves unresolved how relativism can be avoided and value judgements offered. In order to explore this further, a return to ideology is helpful and will be investigated in the next chapter.

# Chapter Two

# DISCOURSE AND IDEOLOGY $\square$

'Discourse' and 'ideology' are not particularly compatible bedfellows. 'Ideology' has increasingly been spurned by cultural critics as being too abstract and rigid to cope with the rapidly changing formations of social thinking in turn-of-the-century western societies. Foucault was especially vocal in his dismissal of its validity, but he is by no means alone in arguing that 'discourse' copes better with a dispersed and volatile model of power. While this chapter claims that Foucault's ideas about the relationship between power, knowledge and discourse provide valuable insights into the *operation* of power through symbolic forms, it also contends that an *evaluation* of this still depends on ideological investigation.

If a concept of ideology is totally abandoned, several aspects of media power become more difficult to explain. Relative degrees of power are hard to account for within a theory of discourse alone. The media's role as second-order processors of discourse, or even as producers of meta-discourse, requires a method of analysis that distinguishes the media's forms of power from those of primary producers of discursive formations. How we define and label critical positions on the media need also to be seen as discursive acts, and consequently open to dispute. Without an appeal to ideology, this not only remains obscure, but the grounds for any resulting criticism become uncertain. As the next chapter demonstrates, a 'tabloidization' thesis in relation to 'serious journalism' has, for instance, been founded on a number of ideological presuppositions. Identifying these, and interrogating them, casts fresh light on the processes at work. To put the dilemma of evaluating contending discourses in extreme form, what discursive reason is there for preferring a discourse of anti-racism to racism, or of feminism to sexism? Without situating the ideological contests at stake, and relating these to material structures of institutional power (including the institutional power of the media), analysis of discourse becomes peculiarly deracinated from agencies of change. Ideology has, however, had an unstable and complex past, and needs to be reassessed in the light of contemporary claims that it has outlived its usefulness.

## REVISITING IDEOLOGY

Ideology has come under cogent attack in recent times from theorists suspicious of its associations with Marxism or its claims to meaningfulness in a postmodern world seen as empty of values and certainties. Yet jettisoning ideology is premature, as Terry Eagleton asserts, considering how many people still commit themselves passionately to a variety of causes. Eagleton sets the late twentieth-century rise of nationalisms, fundamentalist forms of Islamic belief and a powerful religious right-wing in the United States, against the claims of those who assert the death of ideology (1991: xi). What, then, does ideology mean in the current climate? It refers to a systematic framework of social understanding, motivated by a will to power, or a desire to be accepted as the 'right' way of thinking, which has wide (although, as I will argue, not necessarily dominant) support within a particular society or substantial social group. Where ideologies do achieve dominance within a specific culture, they often fail to be recognized as such and pass as 'common sense', or as self-evident truths. Just as we would undoubtedly be more worried about radiation if it were a visible phenomenon or if it turned our hair green, so we would be more concerned about ideology if it drew attention to its own existence. Citing a graphic analogy, Terry Eagleton comments that ideology is comparable to bad breath: we acknowledge everyone else's, but never our own (1991: 2). To western ways of thinking, Islam appears as a threatening ideology, much as communism used to, but the threat that capitalism or Christianity might equally pose is not discussed.

A later section of this chapter will consider in greater detail how discourse might be related to ideology, but a kinship between the concepts may already be apparent. Both refer to systematic frameworks for understanding that are socially formed, but the emphasis in my working definition of discourse is on the *communication* of these, while ideology conjures up more abstract ways of thinking. Ideology is also more emphatically driven by a will to power, or a desire to establish a particular frame of thinking as at least the most valid or even, in its more fanatical forms, as 'the truth'. Discourse always carries latent ideological consequences, but the activation of these depends on specific contexts and conditions. Quiz shows, sports programmes and even some types of cookery programme may all, for instance, provide examples of competitive discourse, but they also vary in their articulation of capitalist relations or in their support for individualistic as opposed to collective endeavour. Without the ability to relate discourse to ideology, these distinctions become blurred and the relative position of discourses in the spectrum of powerfulness cannot be analysed.

In recent decades, the belief that ideology is an outdated concept has been gaining momentum. The era commonly designated as 'postmodern' lacks what Jean Lyotard has called the 'grand narratives' that used to provide some degree of structure to how we made sense of the world (trades unionism, socialism or liberalism, for example). Shared systems of thinking consequently appear too illusory to be sustainable as an object of study. End-of-ideology theorists have also been encouraged by the waning of Marxist influence on contemporary thinking. Marxism gave prominence to ideology as a form of false consciousness that blurred clarity of thought about the mechanisms through which capitalism operated. In traditional Marxist thinking, ideology, as the realm of ideas, was secondary to the material operation of the economy, but in the version of Marxism that became especially influential in media studies, ideology acquired a measure of autonomy. The French thinker, Louis Althusser, whose ideas were especially influential in the 1970s, devised the concept of the Ideological State Apparatus (embodied in, for example, schools, religious institutions, families and the media) to signify how important ideology could be in materially shaping contemporary life.

In the twenty-first century, however, even this formulation appears too rigid and monolithic to do justice to the plurality and diversity of lived experiences of these institutions. What shared systems of belief can we be said to hold in this fractured, highly mobile and increasingly decentred age? Even television, perceived in earlier decades as possessing a 'bardic function' (Fiske and Hartley, 1978: 85–100) and a strongly consensual influence, has become so fragmented in its consumption patterns as to lose any claim to be a means of social cohesion. The digital and multi-media age promises to accentuate this trend. But diversity of viewpoints on the world does not invalidate a concept of ideology, unless we assume that ideology can refer only to dominant frameworks of understanding, and not to those that question the status quo, such as feminism, or environmentalism, or (in many political contexts) nationalism. The survival of ideology does, however, depend on assuming that the contest between different frames of thinking, and the policy decisions they suggest, still has a political purpose, and that the meaningless universe is primarily a figment of the postmodern imagination.

In discussions of the media, irony is often claimed to pose a challenge to all forms of serious discourse. If everything is 'tongue-in-cheek', ideology may indeed become obsolete or at least moribund. But playful irony does not necessarily contest established power. Indeed, as Eagleton claims, 'such irony is more likely to play into the hands of the ruling powers than to discomfort them', acting as a seductive decoy to distract attention from the underlying ideological purpose (1991: 40). The so-called lads' magazines that became popular in Britain in the 1990s may, for example, have been more rather than less persuasive in their sexist impact by being apparently 'jokey' and non-serious in their approach. John B. Thompson also criticizes the attack on ideology for failing to attend to continuing social inequalities, however dazzling the spectacle of diversity in the postmodern world: 'diversity and difference are commonly embedded in social relations which are structured in systematically asymmetrical ways. We must not be so blinded by the spectacle of diversity that we are unable to see the structured inequalities of social life' (1990: 330–1).

Yet, if ideology can be demonstrated to have continuing usefulness, its relationship to power (in itself, a less than stable concept) needs to be spelled out. As Terry Eagleton (1991) warns, it is tempting but misleading to regard all forms of representation as ideological and to see ideology everywhere. He argues that ideology should be reserved for shared ways of thinking that have a specific interest in gaining power. On this distinction, nationalism in stateless nations would qualify as clearly ideological, because it seeks the establishment of power, whereas transcendental meditation in its current manifestations in western society would not, despite being based on an organized set of beliefs and practices. Only those frameworks of thinking with a strong motivation to confirm the status quo or change the structure of our social world satisfy the criteria. This sets a distinction between discourses that (merely) have a strong interest in being heard and those that particularly aim to produce specific political effects. Only the latter, in Eagleton's view, can be properly associated with power. Foucault, as we will see later, muddies these waters by associating power with both types of interest.

Despite their differences of approach, Eagleton and Foucault share the claim that ideologies (or discourses, in Foucault's terms) are not fixed and static, but constantly in process. Eagleton points out that even interests that appear in one context not to be ideological may become ideological in another. The range of cookery programmes on television may seem on the face of it to be relatively non-ideological, compared with news bulletins or documentaries, but their attitudes towards food, and their construction of eating and drinking as a form of discipline (healthy eating), or of risk (food poisoning), or of sensual pleasure may become ideological when they tap into fierce conflicts of interest between differing notions of freedom and consumerism. As Eagleton points out, 'ideology means more than just, say, the signifying practices associated by a society with food; it involves the relations between these signs and processes of political power' (1991: 28–9). The focus on context, and on the relation between signifying practices and power relations prevents any simple prejudging of ideological effect, and requires detailed and specific analysis of how meaning systems operate.

Eagleton differs from a number of other Marxist or neo-Marxist critics in his insistence that ideology is not synonymous with already-dominant systems of thinking. John B. Thompson, on the other hand, is particularly cogent in arguing that ideology should be reserved for those ways of thinking that legitimate dominance. Thompson claims that:

> . . . the concept of ideology can be used to refer to the ways in which meaning serves, in particular circumstances, to establish and sustain relations of power which are systematically asymmetrical – what I shall call 'relations of domination'. Ideology, broadly speaking, is *meaning in the service of power.*
>
> (1990: 7)

As Eagleton points out, and as Thompson himself acknowledges in his response to possible challenges to his approach, this excludes any non-dominant way of thinking that nevertheless has claims to power. Ecologists, anti-globalization protesters, feminists and gay rights advocates would all, on this reckoning, remain on the outside of ideology, despite their commitment to produce radical changes in social, political or economic structures. Eagleton prefers the definition of ideology offered by the political philosopher Martin Seliger: 'sets of ideas by which men [*sic*] posit, explain and justify ends and means of organised social action, and specifically political action, irrespective of whether such action aims to preserve, amend, uproot or rebuild a given social order' (cited in Eagleton, 1991, 6–7). Thompson accommodates the problem by contending that these are not ideologies, but '*contestatory symbolic forms* or, more specifically, . . . *incipient forms of the critique of ideology*' (1990: 68). Thompson's approach offers little scope for a contest *between* ideologies, although the concept of struggle, and consequently the possibility of change over time, is clearly built into his allowance that 'contestatory symbolic forms' act as means of undermining ideology.

Thompson's view of ideology seems unduly restrictive when related to the fragmented culture within which we live. Even though his notion of dominance is tied to the power structure within a particular society, ensuring, for example, that monarchism remains a dominant ideology in twenty-first-century Britain, popular definitions of dominance might also include 'favoured by a majority of the population', which would put Britain's monarchist credentials in some doubt, especially in certain parts of the country. Which frames of thinking are structured in dominance, which in contestatory mode becomes increasingly hard to unravel when so many different and often conflicting interest groups co-exist, intensifying the improbability of consensus. In relation to the media, these problems escalate, as the targeting of specific audiences or readers (what marketing people refer to as 'niche markets') increasingly replaces appeal to undifferentiated, broadly based groups. What counts as a 'dominant ideology' in magazines or television programmes that target a youth readership or audience will be very different from the 'dominant ideology' within society as a whole, especially if the subject matter relates to drugs or sex. Although we may all agree that certain ideologies are structured in dominance within western society and culture (consumerism and capitalism, for example), unanimity about a total taxonomy of dominant ideologies would break down under the pressure of differences of (at least) age, gender, class, ethnic and national identifications.

Within media texts, the ideologies predominantly being advanced are, then, by no means universally aligned with the ideologies structured in dominance within the general society. Once Stuart Hall's 'encoding/decoding' model of meaning production (1980) began to be applied to genres other than news and current affairs, it rapidly became clear that 'preferred readings' or 'dominant decodings' (reading the text in line with its own grain) would not always be consonant with dominant ideological stances, and, equally, 'aberrant' or 'oppositional decodings' (readings 'against the grain') could not be relied upon to challenge the status quo. When white Jewish comedian Sacha Baron Cohen poses as a black man and punctures the pomposity of his famous interviewees in Channel 4's *Da Ali G Show*, audience uncertainty about whether he is making fun of white people attempting to adopt black style, or making black people themselves the target of his mockery becomes part of the show's trademark. Identifying this programme's 'preferred reading' requires the high-wire skills of the trapeze artist and reduces to absurdity any suggestion that reading with the grain necessarily produces a decoding in line with dominant ideologies. Even in less extreme examples, most media texts offer a variety of ideological positions rather than a single 'preferred' reading. Eagleton's model of competing ideologies offers a more satisfactory framework for thinking this through than Thompson's search for ways of thinking that are structured in dominance.

Despite the differences between Terry Eagleton and John B. Thompson, little separates their analysis of the modes of operation of ideology. Thompson lists these as legitimation (through rationalization, universalization or narrativization), dissimulation, unification, fragmentation, and reification (1990: 60–7), whereas Eagleton refers to 'such devices as unification, spurious identification, naturalization, deception, self-deception, universalization and rationalization' (1991: 222). Both see dissimulation or deception (offering false promises) as part of the possible process, but not as the only technique available. In the wake of September 11th 2001, claims that terrorism could be extirpated by waging war laid claim to reasonableness (rationalization) and a unifying goal (unification) that promised apparent salvation. In the process, the necessarily ideological definitions of what constitutes 'terrorism' (defined as sporadic acts by fanatics, but not as premeditated state terror) were detached from any understanding of history (reification and naturalization) and consequently masked from view (dissimulation, deception/self-deception). Both critics stress the diversity and the invisibility (within the host cultures) of the tactics that ideology employs to gain our implicit consent. Although such tactics are clearly discursive, ideology theory presents them as persuasive formulations of preconceived ways of thinking, whereas discourse theory stresses their constitutive role.

While ideologies have tended to be most actively associated with informational genres of the media (news, current affairs, documentaries), their operation through appeals to pleasure has been prominently recognized in feminist-influenced criticism of both popular texts and audience responses. Ideologies exert power not through a process of coercion, but by appealing to our desires, our fantasies and our own sense of self-interest. Antonio Gramsci, the leading Italian Marxist thinker, pioneered the concept of 'hegemony' to explain the magnetic pull that ideology exerts to draw us within its circle. Ideology, for Gramsci as for Eagleton, emerges continually out of a struggle between competing coalitions of interest. His theory of hegemony crucially captures the effectiveness of forms of appeal that speak to our sense of expediency while masking their tendentiousness. The formulations of ideology supported by Gramsci and by Eagleton articulate clearly its relation to power, and yet acknowledge that a simple equation with dominance is insufficient. In his opposition to the rigidity of ideology, on the other hand, Foucault presupposes that ideology necessarily sustains relations of domination. While this brings his thinking into apparent line with Thompson's, he differs from Thompson in rejecting the concept of ideology because it fails to acknowledge that power is activated *through* discourse.

## FOUCAULT ON POWER, DISCOURSE AND KNOWLEDGE

The Enlightenment of the eighteenth century established a clear relationship between power and knowledge. The belief that reason and education guaranteed social progress fitted in with the increasing status of scientific method and became a repeated refrain in liberal philosophical writing. The British radical press of the nineteenth century, intent on extending literacy and political rights to a hitherto disenfranchised body of working-class people, adopted the slogan 'knowledge is power' and incorporated this into the masthead of the indomitable *Poor Man's Guardian*, which survived, despite repeated attempts to close it down, from 1831 to 1835. Adding 'discourse' into this mix may sound like a simple extension of the 'knowledge is power' paradigm. But, far from extending the Enlightenment model, Foucault radically destabilizes it. For the Enlightenment, knowledge was scientifically verifiable, rationally accessible and 'a body of knowledge' that existed independently of our means of communicating it. The contest for power was stimulated by its unequal distribution. Foucault, on the other hand, as we have already seen, denied the ontological status of knowledge. Knowledge, according to him, has no prior state of being, lying in wait for fairer apportioning: it is itself always and continually under (re)construction. Discourse, consequently, is what produces knowledge, and cannot be regarded as a simple means of expressing or communicating already-formed knowledge to others. Instead of conceiving of knowledge as an *object*, Foucault prefers to see it as a *process*, continually evolving through the practice of discourse.

Foucault developed his thinking about the integral relationship between knowledge, discourse and power in the first volume of his *The History of Sexuality* (1981 (1976)), but his ideas about 'knowledge' had already been formulated in his earlier work. By 'knowledge' Foucault was, significantly, referring not to the individual's capacity to understand, but to the continually evolving conceptual frameworks that are necessary to enable understanding. The distinction is one that is readily evident in French, but concealed in the English translation where 'knowledge' becomes a single substitute for two distinct terms: '*connaissance*' (referring to the processes through which we come to know, and therefore implicating consciousness and subjectivity) and '*savoir*' (referring to frameworks of ideas within which understanding can occur). It is important to understand that it is with the latter that Foucault is concerned (1972: 182–4). Although Foucault stresses that these frameworks are perpetually undergoing change, his emphasis on these, rather than on mental processing, contributes to the impersonal and abstract quality of his thinking. In interpretations of the media text, *connaissance*, with its emphasis on cognition and the agency of the reader, has assumed much greater importance, driving the work on audience studies and semiotics, and some approaches to discourse analysis. One of the mismatches between established methods of media analysis and Foucault's work lies, then, in this differing conceptualization of how knowledge occurs. While the role of human cognition and decision-making is played down, Foucault's approach has the advantage of encouraging us to consider how the frameworks of understanding that the media create or reproduce may operate beyond the media also. As the previous chapter indicated, the tendency to see the media as the principal and most powerful originators of discourse obscures this element of interplay.

Foucault reconceptualizes power by insisting that it does not operate by repression alone. A model of power as coercive had been favoured within Marxist thinking, although both Louis Althusser and Antonio Gramsci modified this in varying ways. The Foucauldian argument that power is not synonymous with force is less unique than might first appear, but Foucault's refusal to identify any particular institution or set of practices as a constant source of power distinguishes him from both Marxist and neo-Marxist thinkers. Whatever the disagreements between the latter, they remained united in striving to pinpoint the source of power in order to identify how revolutionary change could best be accomplished. The power of the state and the contested power of class relationships were especially insistent refrains within the Marxist canon.

Foucault rejects any model of power that suggests a universally identifiable point of origin, singling out for particular criticism 'a power whose model is essentially juridical, centred on nothing more than the statement of the law and the operation of taboos' (1981: 85). Exploring what he refers to as the 'polymorphous techniques of power' (1981: 11), he traces, for instance, how historical incitement to talk about sexuality across a variety of domains, including the confessional, medicine and educational practice, encouraged an 'immense verbosity' that drew its *frisson* of excitement precisely from the western world's simultaneously repressive attitude towards this subject (1981: 33). Foucault envisages power as being 'exercised from innumerable points, in the interplay of nonegalitarian and mobile relations' (1981: 94), 'wherein far-reaching, but never completely stable, effects of domination are produced' (1981: 102). This lack of stability means that power and resistance to power are not conceived as opposites, statically ranged against each other, but as fluid force relations that group together, temporarily and uneasily, in oppositional formations: 'where there is power, there is resistance, and yet, or rather consequently, this resistance is never in a position of exteriority in relation to power' (1981: 95).

By proposing the inextricable connection between power and resistance to power, Foucault ruptures the conventional model of polarization between them. His writings offer a number of examples of responses to social phenomena that can be defined neither as intrinsically repressive nor as inherently liberating. He claims, for example, that the rapid rise of nineteenth-century discourses about homosexuality and 'sexual perversions' within professions such as psychiatry and jurisprudence, while intended to control these behaviours, had the effect of enabling discussion of non-traditional sexual desires and practices in terms that challenged the status quo (1981: 101). The apparently repressive was, paradoxically, also liberating. Equally, an appearance of liberation may be deceptive. To take an example that does not feature in Foucault's writing, the rapid growth of gay clubs and pubs, and gay programming on television from the 1980s onwards may on one level seem to be challenging heterosexual power, but at the same time it helped to control the radical potency of homosexuality as a social force. Homosexuality's threat to heterosexuality is diffused and diverted by being associated with the familiar and positively regarded values of consumerism and lifestyle identification. As a consequence, people who are not gay are likely to believe that attitudes to gay people are much more tolerant, liberal and accepting than they actually are, in institutional and legal contexts. Sources of power, then, are not automatically self-evident, according to Foucault, and we need to be alert to a variety of potential origins. Foucault's favoured metaphors for the working of power are those of a net or web: 'power is employed and exercised through a net-like organisation. And not only do individuals circulate between its threads; they are always in the position of simultaneously undergoing and exercising this power' (Gordon, 1980: 98).

Despite outlining these general principles of power's operation, Foucault argues against a generalized theory of power (just as he did with discourse), supporting instead an 'analytics' of power that involves detailed and contingent analysis of specific instances of power's mode of operation (1981: 82). Discourse, as the means through which power and knowledge intersect in Foucault's thinking, plays a vital part in this process. Since power operations cannot be stabilized into binary oppositions, Foucault's model precludes any possibility of ranging one set of powerful or 'dominant' discourses against another set of relatively powerless 'alternative' or 'oppositional' ones. Foucault's warning is explicit on this matter: 'we must not imagine a world of discourse divided between accepted discourse and excluded discourse, or between the dominant discourse and the dominated one' (1981: 100). On the other hand, Foucault acknowledges a need to trace the operation of power in individual instances, and to recognize the process of realignment that is continually going on between these.

Foucault is impatient with the notion that 'recuperation' is the inevitable consequence of a clash between opposing discourses. This concept, together with the cognate notions of 'assimilation' or 'co-option', implies that dominant discourses disarm their opponents by taking on board surface aspects of their formulation without making any genuine concessions to alternative ways of thinking. The feminist concept of women's liberation, in the hands of advertising discourse, becomes reduced, for example, to the freedom to wear sexy underwear, or to save time on the washing up. The group of cultural critics known as the Frankfurt School had been especially frustrated by the inability of alternative discourses to be heard on their own terms. Charlotte Brunsdon agrees that the sting of the oppositional discourse is lost as it is incorporated within dominant ways of talking and thinking, making it misleadingly 'appear as if change has been effected' (1986: 120), but she differs from the Frankfurt theorists in arguing that this process at least allows alternative discourses an airing, and may therefore promote gradual change in popular consciousness.

Foucault rejects the notion of incorporation as too simplistic: 'I don't agree at all with this talk about "recuperation"' (Gordon, 1980: 56). To him, 'recuperation' implies that the dominant discourse swallows up the alternative, eradicating its troublesome ability to fight back, and denying the endlessness of the play for power. Yet, despite his protestation, the example Foucault provides appears remarkably akin to the assimilationist model. Commenting on the rise of society's anxiety about masturbation in the eighteenth century, he notes that 'the response on the side of power' was as much to 'control by stimulation' as 'by repression'. Instead of clamping down on the practice, there was eventually 'an economic ... exploitation of eroticisation, from sun-tan products to pornographic films' (Gordon, 1980: 57). In other words, by distracting erotic attention on to the plane of consumption the sting of a sexual practice that might have posed a challenge to procreation-directed heterosexuality was removed more effectively than would have been possible by repressive means. Where Foucault parts company with critics such as Marcuse is in recognizing 'the indefiniteness of the struggle', and its continuation into perpetuity as 'each move by one adversary' is met by 'an answering one by the other' (Gordon, 1980: 57). Terms such as 'co-option' or 'recuperation' appear to Foucault to freeze this process and consequently to be misleading about the workings of power.

Foucault's thinking on 'recuperation' provides clues about the model of 'ideology' implicit in his writing, and helps to explain why he found the concept so unhelpful. 'Ideology', interpreted as Marxist 'false consciousness', suggests, he argues, an imagined ideal of 'true knowledge' or 'science' but this can only be misleading since even 'science' is discursively constructed. As we have seen, Foucault allows that 'true knowledge' may exist in principle, but it is inaccessible in any pure form to the human mind. Ideology is also suspect, in Foucault's thinking, because it carries the Marxist baggage of being merely superstructural, and therefore very much secondary in significance to economic realities. As such, ideology can contribute nothing to an understanding of how power operates strategically and tactically: 'the longer I continue, the more it seems to me that the formation of discourses and the genealogy of knowledge need to be analysed, not in terms of types of consciousness, modes of perception and forms of ideology, but in terms of tactics and strategies of power' (Gordon, 1980: 77). By linking consciousness, perception and ideology as undesirables, Foucault refuses a model of knowledge that involves negotiation between the individual as subject and a pre-existing body of ideas.

In finding reasons for sidelining ideology, Foucault reduces the possibility of distinguishing between different types of power. The charge of relativism, or treating as equal operations of power that are very different in their consequences, seems difficult to refute. Critics of Foucault have been quick to point out that the logic of his own position is one that even he fails to sustain. As Terry Eagleton asserts, nobody is a relativist to the extent of 'believing that any view of a particular topic is as good as any other' (1991: 169), and even Foucault's disdain for rationalist principles 'does not appear to have prevented him from holding that imprisoning homosexuals is not the most enlightened way of relating to them' (1991: 169). By focusing on strategies and tactics of power, Foucault avoids considering the comparative effectiveness of different types of power in shaping not just knowledge but material change. His ideas also leave us with another conundrum. If power is everywhere, and resistance to power accompanies its every move, how are we to produce any form of analysis or evaluation of the harm or benefits that might ensue from its exercise? While Foucault may be astute in describing the mechanisms of power, he leaves us strangely adrift in reaching any conclusions about its political consequences.

However important it is to stress that our own discursive formulations in everyday interactions help to construct versions of reality, and contribute to the development of knowledge, even Foucault would be unlikely to argue that we possess the same degree of power in this respect as the media. The gap between the media and 'ordinary individuals' in terms of power may be narrowing marginally, thanks to the Internet, but it is still substantial and significant. John Fiske's optimistic notion of the 'semiotic democracy' of active and potentially powerful readers of popular texts similarly falls into the trap of ignoring different levels of powerfulness (1987: 95–9). However actively we may engage with popular culture, and forge our own versions of this in line with our own interests, our power becomes political and ideological only if we translate this into specific campaigns. The 'resistant reader' may just as probably want to push the media further towards rigorous control as to challenge existing strategies of power. Ironically, indeed, the most insistent and powerful audience lobby in relation to the media has come from the political and moral right, not from John Fiske's imagined resisters of state and media power.

Foucault's inflation of discourse 'to the point where it imperializes the whole world, eliding the distinction between thought and material reality' (Eagleton, 1991: 219) also makes political criticism difficult. How are we to argue for change in the media's operation if we are ensnared within the same discursive net, and if we can never escape its meshes? Although all discourses communicate knowledge, it is mistaken to elevate discourse to the position of being the sole originator of knowledge. We also arrive at knowledge through experience, through observation and through the evaluation of one discourse against another. Our experience is, of course, filtered through discourse, but it is not contained by it. As Terry Eagleton acutely points out, when the galley slave protests about his exploitation, that exploitation takes material forms and is not simply a product of discourse (1991: 213). The way we think culturally about the ageing process, likewise, will influence our personal experience of this, but so too will our degree of wealth, our state of health, and our access to leisure or social facilities. While Foucault tends, as we will see, to view contests between discourses as an ongoing, abstract struggle, in everyday life we actively participate in deciding for ourselves which of the available discourses appear to make most sense to us. Without some capacity for agency, as the previous chapter suggested, it is difficult to see how change in dominant ways of thinking can occur.

Foucault is, however, helpful in insisting that models that assume a binary opposition between 'dominant' and 'alternative' discourses simplify the unpredictability of ongoing contests for power and influence. Foucault's dislike of binary oppositions also usefully reminds us that it is facile to assume, as media academics sometimes do, that all 'alternative' discourses have right on their side, and that all 'dominant discourses' are necessarily suspect. While we might happily concur with this perspective when dealing with environmentalists' challenges to capitalist indifference to the future of the planet, we are less likely to support this as an all-embracing model if the dominant discourse is one supporting freedom of expression, and if the alternative is driven by neo-Nazi or racist sentiments. Foucault fails, however, to indicate how we are to evaluate competing discourses once we remove the binary scaffolding. The case study that follows exemplifies the advantages of Foucault's approach for media analysis, but also illustrates this difficulty. The problem of evaluation is one that I will return to in the final sections of this chapter where I develop the case for retaining a concept of ideology alongside that of discourse.

## GREENPEACE VERSUS SHELL: A FOUCAULDIAN CASE?

Between 1995 and 1998, the oil company Shell and the environmental campaigning group Greenpeace fought for control of public opinion over plans to sink a decommissioned oil platform (the *Brent Spar*) in the North Sea. Greenpeace scientists disputed Shell's argument that this was the optimum means of disposal, claiming pollution and damage to marine life. The discursive battle between them erupted into a classic contest for power, with Shell appearing to have the advantage economically and politically. Yet power, as the Foucauldian model suggests, operates in less predictable ways, especially when distilled through the media with their own discursive priorities. The pressure of deadlines, and the need to ensure that television news items can be structured as compelling mini-narratives accompanied by gripping footage, tipped the argument initially in Greenpeace's favour. Using its considerable skills and increased resources devoted to news management (Anderson, 1997: 85, 111–12), Greenpeace targeted key media with graphic video news releases of its occupation of the *Brent Spar* platform. Direct action of this kind has long been part of Greenpeace's consciousness-raising tactics, having been employed successfully in a number of earlier conflicts (see Anderson, 1997: 89 and Hansen, 1993: 160–4). The attraction of Greenpeace's video news release to television allowed the environmentalist lobby to steal an early advantage in the discursive contest with Shell.

As several commentators have observed, this was not uniquely the result of Greenpeace's communicative persuasiveness. Timing and the pre-eminence of particular cultural discourses about 'risk' were also important. Anders Hansen, in a study of the coverage of Greenpeace in the British press between 1987 and 1991, traces the organization's expertise in linking its campaigns to moments of heightened news awareness of environmental concerns (1993: 171). In the case of the *Brent Spar* issue, public opinion had already been turning against Shell because of its publicized disregard of the interests of the Ogoni people in Nigeria. This specific incident consequently resonated with wider public concerns about the ethics of large corporations. The prevalence of a 'David versus Goliath' narrative framework, repeatedly echoed in journalistic and academic coverage of the *Brent Spar* episode (see, for example, Hobsbawm, 1995; Moore, 1995; Anderson, 1997: 6) emphasizes how culturally susceptible we are to the belief that the 'big guy' is likely to be a 'baddie' by virtue of his unfair advantage alone. If this combination of factors produced fertile ground for Greenpeace to sow its seeds of doubt, it was nevertheless a tribute to its news management skills that a well-orchestrated boycott of Shell products quickly ensued, especially in Germany, where Shell reputedly began to lose almost a third of its usual income (Anderson, 1997: 111).

More surprisingly, Greenpeace succeeded in continuing its onslaught on Shell even once inaccuracies in its own scientific evidence came to light. Three months after Greenpeace made its initial claims about contamination of the environment, it admitted that it had overestimated the probable degree of pollution involved. This confirmed the view of many independent scientists who had maintained that, even from an environmental point of view, Shell's plans might indeed have been an acceptable option. Yet, despite the public relations advantage now accruing to Shell, it launched a major review of its intentions, consulted widely with the public, and finally decided in January 1998 to opt for a recycling scheme to turn the dismantled platform into a quayside for ferries on the Norwegian coast. As the Shell spokespeople appearing on a BBC2 programme, *Sparring Partners* (31 January 1998), implied, this decision was based only in part on engineering issues, evaluation of risk and environmental aspects. Belief that a return to the disposal at sea option would be unacceptable to the public provided the primary motivation. In this sense, Greenpeace continued to maintain its discursive lead.

What is clear from this case study is that Shell's status and financial resources gave it no automatic power to control media discourses or to harness public opinion to its side. A powerful and dominant institution, supported in its original policy decision by the British government, was obliged to spend considerably more than its original £4.5 million budget (the estimated cost for dumping at sea) in order to find a solution that would restore some of the gloss on its public image. This example challenges theories of media–source relations, which suggest that the media give automatic preference to the views of economically or socially dominant groups or institutions. The voices of the establishment, dubbed 'primary definers' (Hall *et al.*, 1978: 57–60), are claimed to have first rights of access to the media and consequently to have priority in setting the discourse in which events are framed. In the 1980s John Hartley acknowledged, in his reference to 'accessed voices' (1982: 111–15), that the media grant access to a wider variety of spokespeople, but also emphasized that control over how their remarks are used rests with media producers accustomed to equating public status with authority. Philip Schlesinger (1990) has called for revision of these models to accommodate the more varied patterns that occur. He claims that earlier models ignore potential tensions and disagreements *between* primary definers, and neglect variations in their degree of access to the media. As later chapters will indicate, disagreements between scientists or medical experts on the safety of food or medicines often lead to contests between them as 'definers' of knowledge. Earlier accounts also play down the media's ability to put 'primary definers' on the defensive about their own definitions. The contest for authoritative interpretation of events is, in Schlesinger's view, more akin to the Foucauldian model of power than to Thompson's notion of a stable and definable dominant ideology that will always win through. Schlesinger's claim that '*primary definition becomes an achievement rather than a wholly structurally predetermined outcome*' (1990: 79) acknowledges the element of unpredictability in the process of establishing discursive control, especially in an era when spin doctors, campaigning groups and corporate lobbyists struggle to set the media agenda and establish their own perspectives as the most authoritative. As Schlesinger recognizes, this involves each party second-guessing their opponents' game moves, in order to pre-empt their effectiveness (1990: 82).

In the case of the Greenpeace/Shell contest, Schlesinger's approach makes superior sense than the more static and predictable 'primary definer' thesis. Shell's efforts in the years between 1995 and 1998 were concentrated in combating Greenpeace's influence and in trying to fend off negative reactions from environmentalists and public opinion. Schlesinger draws on the perspectives of media sources as an antidote to what he calls 'media centrism', but he pays less attention than may now be necessary to how both journalists and sources react to what they construe as public opinion. Shell was less yielding authority to Greenpeace than to the impact that it perceived Greenpeace to have made on public thinking. In order to retrieve its commercial position, it was also obliged to counter Greenpeace's challenge on the environmental lobby's terms, ensuring an ongoing struggle where 'each move by one adversary' would be met by 'an answering one by the other' (Gordon, 1980: 57). The conclusion to this conflict became a pragmatic response to a public relations challenge rather than a decisive assertion of rights.

This case study reveals interesting points of contact with Foucault's ideas on power, knowledge and discourse. As the events unfolded, it became increasingly impossible to distinguish scientific 'facts' about the merits of different options from the discursive construction of knowledge about these. Any simple distinction between a prior, knowable reality and discourse was quickly blurred by the media's role as the primary source of information for most interested people. Shell's ability to control the terms of the debate was also foiled by the ease with which Greenpeace could play on public inclinations to believe that any 'David and Goliath' narrative justifiably grants the moral prerogative to the underdog. Foucault's warnings about the unpredictability of power and its multiple points of operation find a clear echo here.

Yet there is also a danger in equating discursive power with political power. Without a concept of ideology, the distinction that needs to be maintained between these becomes fuzzy. In media discourse, on this occasion, Greenpeace led the dance, but this does not mean that the position of these two organizations shifted radically, even in media terms. Shell still commands respectful coverage in the plentiful business pages in the broadsheet press, while Greenpeace has to mount expensive and sometimes colourful campaigns to earn even sporadic attention from the mainstream media. Environmental coverage has increased marginally since Mrs Thatcher, as Prime Minister, gave this non-dominant ideology respectability in a speech in 1988, but no newspaper or television bulletin grants it the regular attention accorded to business news. Shell in addition had a great deal of self-interest in granting some ground to Greenpeace. This was essential not just to restore public confidence, but to maintain consistency with its own advertising campaigns which, from the early 1980s, had emphasized its concern for the environment. The discursive choice manifest in Shell's response to Greenpeace was not entirely, then, due to outside pressures. While the discursive battle waged over this incident may have shifted the balance of power between the two contenders to a minimal extent, the ideological effect of the challenge was less marked. The need to retain scepticism about the synergy and overlap between discourse and ideology is the focus of the final sections of this chapter.

## IDEOLOGY AND DISCOURSE

The evolution of theories of discourse and ideology has tended to marshal critics in support of one or other concept, leaving only a few to consider the possible interconnections between these. Although Foucault, as Sara Mills observes, developed his thinking about discourse in 'open discussion and dialogue with the term ideology' (1997: 32), his preference, as we have seen, is unmistakably weighted in favour of discourse. Other critics, anxious to prop up ideological analysis, have been equally dismissive of discourse theory. John B. Thompson, for example, refers to discourse only in the context of 'discourse analysis': as a methodology for exploring meaning production, not as a theoretical approach to the fundamental links between knowledge and power. Those few critics who have reviewed the connections between discourse and ideology take differing positions on the degree to which discourse is to be regarded as constructing or merely giving expression to ideology, but they do also share some perspectives.

Most agree that ideology is a broader concept than discourse, and that a mapping of discourse (as communication) on to ideology (as abstract thought) cannot be simply conducted. Terry Eagleton, for example, sees ideology as the 'effect' of a variety of potential discourses, with 'bourgeois ideology' being produced through (amongst others) discourses of property rights, the law, and class assumptions in everyday speech (1991: 194). For Teun van Dijk, ideologies emphatically '*cannot be reduced to discourse*' (1998: 317) since they also become manifest in other social practices (such as institutional structures or legislation). With some ambivalence about the role of discourse, he sees it as contributing to both 'the expression and reproduction of ideologies' (1998: 192). The notion of 'expressing' ideology departs substantially from the Foucauldian view that discourse constitutes ways of thinking, but by claiming that it also 'reproduces' ideologies, van Dijk at the same time refuses discourse a purely passive role. When he comments explicitly on discourse, van Dijk tends to downplay its constructionist role in favour of its expressive dimension, but when he goes into detail about how discourse operates he allows it more power to influence the formation of ideologies.

Both critics also assert the need to discriminate between discourses that operate ideologically, and those that do not. This requires attention to context and communicative effect, and cannot be determined by inspecting the discourse in isolation. Van Dijk particularly emphasizes the role of social cognition in both the production and the consumption of discourses. He also comments, significantly for media analysis, on the influence of 'context models' (our expectations about particular modes of delivering discourse, such as specific media outlets) (1998: 83–6). Terry Eagleton welcomes a concept of discourse that gives material form to ideology by embedding it in sign systems. This prevents ideology from masquerading as an abstract and idealist concept that resides in the vague field of 'consciousness' (1991: 194). At the same time, he rejects the subjection of every aspect of our existence to 'discourse'. As we have already seen in the 'revisiting ideology' section of this chapter, Eagleton reserves ideological resonance for discourses intent on producing a strong impact on the ways in which we organize our social and political structures. Both critics would argue, for example, that 'confessional modes of discourse' (identified by Foucault (1981) as contributing to the policing of sexuality in previous centuries) cannot be assumed to operate in an identical ideological manner in twenty-first-century women's magazines and on contemporary talk shows. Sara Mills, indeed, suggests that confessional discourse can become a means of resisting oppression by 'locating oneself within a larger interest group or political group (such as feminists, or working-class women or lesbian women)' (1997: 82).

Van Dijk's approach is helpful in allowing a role for human agency in the reproduction of ideologies through discourse, by stressing the processes of social cognition. His definition of discourse is, however, limited in being confined to verbal expression and interaction. Although this is a common approach amongst linguists, as I outlined in the Introduction, van Dijk justifies his exclusion of image and other semiotic codes by arguing that 'there is no semiotic code as explicit and as articulate in the *direct* expression of meanings, knowledge, opinions and various social beliefs as natural language (and of course in various sign languages)' (1998: 192). Why directness in the expression of meanings should be a necessary qualification for discourse is less clear, especially as van Dijk admits that images can be more persuasive than words. As the case study on racism that follows makes clear, the role of image in the construction of discourses is too crucial in the contemporary media to be sidelined in this manner. Racism, as an ideology, has appeared through a number of different discursive manifestations. These, as van Dijk points out (1992), include the 'denial of racism', leading to an interesting philosophical dilemma for an analysis that focuses on discourse alone. In the examples to be considered (coverage of the O.J. Simpson trial and its aftermath in the United States, and the media's belated response to the murder of Stephen Lawrence, a black teenager, in Britain), the importance of retaining a concept of ideology alongside that of discourse will be examined.

## DISCOURSE AND DENIAL: THE CASE OF RACISM

In the 1990s, racism surfaced as a significant issue for the media in both Britain and the United States. In the aftermath of the Rodney King beating by members of the Los Angeles Police Department, captured on videotape and relayed to the nation in 1992, the O.J. Simpson murder trial in 1994/1995 reactivated debates about discrimination on the grounds of race in the administration of American justice. In Britain, concerns of a similar nature centred on the police investigation into the murder of a black 18 year old, Stephen Lawrence, in April 1993. While media interest in this case was slow to emerge, it eventually became sufficiently prominent to turn Stephen Lawrence into a household name and to prompt the government to set up an official inquiry into the police's handling of his murder. Despite the differences between these cases, they both raise questions about the sufficiency of analysing media coverage in terms of discourse alone. In evaluating their positioning on racism, especially, reference to ideology becomes inevitable. Borrowing Eagleton's model of ideology as the effect of a variety of discourses, racist ideology is perpetuated through multiple discourses, many of which work to obscure the attribution of superior value to whiteness and the various forms of discrimination that ensue. Many of these discourses operate through visual rather than verbal conventions. For example, differing shooting styles in film or still photography have been used to celebrate the purity of whiteness while animalizing the black body (for further discussion of this, see Richard Dyer's discussion of lighting techniques in *White* (1997), and Mercer (1988) and Carrington (2001–2) on photographing the black male body). While it makes sense to place discourse at the centre of an analysis of processes of signification, reference to ideology reminds us that discourses contributing to racist perspectives are only part of a larger picture of institutional and organizational behaviours that impact on people's lives in direct and tangible forms (through, for example, income levels, educational and life opportunities, housing policy and the legal system).

In western cultures where there is a growing sensitivity to 'race issues', racist discourses rarely now appear with full-frontal blatancy. Instead, as van Dijk (1992) points out, they tend to operate via the denial (explicit or implicit) of racism. As a result, ideological analysis that seeks direct evidence of 'racism' in media texts may be disappointed. In the O.J. Simpson case, a contest between 'black' and 'white' perspectives was highly visible, whereas in the Lawrence case this was masked from white view. Competing constructions of 'knowledge' were differently articulated in the media in both instances. For these to be revealing of macro-structures of power, analysis needs to move beyond the particular discursive contest to an evaluation of the thinking and behaviour that constitute an ideology of racism. As Robert Miles argues, 'the expression of racism is an integral component of a wider, historical process of racialisation which is interlinked with exclusionary practices and with the expression of other forms of exclusionary ideology' (1989: 98).

The arrest of the African-American celebrity O.J. Simpson as suspect for the double murder of Nicole Brown Simpson and Ron Goldman in Brentwood, California, in June 1994 was in itself a media event. The now legendary chase of the white Ford Bronco in which he seemed to be attempting to escape was watched live by an estimated 75–100 million viewers, some of whom were also simultaneously present on the scene (Fiske, 1996: 255–64; Glynn, 2000: 89; McLaughlin, 1998: 71). This spectacle already set in process the racializing of responses, as African-American spectators found themselves caught between incompatible viewing positions. As one black man interviewed by John Fiske put it, 'My eye was in the helicopter with the police ... but my heart was in the Bronco with O.J.' (cited in Fiske, 1996: 260). White viewers, on the other hand, had the opportunity, as Fiske sees it, to identify more wholeheartedly with the pleasures of the panopticon vision, untroubled by the negative associations of surveillance common among heavily monitored groups (1996: 259–60).

When O.J. Simpson's 474-day trial got under way, this racializing process was accentuated. Opinion polls in the course of the trial demonstrated that white Americans overwhelmingly thought Simpson to be guilty of murdering his ex-wife and her friend, while African-Americans were equally strongly inclined to believe in his innocence. In the aftermath of the verdict these convictions strengthened (Fiske, 1996: 267). Particular controversy surrounded taped evidence, made available towards the end of the court proceedings, of the overt racism of detective Mark Fuhrman, who was accused by defence attorney Johnnie Cochran of planting crucial evidence against O.J. The charge of framing an African-American suspect was one many black Americans found instantly credible, while white commentators accused Cochran of 'playing the race card' to his team's advantage. When Simpson was found not guilty of the murders by the criminal court in October 1995 (he was found culpable following a private prosecution in the civil court a year later), exultation or despair at the verdict split largely along racial lines.

Media discourses were inflected by further considerations. Since viewers had access to the trial as an unfolding spectacle on CNN and Court TV, the key players were performing not merely to those present in the courtroom, but to the much wider audience of the viewing public. Dramatic timing, humour, visual symbolism, playful performance, were used by both sides in an attempt to gain advantage in the argument. In this sense, the presence of the media helped to shape the very performance that was then being 'reported'. Equally, the media were aware that whatever commentaries they offered had to be consistent with what the audience was seeing. While the media could not ignore the role of racial issues in this trial, they frequently subordinated this to other discursive constructions, particularly of class and of gender. For the tabloid press, O.J. Simpson hovered between being seen as a victim (hunted by an unfriendly police force) or as a celebrity exploiting his position, and justifiably now being cut down to size (Glynn, 2000: 73). The tabloids, together with popular talk shows, also pitted alternative forms of knowledge against science to question the court's reliance on DNA evidence. As Glynn indicates, the evidence of psychic John Monti was especially deployed to question the implication of O.J. Simpson in the murder (2000: 69). Domestic abuse surfaced to a limited extent in media accounts of the trial, as evidence of O.J. Simpson's earlier beatings of his former wife emerged. A recording played in court of Nicole summoning the emergency services as she was being terrorized by O.J. in 1993 served as a stark reminder of the gendered violence at the heart of this case. But media attention to domestic abuse, where it occurred, tended to ignore the 'mutually constitutive' nature of gendered and racial abuse, thereby proposing for black women a choice between racial solidarity or antagonism to domestic violence (McLaughlin, 1998: 85).

The predominantly white, 'respectable' American media were obliged to acknowledge the degree to which this criminal trial had come to be seen as the trial of a black man for the murder of a white woman (in the mythologizing of this narrative, with its appeal to deep-seated fears about miscegenation and the black rape of white women, the death of Ron Goldman was also marginalized). Race was consequently a profiled issue, but through the eyes of a predominantly white perspective. The racial composition of the jury (overwhelmingly black) drew extensive comment. Johnnie Cochran's 'playing of the race card' both depended on the credibility (to a post-Rodney King white audience) of elements of racism within the police, and on perceptions that 'playing the race card' implies 'trying to gain advantage for black rather than white perspectives'. Perceived through white eyes, Cochran was at times accused of 'inverse racism', which, as will become clear below, is one of the standard techniques for denying racism.

The credibility of police racism was also contained. Neither the Rodney King case nor the evidence presented in the O.J. Simpson trial served in media reports to suggest endemic racism. Instead, the individualizing of the problem (especially laid on the shoulders of Mark Fuhrman in the O.J. Simpson case) supported a white interpretation of sporadic difficulties that denied a systemic problem. The racial elements of this trial and its verdict could, in this manner, be partly admitted without involving a wider interrogation of the racism of society. As John Fiske comments, 'the media . . . consistently constructed the racial question as an exclusively Black one' (1996: 272). If corroborating evidence were needed that white society (or at least its male half) was ultimately untroubled by the case, it lies in the continuing fascination with accounts of the trial and the background to it, the growth of an industry of joke-telling around it, and the chilling fact that 'in 1994, some of the most popular Halloween costumes in Los Angeles featured the likenesses of O.J. and Nicole' (McLaughlin, 1998: 72).

Stephen Lawrence's murder and its aftermath differed from the O.J. Simpson case in a number of key respects. Instead of celebrity involvement, the central players were distinguished by their ordinariness. Stephen's death arose not from the intensity of a personal relationship turned sour, but from an act that would have been totally arbitrary but for the involvement of racial hatred. Whereas Nicole and O.J. could both be variously demonized in aspects of media coverage because of their association with drugs and their allegedly voracious sexual appetites, even the scandalmongering British tabloid press could find no grounds for disparaging Stephen or his family. In contrast to the ready-made ingredients of tragic drama with the added spice of thriller attaching to the death of Nicole Brown Simpson and the suspicion of O.J.'s involvement, there was no obvious narrative or dramatic framework into which to slot the murder of Stephen Lawrence. While the murder of Nicole and her friend received instant media attention, Stephen Lawrence's murder activated the interest of the British media only after a lapse of almost four years. Yet, despite these differences, the media's difficulties with the growing implication of racism in both the murder itself and the police behaviour following the attack echo the Simpson case.

As Teun van Dijk explains, the media have moved away from overt expressions of racism (visible in earlier periods, as Hartmann and Husband (1974) demonstrate) and increasingly engage instead in tactics that amount to a 'denial of racism' (1992). In the case of Stephen Lawrence's death in April 1993, the denial was initially almost total in the mainstream media, with scant recognition beyond the black press of the significance of another racist murder on the streets of Britain. There was nothing unusual about this. Indeed, given the number of racially motivated murders taking place in Britain around the same time, the puzzle is more why this particular case was singled out for eventual media attention. Police pursuit of the likely suspects was dilatory. Belated arrests were made, but those accused were either found not guilty or were never taken to court because the evidence against them was claimed to be insufficient. A private prosecution initiated by the family also failed. In February 1997, almost four years after the murder, an inquest jury finally returned the verdict that Lawrence had been unlawfully killed and was the victim of a 'completely unprovoked racist attack by five white youths'. It was only at this point that media apathy was replaced by intensive coverage. The following day (14 February 1997) the *Daily Mail* ran its surprising front-page spread accusing five white youths of murdering Stephen Lawrence. Challenging the accused to sue if they were innocent, the *Daily Mail* risked legal retribution for breaching Contempt of Court legislation. The British media now rushed to give unprecedented coverage to a declaredly racist attack: between 1997 and 1999 at least three major television documentaries, a drama-documentary and the first edition of ITV's new current affairs series *Tonight* filled the earlier gap, alongside extensive newspaper comment. Whether the discursive strategies deployed in marking this apparent change of heart helped to contest racist ideologies is a different matter.

On the same day as the *Daily Mail* ran its front-page 'MURDERERS' allegation, its editorial took care to avoid endorsing the view that police behaviour following the murder had amounted to 'racism'. Two charges had been advanced by the family, their lawyer and the Anti-Racist Alliance who were supporting their campaign: first, that on the night of Stephen's murder the police had wasted time pursuing their suspicions that Duwayne Brooks, the friend who was with Stephen when he was attacked, and Stephen himself were involved in criminal activity; and, second, that the police had been exceptionally slow to follow up leads that might have led to early arrests of the suspects. Both charges were later upheld by the Macpherson Inquiry, set up by the government in 1998 to examine police procedures (*The Stephen Lawrence Inquiry Report*, 1999). In the *Mail*'s editorial, however, a variety of tactical devices were used to ensure that the emerging discourse was one of a miscarriage of justice, but not of racism.

Amongst the techniques used to deny racism van Dijk includes positive self-presentation (making a charge of racism implausible), mitigation of the problem (defining it not as racism, but as some more minor and treatable difficulty), and distancing from any association with racism or charges of racism. All were visible in the *Mail*'s comments. Headed 'A tragic failure of British justice', the emphasis was on precisely that: the inability of the judicial system to deliver justice to a wronged family. This, the *Mail* suggests, 'diminishes us all', implying the centrality of principles of justice to British national identity. More subtly, the paper presents charges of racism as pathological, both in defining the accused youths as being '*almost insane* with hatred of people they call "Pakis and coons"' and in approving the coroner's verdict that 'society must increase its efforts to rid itself of the *paranoia of racism* and its intolerance' [my italics] (14 February 1997). Right-thinking *Mail* readers cannot, then, be aligned with such views. Although the paper does cite the judgement of the inquest jury that Stephen Lawrence was killed in a 'completely unprovoked racist attack', the editorial diminishes the seriousness of this verdict by emphasizing the peculiarly thuggish characteristics of the attackers. They are variously described as a 'gang', 'a pack of bigots' and as 'moronic thugs who make a habit of racial abuse'. By particularizing their extremism, worries about more endemic racism in society can be allayed. In a distancing move, the editorial also disputes the allegation of racism made against the police by Mrs Lawrence, while still appearing to respect her position. Her 'lash[ing] out' is attributed to her grief, and is seen as both 'misplaced', and yet wholly understandable. The paper further undermines the plausibility of accusations of endemic racism by transforming the Lawrences into an archetypal *Daily Mail* family, upholding values of hard work, aspiration and decency.

The sharply contrasting pictorial representations of the Lawrence family and of the accused youths became central tropes in producing a narrative of good/justice as against evil/contempt for justice. Images of Stephen's parents, grief-laden but emotionally contained (Figure 2.1), contrasted with the pictures of five young white men behaving aggressively (Figure 2.2), their faces distorted with apparent hate and contempt. This visual distinction reinforced another opposition: between the restrained but assertive articulacy of the Lawrences and the contemptuous insistence of the youths on their right to silence. The Anti-Racist Alliance acknowledged that the Lawrence family image (unlike that of other families of murdered black youths) was one that could be sold to a white media (on the *Black Britain* special, 'Why Stephen?', BBC2, 13 February 1999). Like the Huxtable family in *The Cosby Show*, their respectable appearance and their adherence to values similar to those of the white middle classes, made them appear unthreatening to the majority audience. Justin Lewis has demonstrated that many of the white viewers of *The Cosby Show* forgot that this was a show about black characters (1991: 173–84). Frequently reproduced, key images of both the Lawrences and the white youths became the prisms through which many of the developments in the case were perceived.

Two sets of pictorial representation of the accused men emerged, from quite different circumstances. One was from a police surveillance video, and represented the youths engaging in racist dialogue and demonstrating how to inflict serious knife wounds on their victims, and the other was taken as the five were pelted with eggs and other missiles as they left the public inquiry in June 1998. Their insolent and contemptuous attitude had provoked

Figure 2.1   Stephen Lawrence's parents, the *Guardian*, 25 February 1999. Photo by David Cheskin, by kind permission of the *Guardian* and PA Photos.

the waiting crowd's anger, but the most frequently reproduced image (selected despite technical flaws, see Figure 2.2) acquired different discursive significance. Although the captions accompanying this picture were careful to provide an accurate account of the context ('under attack', 'running the gauntlet', 'pelted with eggs' were recurring phrases), the image became indexical of the youths' aggression and viciousness. The possibility of reading this image as a picture of victims of a hostile crowd was denied by the accompanying stories and their headlines, which stressed the youths' stonewalling of the inquiry. The contrasting images endorsed the narrative structure of the developing saga – that this was a conflict between a wronged family and a contemptible bunch of young British thugs.

The issue of racism, raised repeatedly by Stephen Lawrence's mother and the family's legal team, was consistently downplayed by most of the media. Also written out of this script was Duwayne Brooks, who, as the Macpherson Report makes clear, was himself a victim of police malpractice. His confrontational allegations of racist treatment gained little space in the media narratives, and indeed were undermined by his image as a stereotypically aggressive black male youth. Duwayne Brooks, unlike the Lawrences, could not become an unchallenging, surrogate 'white' icon. The role of the BNP (the extreme right-wing British National Party) in stirring up racial hatred in the area in which the murder was committed was also given scant attention. Had this attracted more prominent comment, the personalized narrative would have been undermined by overtly political considerations of the operation of power and its racist characteristics.

Figure 2.2  Stephen Lawrence's suspected killers, widely reproduced in the press, 1 July 1998. Photo by Paul Hackett, by kind permission of Popperfoto.

The difficulty of sustaining this denial-of-racism approach intensified when *The Stephen Lawrence Inquiry Report* (popularly known as the Macpherson Report) was published in February 1999. Despite being chaired by a former judge not known for his lenient sentencing, and thought to be sufficiently illiberal to be initially challenged by the Lawrence family lawyers as an unsuitable choice, this detailed report into police incompetence in the handling of the murder investigation became notable for its assertion that institutional racism existed, not only in the Metropolitan Police Force but more widely in British society. The definition that Macpherson offered of 'institutional racism' has some affinity with Stuart Hall's account of modes of '*inferential* racism', which he describes as 'those apparently naturalised representations of events and situations relating to race ... which have racist premises and propositions inscribed in them as a set of *unquestioned assumptions*' (1981: 36). According to Macpherson, institutional racism involves:

> ... the collective failure of an organization to provide an appropriate and professional service to people because of their colour, culture or ethnic origin. It can be seen or detected in processes, attitudes and behaviour which amount to discrimination through unwitting prejudice, ignorance, thoughtlessness, and racist stereotyping which disadvantages minority ethnic people.

> (*The Stephen Lawrence Inquiry Report*, 1999: 6:34)

The official recognition that racism can occur even when it is not deliberate or consciously promoted marked a significant departure from the earlier Scarman Report into riots in Brixton in 1981, which concluded that 'institutional racism does not exist in Britain' although it admitted that 'racial disadvantage and its nasty associate racial discrimination have not yet been eliminated' (1981: 9:1). British press reaction to the Macpherson Report demonstrated considerable resistance to his analysis and the self-critical approach it invited. Once again, a number of strategies of denial were in evidence.

Relying on positive self-presentation, the argument that Britain is a decent, harmonious and tolerant society is used in a number of editorial columns to counter the charges of institutional racism. The *Daily Mail* reminds its readers that Sir William Macpherson 'seems to have forgotten that Britain – despite some appalling crimes and the faults of its individual citizens – remains a fundamentally decent and harmonious country', and goes on to conclude that 'it is difficult to escape the conclusion that some of what [is] being proposed will inspire resentment rather than goodwill' (25 February 1999). According to the *Daily Telegraph*, the proposals 'represent an attempt, inspired by the worst excesses of American academe, to make life intolerable for the defenders of bourgeois democracy' (Editorial, 26 February 1999). The spectre of 'political correctness' (implicit in this quote) is frequently raised to discredit the report's conclusions and recommendations. The *Daily Mail* warns that Britain is in danger of making 'the politically correct mistakes which the

Americans are now trying to undo' (Editorial, 25 February 1999), and goes so far as to assert that suggestions that 'the whole country is institutionally racist' amount to 'political correctness gone mad' (Editorial, 24 February 1999). 'Political correctness' has become a particularly effective means of disarming ideological opponents. A corruption from 'politically correct', a term conceived in ironic playfulness by left-wing thinkers in the 1970s, the noun form has acquired definitive connotations of censorship by some ill-defined thought police (for an interesting account of the term's development, see Deborah Cameron, 1994). Its use achieves what van Dijk refers to as the 'strategic move of reversal: *we* are not the racists, *they* are the "true racists"' (1992: 104). In the process, an accusation of 'political correctness' forecloses debate and stifles open discussion.

Yet the papers are careful to distance themselves from the charge that they are insensitive to specific acts of racist injustice. The *Daily Mail* is insistent on this point: 'Few will be tempted to quarrel with the judgement that where racism exists, it must be rooted out' (Editorial, 24 February 1999). In *The Times*, the Editorial asserts that 'the police's failings are not best understood when viewed solely through the prism of race'. It argues that 'reform must concentrate on enhancing the operational effectiveness of the police rather than seeking to conciliate every interest group with a grievance' (Editorial, 25 February 1999). Those alleging institutional racism are diminished by being presented as a whining lobby. The liberally minded broadsheets, such as the *Guardian* and the *Independent*, were less reluctant to acknowledge institutional racism in their comment columns, but even they hedged around acceptance of Macpherson's conclusions with qualifications, producing an uneasy heterogeneity in their discourse. Although the *Independent*'s Editorial bears the heading 'This report places a responsibility on the whole nation', it regards the concept of 'institutional racism' as unhelpful because, it claims, 'it allows those "unwitting" racists among the police to avoid taking personal responsibility for their actions by attaching a value judgement to the force as a whole'. It also qualifies its concern about remaining inequalities by reminding its readers of the lack of a white supremacist movement in Britain (25 February 1999). Confronted with the charge of racism in Britain, the press that had been so highly supportive of the Lawrence family's campaign for justice drew in their collective horns. Allegations of endemic racism were, in a variety of ways, allied to forms of extremist thinking and disarmed by pledges to root out such (limited) signs of this scourge as the media were prepared to recognize.

## CONCLUSION

In both these cases, discourses paid lip-service to the racial aspects of both the crimes themselves and the judicial processes that followed, but stopped short of admitting that racism was an intrinsic problem in either society. Within the bubble of discursive analysis, the contest of perspectives – between African-Americans and white Americans in the O.J. Simpson case, or between the Lawrence family/their lawyers/the Anti-Racist Alliance and white Britain in the second case – can be sharply and effectively delineated. This kind of detailed analysis misses, however, the broader picture of how power relations are being aligned or realigned, and how ideological formations are being reproduced or restructured. Discourses that, paradoxically, work primarily through denial need an ideological touchstone with especial urgency. As Robert Miles explains, 'there are circumstances where an explicitly racist discourse is modified in such a way that the explicitly racist content is eliminated' (1989: 84). The benefit of approaching the media through a discursive analysis remains one of exploring the varied and often subtle guises that the power/knowledge relationship adopts, but an analysis of the implications of this invites a return to ideology. Resurrecting ideology's profile in media analysis also prompts alertness to the 'unsaid' of discourse that, as the case studies presented in this chapter demonstrate, remains one of its most effective mechanisms of power.

Section

# Changing media discourses

# INTRODUCTION

The media, as part of the fabric of our social world, participate in constant discursive change. How we describe this process frames our thinking about it, and becomes in itself a form of analytical discourse. The next two chapters examine some of the constructions that academic critics (and, to a lesser extent, journalists) have erected around shifts that are thought to be under way in media discourse. Because of our habit of thinking in binary pairings, these have most often been articulated in oppositional terms. The media are seen as abandoning their public service ethos in favour of entertainment, and as moving steadily away from public concerns towards the private and the personal. Although critics are not unanimous in viewing these as wholly negative developments, the terms in which change is expressed tend to predetermine the conclusions that will be reached. Concepts such as 'tabloidization', 'infotainment' and 'dumbing down', applied to the media's informational genres, imply a dereliction of educational duty, while claims of 'democratization' or 'feminization', applied to popular genres such as the quiz show or the talk show, suggest potential benefits.

Both types of change to be considered in the next two chapters depend on the assumption that the media have traditionally formed part of a public sphere, with a commitment to public service. Even though commercial pressures modulated this in varying ways across British, European and American media, and inflected it differently in print and electronic media, the belief that at least informational genres have an obligation to foster citizenship and civic responsibility used to be remarkably constant. Since the 1980s, this certainty has lessened under pressure from a range of commercial influences, including intensified competition from cable and satellite outlets, the growing internationalization of the information industries, and a loosening of state or government regulation (Dahlgren, 1995: 49). Under these circumstances, television schedulers and programming commissioners have been reluctant to sustain a public service ideal against the consumerist tide. In Britain a shift from nurturing citizens to appeasing consumers was sharply accentuated by Thatcherism during the 1980s across a range of public services, including education. A consumerist model of media audiences and readers, typifying them as impatient pleasure-seekers, has become such an accepted mantra that questioning its assumptions may seem perverse. Yet the chapters that follow will investigate how oppositions between 'information' and 'entertainment' or between 'public' and 'private' obscure and simplify the complexity of the changes taking place in media discourse. Instead of characterizing these as a pendulum swing from one extreme to another, I argue that we need instead to reinvestigate them against a model of citizenship that is inclusive, engaged, and open to challenge and debate.

Presumptions about the public's lack of tolerance for information can become a self-fulfilling prophecy: scheduling decisions, for example, may make informational programming increasingly inaccessible on television. In the weeks following September 11th, books on Islam were in sharp demand, and even some popular papers offered mini-guides to the central tenets of the Muslim faith. Television stations, which in calmer times would have balked at devoting airtime to a remote country such as Afghanistan, opened up space on their schedules in an expectation of viewer interest. The consumer had, however briefly, become *also* a citizen. Chapter 3 will explore how this duality of identity might be addressed through some of the forms of presentation that have been denigrated in the tabloidization thesis.

In Chapter 4, the focus shifts to the evolving relationship between concepts of 'public' and 'private', evident in popular television genres such as the talk show, the 'reality TV' show, and in media coverage of celebrity scandals. This chapter will consider how far this perceived destabilization of previous norms *is* leading to a restructuring of the relationship between these historically constructed binaries. While much critical attention has centred on the implications of change for a 'public sphere' conceptualization of the media, my discussion will investigate whether it is also reshaping our understanding of 'the private' and 'the ordinary', especially in the context of the performative demands of the media. While in Chapter 3 my argument urges caution about the exaggerated negativity of a 'tabloidization' thesis, in Chapter 4 it warns against an unduly euphoric interpretation of an alleged loosening of exclusionary boundaries.

The habitual discursive definitions of the changes being discussed in both these chapters depend on an Enlightenment discourse that privileges rationality, abstraction, analysis and the 'public' world over emotion, instantiation, experience and the 'private' world. With roots in the eighteenth-century promotion of science as the basis of true knowledge, this form of polarized thinking acquired strongly gendered connotations. A masculinized public world was supported by male-dominated forms of logic and reasoning, just as the feminized world of the home became associated with feelings and intuitions. Feminist criticism provides a useful basis for reviewing the presumptions on which this thinking is founded. In Chapter 3, feminist approaches to experience and subjectivity play an important role in discriminating between the varied forms of personalization that characterize contemporary journalism. A focus on personality and personal interest is one of the recurring complaints of 'tabloidization' theorists, but Chapter 3 will argue that such a view can be sustained only if personalization is narrowly conceived as a singular process. In Chapter 4, feminist reviews of the work of Jürgen Habermas, the German thinker who has been especially influential in current thinking about the 'public sphere', similarly provide a useful basis for rethinking what we mean by the 'public' and the 'private', and the shifting relationship between conceptualizations of both.

Although both chapters are related in terms of theoretical approach, they focus on different media genres. Chapter 3 concentrates on evolving discourses in news, current affairs and documentary – traditionally seen as the 'informational' genres of television. Chapter 4 considers representations of the apparently 'private' life of politicians (especially in relation to the political 'scandal'), and examines the role of the talk show and 'reality TV' in producing diverse ways of performing the personal.

# Chapter Three

# RETHINKING □ 'PERSONALIZATION' AND THE 'INFOTAINMENT' DEBATE

When David Beckham, the captain of England's football team, broke a bone in his left foot on 10 April 2002, concern about his injury dominated the news in Britain. The conflict in the Middle East, simultaneously reaching such depths of degradation as to prompt even American concerns about Israel's aggression, struggled to compete for attention. Ten days later, it was the English football manager, Sven-Goran Eriksson who captured the headlines as the press became obsessed with allegations of his affair with the UK television celebrity Ulrika Jonsson. This mesmerizing preoccupation with celebrity personalities and human interest is one of the central complaints of those who allege that the media are 'dumbing down', or indulging in 'infotainment' or 'tabloidization' at the expense of serious news. Claims that the intensifying competition for viewers and readers is encouraging timidity in pursuing analysis of home or international affairs appear incontestable in the face of numerous other examples of this kind. Documentary-makers, too, have been accused of diluting their agenda and abandoning 'discourses of sobriety' (Nichols, 1991: 3–4) to meet the requirements of commissioning editors and schedulers for entertaining programming. Current affairs programmes, increasingly shunted around the schedules, parade populist titles such as 'Frankenstein Foods' and 'Nicking the Neighbours' (both from BBC1's flagship series *Panorama* in the 1990s) to signal their relevance to a supposedly apathetic audience.

The concerns of the critics of 'tabloidization' extend beyond these quantitative arguments to qualitative worries. Information that aims to be entertaining becomes what Bob Franklin calls 'newszak': 'a product designed and "processed" for a particular market and delivered in increasingly homogenous "snippets" which make only modest demands on the audience' (1997: 4–5). This commodification of news also attracts the disapproval of the French cultural commentator, Pierre Bourdieu. 'The focus,' he writes, 'is on those things which are apt to arouse curiosity but require no analysis' (1998: 51). This feeds a style of reporting capable of mobilizing prejudice against those who are already stigmatized (recent examples might include paedophiles or asylum-seekers). The resultant emotion can become 'aggressive enough almost to qualify as symbolic lynching' (1998: 52). The audience or readers cease to be addressed as citizens or active participants in democracy, and are perceived instead as mere consumers, eager to be diverted by gossip or scandal. Colin Sparks expresses particular antipathy to the personalization of news, arguing that it makes 'the personal' 'not only the starting point but also the substance and end point' (1998: 9). This leads to what he earlier called a 'depoliticization' of understanding (1988), as individual actions and experiences are detached from social processes and appear purely random, driven by chance or luck (Curran and Sparks, 1991). Human intervention and agency appear pointless, and the sole satisfaction on offer is reduced to the pleasure of consumption.

The 'tabloidization' complaint has, however, been contested by a number of other critics. Those who have conducted quantitative analyses of the changing content of news (both in newspapers and on television) have found a more varied picture of developments than a full-blooded 'infotainment' thesis implies. A content analysis of two broadsheet and three popular British newspapers from 1952 until 1997 suggests, for example, that the growth of personalization in the British press may be less dramatic than is sometimes thought. This study differentiates between the human-interest story and 'entertainment news stories' (stories about celebrities and the entertainment industries) and finds that while in the popular papers content devoted to human interest, expressed as a percentage of total stories, 'remained relatively constant over the forty-five-year period, rising only from just over 10 percent in 1952 to 11 percent in 1997', 'the percentage of entertainment news stories has increased dramatically over this time period, from just over 6 percent in 1952 to 17 percent in 1997' (McLachlan and Golding, 2000: 84). In the broadsheet press change is more visible, with a steady rise in both categories, especially from 1987 to 1997. At the same time, political stories have not declined markedly, and indeed formed a higher percentage of total stories in 1997 than they did in 1952 (McLachlan and Golding, 2000: 85–7). Without considering external factors such as general election campaigns, such statistics may be misleading, but they do suggest that a growing human-interest emphasis in the broadsheets is not necessarily at the expense of 'serious' news. Newspapers, and especially broadsheet newspapers, have grown in size since the widespread introduction of computerized technology in the 1980s, and declining percentages of total space may not equate with declining coverage.

A content analysis of British television news from 1975 to 1999 also remains guarded about the degree of change in content. Although it finds that all the major terrestrial broadcast channels spent less time on 'broadsheet' (or 'serious') news stories in 1999 than in 1975, percentage coverage of international news remained at similar or even increased levels. The authors admit that this may have been partly explained by the predominance of the Kosovo conflict in 1999, but they remain confident that charges of 'tabloidization' are excessive. In particular, even though the number of 'tabloid-style' stories has risen in early-evening bulletins, they point out that this type of story still comprises only a third or less of the items covered (Barnett *et al.*, 2000). This study does, however, express wariness about complacency, arguing that in 1999 consumer news, crime stories and sport were showing signs of increasing prominence, and might 'represent the beginning of a trend rather than a blip' (Barnett and Seymour, 2000). The relative crudity of the content analysis approach may also, the authors admit, disguise the degree of change that might be revealed by investigating shifts in presentational style. They also argue, however, against interpreting the changes as a purely negative sign, remarking that earlier news formats were bland, standardized and often limited in their appeal. Now, the demands of the market ensure that broadcasters rethink how they can communicate most effectively with a diversified audience. International comparisons endorse this variegated picture. While some studies (e.g. Turner, 2001; Nahra, 2001) suggest that commercial pressures in Australia and the US broadcasting industries parallel, or even exaggerate, trends within Britain, a multiplicity of divergent national factors ensures that, globally, there is 'no uniform process of tabloidization . . . going on today' (Sparks and Tulloch, 2000: 21).

Even critics who acknowledge that a worrying drift is occurring from 'serious' to 'entertaining' news, reach differing verdicts on this development. Some perceive democratic possibilities in journalistic approaches that value the ordinary. John Fiske (1992), for example, argues that the forms of popular knowledge offered by the tabloid press (including fantasy, superstition and humour-inspired scepticism) provide an alternative to 'official' or 'power-bloc' knowledge, even if the impact of this may only infrequently feed through into political action. Extending this argument into a postmodern approach, Kevin Glynn (2000) pursues the possibility that 'tabloid television' (which includes in his analysis popular current affairs shows, talk shows and 'reality TV' genres) breaks down the hierarchies of discourse typical of established journalism and allows space for a heterogeneity of voices and points of view. In this process, white, masculine, middle-class authority is subject to the challenge of perspectives previously excluded from journalism. Glynn comments that non-conformist, black and women's perspectives often gain greater authority through the tabloid media than through official reports (see, for example, 2000: 96–7, 132–3). Cultural studies' approaches to the news have additionally emphasized the value of what John Langer (1998) calls 'other news' (everyday stories about accidents or the weather, for example, that make no claims to be politically or socially significant). By allowing ordinary people's concerns to impinge on criteria of newsworthiness, a challenge may be presented to dominant ideologies, especially when the perspectives provided are those primarily of the subordinate or the marginalized. Feminists, reacting to the belittling of female voices and perspectives that has characterized much of the practice and discourse of news and current affairs, have also investigated the possibility that some of the changes disdained as 'tabloidization' may be beneficial to women (see, for example, Holland, 1998; van Zoonen, 1998).

Other critics, however, regard this approach as the wishful thinking of '"popular culturalists" . . . who seem disposed to applaud almost any cultural form so long as it is popular' (Blumler, 1999: 246). Even those so described express a number of reservations. While Langer stresses the positive and counter-hegemonic aspects of 'other news', he admits it can also serve to reinforce compliance: 'such news can be crucial within the totality of television news both for winning consent, and for offering pleasures which might work against the production of such consent' (1998: 159–60). Equally Glynn warns that the expansion of voices to be heard through tabloid television news should not be 'taken to imply that the "New News" provides "equal representation" to all of the voices competing to be heard within the din' (2000: 232). The pitfalls of classifying as 'feminized' informational media that are more responsive to women's concerns and perspectives are also acknowledged. Subscribing to this discourse may reiterate and reaffirm the very process of devaluing women's interests that it is designed to counter (van Zoonen, 1998). As the exchanges between Kees Brants (1998; 1999) and Jay Blumler (1999) in the *European Journal of Communication* demonstrate, academic opinion on tabloidization remains divided.

Investigations into viewers' understanding of news query remaining assumptions that traditional news values and impersonal modes of presentation are the best means of communicating with audiences. Elizabeth Bird's research into responses to news and current affairs programmes in the United States suggests that people find it easy to discuss and remember human-interest and supposedly 'trivial' topics whereas they recall foreign news stories with difficulty and discuss them without enthusiasm or conviction (Bird, 2000: 216–21). Their ability to relate personalized stories to their own experience ensures that 'personal narratives, with a clear structure, moral point, and vivid imagery, are memorable' (Bird, 2000: 217). Findings from the Pew Research Center into public responses to news in the USA endorse Bird's research. In 2000, the only story to gain the 'very close attention' of the majority of the US public was the rising price of petrol (gasoline). A total of 61 per cent of those questioned named this as a story that they followed with particular attention, whereas the presidential election outcome (10–17 November) gained a devoted following of only 38 per cent (Pew Research Center, 2000). Even more significantly for the future of news programming, this research centre also discovered that it was only in the 50+ age bracket that a majority 'enjoyed keeping up with the news a lot'. Amongst the 18–29 age group, only a third described themselves in this category (Pew Research Center, 1998a), although this was also the age group most likely to be following news stories on the Internet, where immediacy was valued even above entertainment value (Pew Research Center, 1998b). Bird's study indicates that news presented in a personalized way is still more likely to be mulled over and talked about, producing a greater degree of involvement from viewers.

We need, then, an alternative to a critical model that opposes 'entertainment' to 'information', or, in John Corner's terms, sets 'popular culture' against 'public knowledge' (1991). This binary tradition dates back, as the introduction to this part of the book explains, to eighteenth-century Enlightenment thinking about the contest between rationality and emotionalism, between abstract analysis and individual instance and anecdote. While in a Foucauldian universe the struggle towards knowledge inevitably involves intensive and ongoing discursive contest between competing ways of thinking, in Enlightenment philosophy rationalism and a scientific methodology are privileged as the keys to the truth. Much of our thinking about media discourse falls within a pattern of pendulum-like swings between such polarized extremes. Yet if the need to *interest* a range of potential audiences (which is, after all, what current commercial pressures ultimately require) replaces the stark alternatives of *either* 'informing' *or* 'entertaining', different conclusions might be drawn. Media practitioners, like all communicators, have to find ways of attracting and engaging their intended publics. Serious and worthy output that fails to involve its intended audience may have purity of purpose, but not much else to recommend it: even academics have had to adjust their pedagogy in response to a widening range of students. This may, of course, produce 'dumbing down', but it does not necessarily do so. As Peter Dahlgren puts it, 'at some level the criteria for "good journalism" must in part depend on its capacity to attract and engage the audience, to stimulate the processes of meaning-making and critical reflection' (1995: 50).

The remainder of this chapter concentrates on how personalization, or a growing dependence on subjectivity and human interest in news presentation, might be thought through without assuming that it involves an inevitable rejection of knowledge-forming values. Although personalization is by definition identified as a singular abstract process, it needs to be re-examined in its variety of differing forms if its discursive force is to be assessed. Personalization sometimes results from lazy journalism and inadequate research (encouraged by tightening resources); but at other times it indicates a serious attempt to find effective ways of engaging and holding the attention of the reading or viewing publics. The formation of knowledge depends on understanding, on openness to fresh insights and a willingness to re-examine existing hypotheses. Journalism's task in an era of readily accessible if loosely sourced information via the World Wide Web is not to replicate that facility, but to involve us in the formation of an active and engaged citizenry. Social and political activism rarely emerges out of intellectual conviction alone but is most often prompted by emotional as well as rational response to some moment of insight. For the informational media to provide such stimulus, they need to cross the artificial divide of the Enlightenment model. When Bill Nichols criticized news reporting for 'urg[ing] us to look but not care, see but not act, know but not change' (1991: 194), he was writing not about 'tabloid journalism' but about its serious counterpart. Analysts of the media, and practitioners, need to rethink some of the critical categories that have become discursive habits if helpful aspects of current trends are to be identified.

## RETHINKING 'HARD' AND 'SOFT' NEWS

Journalists, and to a lesser extent critics, classify news and current affairs topics into oppositional categories of 'hard' and 'soft'. Within this discursive framework, a clear hierarchy prevails. International news stories, rich in information and appealing to our citizenship identities, are highly valued, whereas 'soft' categories are often demeaned as snippets of gossip or human interest that kill an idle moment and address our consumerist selves. Somewhere in between, categories such as consumer affairs and health or welfare stories perch uneasily, regarded as socially important but lower down the 'pecking order' than business news or politics. The 'hard' and 'soft' binary is also strongly gendered in both production terms and assumed consumption patterns. Women journalists still predominate in the latter area of news production, and politics in the female-oriented sections of newspapers is frequently reconstructed as being a matter of fashion or personal style (Adcock, 2002). During her research into child sexual abuse and the media, Paula Skidmore cites journalists' own expectations that 'the women in the office were always so much better at dealing with those things than the men' (1998: 204). None of these are natural classifications or expectations, but depend on deeply engrained ideologies of masculinity and femininity.

Given this background, worries about a shift from 'hard' to 'soft' news topics might cause less justifiable consternation than some critics suggest. Franklin (1997) deplores the decline in parliamentary news and reports of House of Commons debates in the British broadsheet press without giving adequate consideration to either innovations in broadcast coverage (especially the introduction of cameras into the houses of parliament) or, more significantly, whether parliamentary reporting was ever the optimum means of exploring and dissecting politics for the majority of British citizens. Within a public-school, masculinized tradition of confrontational rhetoric, proceedings in the House of Commons often resemble the rugby field more than a policy-making forum. Potentially alien to the majority of non-white, female and working-class citizens, Westminster's spectacle of politics seems remote from the debate that does need to be held about policy direction on a range of issues. Franklin's concern would have been better placed in investigating how adequately the press encourages this, and whose perspectives are granted authority and legitimacy in the process. It is not only the style of Westminster politics that seems remote, but also its failure to countenance a sufficient diversity of views. A model of political reporting that is responsive merely to the parliamentary agenda makes the media complicit in a form of political dialogue that leaves most citizens either on the outside or, at best, on the touchline. Franklin's presumption that democracy was, in the past, well served by the traditional parliamentary diet of broadsheet newspapers is based on an acceptance of 'hard news' definitions of what politics is about.

Equally, deriding the extremes of gossip and titillation stories often casts aspersions on 'soft news' and human-interest stories in general, without due discrimination between the differing approaches or achievements of these. 'Consumer' stories and investigations, for example, are often included in this derogation: their increase in the serious informational media (including current affairs programmes and documentaries) serving as evidence of a lowering of standards. Graeme Turner comments on the 'shift towards consumer affairs and away from politics' as part of the 'move towards the entertaining and the sensational' and 'a retreat from the news agenda of the day' (2001: 52). Yet consumer affairs can be presented in a way that asserts their political relevance. Even cosmetic surgery, often derided as a trivial and 'women's magazine' type of topic, becomes a political issue if we ask whether this is a legitimate form of treatment under the National Health Service in Britain. Television programmes exposing the use of sweated labour in the production of clothing for branded high-street stores may activate more political awareness than hours of debate on globalized economics in reported parliamentary discourse. Photographs in *Life* magazine in June 1996 of Pakistani children who were being paid poverty wages for producing balls carrying the

Nike swoosh, triggered extensive protests and awareness of the human cost of capitalist exploitation (Klein, 2001: 328). As Chapter 6 will make clear, worries about the safety of food have led to heightened concern about the potential environmental harm that might be wrought by genetic modification. The discursive categorization of such stories as 'soft' or 'feminine' is hard to sustain. Not all consumer stories, of course, have such clear political ramifications, but there are few areas of consumption that lack the power to reveal insights into the structures of the global economy.

Stories about the sexual activities of celebrities have less capacity to stimulate political insight, although they do reveal a great deal about how we construct sexual norms, and how we differentiate between norms thought appropriate to showbiz celebrities as opposed to politicians (the political scandal will be considered further in Chapter 4). The gossip-style 'other news' of human-interest trivia that forms part of the daily diet of the British popular press has a ritualistic function that provides passing amusement or moralistic indignation, but in its atomized repetitiveness offers no fresh insights. Yet this genre of human-interest *story* remains specific to the tabloid press, and has not yet infiltrated the world of serious journalism. Human-interest *modes of presentation*, on the other hand, are widely in evidence across the informational media.

## PERSONALIZED STYLES OF PRESENTATION

Concerns that personalization's steady progress into journalism is diverting it from its serious purpose accentuate general worries about tabloidization in two distinct ways. First, the central attention to people in news, current affairs or documentary output intensifies anxieties around 'the isolation of the person from his relevant social and institutional context, or the constitution of a personal subject as exclusively the motor force of history' (Hall, 1973: 183). By focusing on individual people, reporting can fail to explore relevant structural factors. If news or current affairs stories about floods, for example, look no further than the human misery involved, they neglect the policy decisions that might help to prevent these occurring, and sidestep their environmental implications. Although 'ordinary people' may feature at the centre of these stories, they appear as the powerless victims of forces beyond human control. Questions of the typicality or representativeness of the individuals represented also arise. To give them, or us as readers/viewers, a sense of potential agency, connections between the 'personal subject' and the 'motor force[s] of history' need to be activated. Without this, ordinary people can appear as objects of spectacle, offered for a voyeuristic gaze. The second specific concern relates to the obtrusion of the personalities or subjectivities of reporters or presenters into their own reports. The increasing foregrounding of the presenter or reporter as a personality jars with the western belief that journalism's commitment to objectivity should be supreme.

These worries emerge from the Enlightenment tradition of binary thinking mentioned earlier. The valuing of rationality and scientific methods of discovery encouraged a naive belief that, even if it could not be wholly attained, objectivity was and is a principle worth striving for. As we saw in Chapter 2, the notion of objective access to 'the truth' is challenged by the Foucauldian concept of discourse, and has increasingly been queried by media critics who underline the inevitable selection, and therefore partiality, involved in any mode of representation. From choices of words or sound effects to camera positioning and angles, journalistic producers construct and shape rather than merely re-produce 'the real'. From the perspective of feminists, gay rights activists or anti-racism campaigners, objectivity has been depicted as a euphemism for conventionalized and naturalized discrimination against ways of thinking that challenge dominant ideologies. Stuart Allan (1998) interestingly argues for a gender-sensitive reworking of Bakhtin's (1984) notion of a 'dialogics of truth' as a means of rethinking the monocular vision inscribed in a fetishization of objectivity. Instead of reifying a singular version of truthfulness, Bakhtin's dialogism acknowledges that 'truth . . . is born *between people* collectively searching for truth' (cited in Allan, 1998: 124). By stressing the need for open dialogue and a recognition of the contested nature of any truth-claim, Allan's perspective also suggests that the current demeaning of particular perspectives (whether of class, gender, religion or sexual orientation) cannot be rectified by merely reversing the existing pattern to grant these voices, in turn, exclusive ownership of an equally monocular 'truth'. John Corner advances a related, although differently grounded, argument when he rejects 'objectivity' as an impossible goal in favour of a 'multivocal' impartiality that recognizes the desirability of plurality in constructions of perspective in news reports and features (1995: 64–74).

Both these criticisms of objectivity acknowledge the importance of discursive contest, but Allan's appropriation of Bakhtin is especially helpful in emphasizing a role for human agency. As we saw in Chapter 1, Foucault's indefiniteness about agency remains one of the difficulties in applying his thinking directly in media analysis. In addition, feminist thinking about the importance of subjectivity and experience challenges the Enlightenment binaries by regarding the personal as potentially political. 'Subjectivity' becomes more than 'a mere expression of the self' (Trinh, 1991: 113). Instead, it becomes a means of perceiving our own experience 'while soliciting at the same time [our] ability to reflect on [our] social conditioning or on the ties that bind [us] to other social selves' (Trinh, 1991: 113). Where the Enlightenment devalued 'experience' as the antithesis to the preferred virtues of rationality and abstraction, feminist theory argues that its contingent, multi-layered quality takes us inevitably, and often acutely, into the realm of power relations. Recent feminist thinking refuses the model of experience that casts it as a fixed state of being, preferring instead to perceive it, in line with poststructuralist thinking, as always in process and continually being re-formed. Its exploration therefore provides an ideal means of exposing the complex workings of power, and the contest between social structures and individual agency. Elspeth Probyn, writing about autobiography, comments that it provides 'a critical tool to analyze and cut into the specificity of the social formation' (1993: 29). Similarly, Annette Kuhn observes that by peeling back the layers of the past in memory work, it is possible to link '"public" historical events . . . and "personal" memory' so that 'histories outer and inner, social and personal, historical and psychical, coalesce; and the web of interconnections that binds them together is made visible' (1995: 4).

In exploring how personalization operates within the media, feminist theory's conceptualization of the link between the personal and the political acts as a useful criterion for evaluating its claim to compatibility with serious journalism. As feminist thinking explains, 'not every personal event is political, but all personal events certainly have the potential to be political' (Trinh, 1991: 113). The discussion that follows concentrates on three possible propositions regarding personalization in relation to informational discourse:

- that it merely provides an affective or illustrative aid to journalism's principal objective of exposition
- that it detracts from informational objectives by substituting spectacle and encouraging a voyeuristic gaze
- that it takes us inside experiences that cut through the defences of familiarity and ritual discourses to offer fresh insights into social or political processes.

In exploring these possibilities, the 'making visible' of a movement between personal and social, and of power relations, becomes of especial interest.

## AFFECTING AND EXEMPLARY TALES

The ability of personal stories to add colour and interest to information has been a central tenet of professional practice since the beginnings of popular journalism. The instruction given to his staff by Arthur Christiansen, editor of the *Daily Express* newspaper from 1933 to 1957, that 'there is no subject, no abstract thing, that cannot be translated into terms of people' (Williams, 1958: 220), underlined this approach. Yet even in the early decades of popular journalism in Britain this took the form of both sensational melodrama and the formation of a 'demotic radicalism' (Smith *et al.*, 1975: 241), which set itself the task of campaigning for 'the people'. Both trends were vividly combined in the *Daily Mirror* of the 1940s and 1950s. As Cecil King, the chair of the company later put it, 'if the *Mirror* was sensational and sexy, it also had a nagging social conscience. It was firmly on the side of the under-dog' (Granada Northern Lectures, 1966, cited in Smith *et al.*, 1975: 140–1). The capacity of human interest to be both a diversion from serious journalism and yet an effective means of exploring social injustices had been discovered. John Corner refers to television news as exhibiting a 'dual aesthetic': producing stories with strong 'appeals to deep and subconscious cultural patterns of fear and fantasy' while also offering exposition and explanation that aims to develop cognitive understanding (1995: 57–8). Human interest, together with the principles of story-telling, becomes a powerful means of attracting and holding audience or reader interest. A common approach is to develop personalized narratives around particular people's life experiences, in what I have elsewhere referred to as the 'case study' (Macdonald, 1998; 2000).

Case studies are intended to engage our attention, provide evidence of the issue being examined, and illuminate aspects of the necessary exposition. They have potential merit in drawing us into stories that we might not otherwise care about (especially if geographical or cultural distance intervenes) but potential dangers also surround their use if they are deployed too selectively to justify a monocular thesis, or if personal experience becomes the sole source of evidence. In ordinary exchanges, the dangers of 'argument by anecdote' are manifest. Accounts of direct experience carry apparent authority and persuasiveness despite their contingency on particular circumstances. In order to analyse this form of personalization, we need to ask whether the affective quality of the case study is taking us into a developed understanding of the complexity of an issue, or whether it is being used to stir strong emotions without supplying the dialogic prompts that might stimulate awareness of a discursive contest between differing frames of understanding. Here, as in other areas of informational reporting, the quality and extensiveness of research impacts on the presentational style. As budgets for informational genres tighten, producers are often forced to mask the poverty of their investigation by presenting plausible, but not necessarily typical, case material. Typicality is, of course, in itself a difficult concept, particularly in relation to observational (as opposed to fictive) genres. As the critic Lukács (1972) pointed out, sharper insights into social processes in the realist novel are offered by the use of telling examples than by ranging up a number of 'average' cases. But in informational genres, where the cases are actual rather than imaginary, the telling instance needs also to be statistically credible. Where research is inadequate, the case study is likely to be a dubious means of exploring significant issues.

The case study appears mainly in current affairs and documentary genres, where there is sufficient time to consider particular experiences in some depth. During the 1990s, the BBC's flagship current affairs programme, *Panorama*, ran a number of editions that examined the changing pattern of British motherhood, and its relation to welfare policy and the educational achievements of children. These programmes illustrated both the advantages and the limitations of the case study. In each case the emphasis was on *mothers*: although the policies or educational issues related to *families* and *parents*, caring was transformed, in line with dominant ideologies of both gender and the family, into a women-only role. It was not accidental that these programmes appeared in the 1990s. During the early part of that decade, unemployed single mothers became a particular target of hostility from a Conservative government anxious to encourage a work ethic and reduce its welfare bill. The 'backlash' against women's progress that Susan Faludi (1992) identified as a 1980s' phenomenon, especially in the United States, became even more evident in 1990s' Britain. In addition, growing anxieties about child welfare, stimulated by rising street crime and poor educational achievement, especially in the inner cities, placed the family under intense scrutiny. Two *Panorama* programmes, four years apart, set out to examine the link between welfare provision and single *mothers'* attitudes to work. Throughout the decade, work was being fetishized as the solution to problems in the economy, but, perhaps more significantly, as the answer to the low self-esteem of the urban underclass. The transition from a Conservative to a Labour government in 1997 did not disrupt this discourse. At the same time, the importance of 'family values' was being emphasized as the basis of a sound society, with the family conceived as a secure unit, where care of children, and nurturing of their social and moral development were primary. The lack of fit between discourses that promoted self-reliance and work for each individual, while simultaneously imagining a family that looked and behaved like those in 1950s' advertising, attracted some criticism from political commentators but little popular attention. *Panorama*, too, ignored the anomaly.

The first programme, 'Babies on benefit' (*Panorama*, BBC1, 20 September 1993) reiterated the Conservative charge that single women were deliberately and irresponsibly getting pregnant in order to obtain welfare support and live at the taxpayers' expense. Its argument was built around a series of case studies of single mothers living on the very estate that had been chosen as the site for the Conservatives' high-profile original attack. After complaints, on the mothers' behalf, from the National Council for One-Parent Families, the BBC was forced by the Broadcasting Complaints Commission to acknowledge that its account had been unduly partial (although this admission was later withdrawn on a technical appeal). Images of the women's fun-loving, leisured lifestyles, and of their well-equipped and comfortable houses underlined the dominant discourse that these women were exploiting and manipulating the taxpayer. The programme opened with a scene of a mother and her children enjoying the delights of a funfair, even although the voice-over cautioned 'birthday treats, like this visit to the fair, are rare'. The woman being represented was, we were also told, pregnant with her fifth child at the age of 22; two men had fathered her children, and she relied on the taxpayer to provide for them.

This edition of *Panorama* was fiercely criticized on BBC's feedback programme, *Biteback* (BBC1, 10 October 1993), for misrepresenting and exaggerating the problem it was exemplifying (single, never-married women then accounted for only 32 per cent of lone parents in Britain, with only about half of these falling within the *young* single women category featured on 'Babies on benefit'). Alan Yentob, then controller of BBC1, was forced to admit that *Panorama* might not have succeeded entirely in 'a tricky area, this area of marrying issues with human interest' (*Biteback*, 10 October 1993). By feeding already-stimulated prejudices, the case studies on this programme raised no new considerations for the audience to ponder: instead, viewers (predominantly consisting, for *Panorama*, of present or past taxpayers) were encouraged to set themselves against a group of exploitative 'others'.

A later programme on single mothers and welfare, broadcast on 29 September 1997, which queried the new Labour government's intention to encourage single parents back to work, adopted a more productive approach to the case study. The women featured in this programme differed radically in their attitudes to the policy, with one taking the view that single mothers were performing an important social role in bringing up children and were consequently entitled to full state support, while another wholeheartedly endorsed the need to become self-sufficient, even on a low income. The women also had differing experiences of employment and the difficulties of obtaining it, with one stressing the need for training and appropriate child-care facilities if single mothers were to be enabled to return to work, and another claiming that she had tried work but abandoned it when she discovered that she was less well off working than unemployed. A woman introduced to the viewer as 'a model single working mother' demonstrated how her model status depended totally on the exceptionally good after-school care available in her neighbourhood. A comparative assessment of a policy introduced in Wisconsin in the United States to force single parents into work also provided variable evidence of its benefits and drawbacks from the women interviewed there.

Despite the gender discrimination, this diversity of personal accounts raised a number of complications in the government's thesis, including: the currently patchy provision of quality child-care provision; problems of low pay in work; the need for adequate training for work; the difficulty of providing a safety net that avoids becoming a way out for work-shy parents. These issues not only emerged from what the women were telling us about their own experiences; they were also taken up and deployed by the presenter to challenge official spokespeople. The case of the 'model single working mother', enabled to continue work because of the after-school club her son attended, prompted the presenter to point out that 'only 2 per cent of children of primary school age have access to an after-school club like this', and allowed him to elicit an admission from the spokesperson from the relevant government committee that there is 'a child-care gap' in Britain.

Instead of endorsing a univocal and dominant discourse within the commentary, the case studies were used to confront the government's ideological stance with a number of different discourses concerning welfare, the importance of the family, and the nature of paid and unpaid work. Experience became the mechanism for triggering a deeper analysis of the issues, and the equal status granted to the different women to express their points of view provoked thought by leaving the issue open. There was no sense in this programme that we were being invited to identify with one line of thinking only. At the same time, of course, the case study choices reiterated and re-emphasized the responsibility of women rather than men for juggling often conflicting commitments.

Two further *Panorama* programmes ('Missing mum', 3 February 1997, and 'Back to the kitchen sink', 24 January 2000) drew on research into the impact of working *parents* on children's education, but each (as their titles indeed suggested) again profiled *mothers*. Evidence from both Britain and the USA that children of parents who are both working perform less well at school than children of parents where one of the parents is at home part-time was used in the first programme to castigate full-time working mothers for impairing their children's (and especially their sons') life chances. The research studies were poorly contextualized, with one of the researchers subsequently complaining about oversimplification: 'while academic research practices usually try to display complexity, media practices tend to be more reductionist' (O'Brien, 1997). In one of the case study families, it was the father who had returned to employment after looking after the children when they were young, but it was his wife who was featured as blameworthy: 'she doesn't accept that her absence is affecting Rob's [her younger son's] schoolwork'. The mother involved later complained that both she and her family circumstances had been misrepresented in *Panorama* (*Biteback*, BBC1, 2 March 1997).

silent objects of the constructions of others. In the O.J. Simpson case, the defendant's legal team was highly sensitive to the importance of the spectacle of the accused in the formation of public opinion. As the coroner was providing evidence about the wounds on the victims' bodies during the pre-trial hearing, defence counsel Robert Shapiro strategically inserted his own body between O.J. and the camera to ensure that his client's distress could not be seen by the viewing public (*Late Show* on the O.J. Simpson case, BBC2, 1994).

The voyeuristic object of study, by primarily being spectated rather than listened to, becomes a receptacle also of a range of viewer responses and interpretations. When Louise Woodward was convicted of second-degree murder at the end of October 1997, the still image of her raising her head in anguish, captured by photographer Ted Fitzgerald of the *Boston Herald* and sold around the world, was appropriated differently by those who thought her guilty and by British papers convinced of her innocence. The capacity of that image, when anchored by appropriate verbal text, to operate as a powerful symbolic sign of a wrongful verdict led the Eappen family in turn to release to the media a distressing photograph of their injured son. In the contest over discourse, images again became evocative players for control. In Britain, at the time of writing, filming in court is forbidden, although experiments have been conducted in Scotland. In the argument between broadcasters and the authorities about the ethical and practical consequences of allowing this development, the broadcasters claim their incentive to be primarily that of enabling public understanding of court procedures. Those who contend that the aim is primarily to emulate the ratings achieved by the big trial spectacles in the USA treat this assertion with scepticism. There is, however, no equivalent campaign for the broadcasting of court proceedings on radio, where the public service objective could be equally satisfied but where the drama of personalization would be lost.

News, current affairs and documentary programmes all treat cameo performances of emotion as standard ingredients in dealing with tragedy, whether on a personal or social scale, or with reactions to injustice. Because the emotional display that is offered to us is usually carefully controlled in terms of its timing (faded out, for example, when it hovers on the edge of embarrassing us), and because it fits in with our conventional expectations (people in distress will cry; people guilty of antisocial behaviour will look and behave shiftily; in reality, of course, neither is necessarily true), the spectacle often feels ritualized and manipulative. Apparently filmed and edited in accordance with audience expectations, the visualization of emotion merely confirms that which we already know, and can therefore be a powerful reinforcer of ideology (especially in relation to the identification and characterization of 'victims'). Victims are often female, confirming rather than challenging dominant notions of gender. Although audiences may also have the impression of spontaneity and naturalness in the behaviour of the person being spectated, this is often as illusionary as the seemingly natural expression of personal experience in the case study. An interviewer for *Man Alive*, the BBC programme (1965–81) that pioneered many of the techniques of the human interest interview, explains that silence on the interviewer's part could be tactically useful in extracting additional narration from a distressed interviewee:

'if somebody was in a poor way and the tears were rising ... and you did a bit of nodding and didn't say anything, then they felt that they had to help *you* out, so they'd come out with much more of the ghastliness. ... We all got quite good at knowing how to deal with them when they began to glitter' (cited in Holland, 1997a: 168). Although the 'glitterer' is not explicitly gendered, many of those contributors of 'ghastliness' would have been women.

There are circumstances in which the personalization of emotion breaks through the conventional rhetorical confines. These instances achieve the status of what I refer to in the next section as testimony. In particular, as I have explained elsewhere (Macdonald, 1998: 118–19) a focus on human emotion can become the only way for television to communicate the magnitude of events that remind us of the gap between discourse and history. Even here, however, familiarity with a widening repertoire of affecting spectacle diminishes its power to break through the protective shield of expectation.

## EYE-WITNESS REPORTS AND TESTIMONY

Expressions of subjectivity that can be perceived as spectacle may, on the surface, seem to be identical to eye-witness reports and testimony. Each, after all, involves individuals articulating their experiences in their own words. Yet, in evaluating different modes of personalization, the distinction between self-presentation as spectacle and as testimony is crucial. In the former, the speakers are presenting their subjectivity and emotion as performance, whereas in the latter the self is both positioned within, and establishing links with, the social. As I have argued elsewhere (Macdonald, 2000: 261), the conditions for televisual testimony are met when:

- the connection between the social and the personal is made apparent to the audience
- the expression of emotion and experience is clearly contingent on circumstances beyond those of the speaker's own making or temperament.

In addition, testimony often refuses closure by opening up questions that might challenge viewers to inspect their own assumptions and preconceptions. The predictable pattern offered by emotional spectacle is replaced in the most effective testimony with edginess and rawness.

On the day that the twin towers of the World Trade Center collapsed, the unimaginable magnitude of what had occurred, completely without warning, set a challenge for broadcasters and journalists (the coverage of this event is discussed further in the final chapter). Faced with the dilemma of finding an instant language capable of communicating the scale of what was happening, and of breaking through the sense of unreality produced by the spectacular filmic images of the burning and then collapsing towers, eye-witness testimony became a crucial bridge to re-insert us in a world where hostilities and ideological divisions had acquired new political urgency. Unlike the forms of recollected testimony that characterize many documentaries, the articulation of experience here was incomplete and in process, as people caught up in developments that they had scarcely begun to comprehend were still struggling with their own bewildered reactions. The incompleteness of what was being witnessed may have produced 'theatre', but this was a theatre that dragged the audience into the performance, and denied the safe and distanced viewing position of the voyeur. A woman eye witness in a palpable state of shock tells how people were jumping out of windows, but then adds with intensifying horror in her eyes: 'And if you go over by there you can see the people jumping out the window. They're jumping out the window right now. Oh my God!' (ITV early evening coverage, 11 September 2001). The awareness of a continuing nightmare that is still unfolding denies the comfort of containment.

The contingency of witnesses' emotions is in this situation highly evident, underlined by the backdrop of a New York in turmoil, by the shock visible in their eyes, facial expression and body movements, and by the frenetic and fragmentary mode of delivery of their accounts: 'Smoke; I dragged a guy out; his skin was hanging off' (Channel 4 News, 11 September 2001) or 'It was complete dark, complete dark. There is no light so thank God someone with a light came out 'cos we couldn't even see what was happening you know there's dust and debris and . . .' (BBC News 24, mid-evening, 11 September 2001). Instead of emotion contained by the conventions of representation discussed in relation to spectacle, here the emotion spills over to leave unfinished narratives. Time after time, witnesses break off their accounts mid-sentence and turn away from the camera, or articulate through their body language that they have reached the limit of their capacity to put their feelings into words. A man in Times Square comments, 'I've never had a feeling in the city like this. Everybody is like frozen. I mean this is like if they can do this what's next? I . . .' (Channel 4 News); his verbal articulacy at this point gives way to a hopeless shrug. One woman, who had been in the World Trade Center when the bomb exploded in 1993, mocks her American interviewer's question as to whether she had seen any people bleeding: 'Do you want blood? Here's blood [lifting up her dress to reveal a leg covered in blood]. Everybody's bleeding . . .'.

It is a characteristic of testimony that it takes us by surprise, breaching the codes of emotional expressiveness that we expect from a television journalism that has taken its emotional cue from film and television drama. The injection of a raw form of personal experience into the routinely familiar can be a powerful means of re-establishing what Bill Nichols in a different context refers to as 'vivification': the bringing to life and significance of events that cannot be wrapped up and disposed of in their representation. In this process, history (what Nichols, citing Fredric Jameson, refers to as that which is capable of really hurting) remains on the agenda (Nichols, 1991: 230–7). In the eye-witness testimony from Manhattan on September 11th, accounts moved constantly between self and others, between the seen and the unimaginable. Despite the singular delivery of the reports, the repetition of similar, and similarly incomplete, narratives produced an effect of shared witnessing.

This kind of testimony does, of course, have its limitations in terms of delivering an analysis of events. None of the eye witnesses could begin to address the question of who might have been responsible for this atrocity, or why. But it would also be mistaken to conclude that personalization can therefore only stir our emotions, or haunt us with recurring fragments of narrative, while television has to look elsewhere – to experts, politicians and experienced journalist commentators, and their capacity for abstraction and reasoned analysis – to make sense of events. In the weeks that followed September 11th, current affairs and documentary programmes in Britain gave unprecedented attention to the voice of 'ordinary' Muslims articulating their experiences and perspectives. This often gave sharper insight into the origins of fear-fuelled anger against the United States and the West than could be achieved by more dispassionate analysis. From the Afghan woman demanding an explanation of American action in backing the *mujahidin* terrorism that destroyed her family house in 1989 (replayed in *Panorama*, 7 October 2001) to the Muslim speaker at an anti-war rally in Birmingham (*Panorama*, 'Koran and country', 14 October 2001) who narrates how she was spat on in the street and how no one came to her aid, we are exposed to speaking positions that, at least for the non-Muslim viewer, 'entail a defamiliarization of the taken-for-granted' (Probyn, 1993: 80). This means of 'speaking the self' was advocated by Probyn as part of a feminist strategy for encouraging 'lines of analysis that move from her experience to mine, and mine to hers' (1993: 4). In remarking that 'it was the indifference of those people watching which was more demoralizing than what that person actually did', the Birmingham woman confronts the indifference of the spectator of spectacle.

Testimony, at its sharpest, refuses us a purely spectatorial position and involves us in reviewing familiar discursive positions. Its unsettling capacity makes it both haunting and memorable. Even if we still need additional information to make sense of these experiences, this form of personalization can at least stimulate the curiosity that may encourage us to seek additional information. The 'news we can use' that Elizabeth Bird found to be demanded by audiences was also a plea replicated in a survey conducted by the BBC in 1998 into their news coverage. Nervously anticipating a demand for more popular forms of presentation, they found instead that the British public wanted news from the BBC to be expressed in terms that they could understand and to which they could relate (*Guardian*, 7 October 1998). What was being sought was not a change of style but a shift in modes of presentation. Personalization can be a powerful discourse through which to generate talk about news, and this talk in turn helps to produce interest and continuing analysis.

## SUBJECTIVE REPORTING

A growth in subjective modes of reporting is a further source of anxiety about 'tabloidization' in the informational media. In part these anxieties centre on the commodified and celebrity status of newsreaders and presenters, and the growing temptation for information genres to use presenters with a track record in entertainment.

a simple reading by reflexively commenting on her own involvement as a westerner in Rwanda at the time:

> In the first few days of the genocide my phone worked and a lot of Tutsis I know rang me and asked me to come and save them, and I failed to do that because I didn't have any petrol in my car, and because I wasn't sure where they lived, and I didn't think that I could reach them. Now that means that I'm like a lot of Rwandans who might have wanted to save people or protect them but I didn't have the means, or maybe I wasn't brave enough, or I wasn't strong enough, or I wasn't good enough, and I didn't do it.

By putting her own dilemma into the frame, Hilsum obstructs our capacity to bracket the Catholic Church's actions off from the wider moral conflicts facing human beings in life-or-death situations.

Reflexivity of this kind by journalists about their own role and feelings can, of course, be seen as a form of confessional, serving merely to lighten the burden of guilt. If this were all it achieved, it would indeed be self-indulgent. But it can also effectively add to our awareness of the ideological locatedness and contingency of reporting, and alert us to the discursive gaps and silences that are otherwise hard to detect. On the other hand, in current affairs and documentary programmes the personalizing and profiling of the presenter to the extent that s/he takes centre frame can distract from the processes of knowledge formation. Although Fergal Keane, another British correspondent whose work spans the broadcast and print media, has produced moving and harrowing accounts through a personalized and sometimes self-reflexive voice, he has at times crossed the borderline into making his own role in the narration a primary source of interest. In a *Panorama* programme on the post-apartheid South Africa, broadcast in January 1999 and entitled 'In search of Cynthia Mthebe', Keane engages on a quest to track down the mother of seven children whom he had filmed five years earlier in a squatter camp. His search for her supplies the initial narrative interest, casting Keane as the investigative journalist with a mission. Appalled to discover that Cynthia's living conditions have improved little since the ANC victory in the 1994 elections, he visits the local housing officer with her to plead her case. This crossing of the line between investigation and advocacy, visualized on screen, turns the presenter's role into that of a personality performing as a bit player in a drama he himself has scripted.

Similar problems, on a more developed scale, are becoming manifest in documentary where the personality of the documentary-maker becomes a focal point of our interest. Playing the role of a contemporary urban sleuth, the film-maker Donal MacIntyre, who began life as an investigative reporter, has made a series of undercover documentaries since the late 1990s exploring the seamy underbelly of contemporary urban society. In each, his own research tactics form much of the interest, and the narrative drive comes from the thrill of the chase and the suspense generated by the possibility that his cover might be blown. Despite offering insights into aspects of life that normally remain hidden from view, the personalization of the presenter pushes these documentaries towards celebrity interest, and threatens to replace social exposure with a psychological battle of wits.

## CONCLUSION

When analysing media genres that claim to be knowledge forming, we need to inspect closely how adequately they achieve this aim. This chapter suggests, however, that a discourse of tabloidization, or infotainment, built around constructed oppositions between information and entertainment, sidetracks this investigation. Because of its association with categories and forms of classification that are themselves ideologically weighted in favour of Enlightenment principles, it can blind us both to problems with conventional methods of communicating information and to opportunities in some of the movements away from these. Personalization, in particular, is worthy of closer inspection as a multi-dimensional rather than a singular process. In discriminating between forms of personalizing the news, or between types of subjectivity, the validity of some of the worries of tabloidization theorists do nevertheless require to be taken into account. There are dangers in univocal absorption within subjective ways of thinking, particularly if these remain unchallenged and closed to scrutiny. Modes of presentation that encourage dialogic interaction and multivocality, on the other hand, provide a sharper sense of discursive contest, and of the blinkered nature of our own vision, than can be achieved through the frequently closed discourse of 'objective' analysis. Within a different discursive framework, critical questioning might focus more acutely on the degree to which forms of accessible communication are founded on painstaking, multi-sourced and cross-examined research. Some of the least enlightening forms of personalization and subjectivity are open to criticism less because of their presentational style than because of their shoddy and inadequate research base.

In the age of the World Wide Web, those of us with access to this technology live in a world that is far from starved of information. As we struggle to cope with its overflow, we may, paradoxically, be more inclined to retrench our curiosity about other frameworks of thinking and seek refuge in solipsism. Traditions of journalism that disguise interpretation as a singular form of the truth provide little encouragement to do anything else. In the ongoing crises in the Middle East, it may be comforting to identify with the discursive position of either Palestinians or Israelis. But even in forming the discussion in these terms, we leave aside the questions of which Palestinians? which Israelis? To open up our understanding, to construct 'news we can use', we may need to be taken on the messier journey of involving ourselves in a variety of dissonant perspectives. At one time, we would have looked to literature to take us on this trail of imaginative discovery. Encouraging a popular journalism that can help in this process may seem a utopian vision, but scorning all forms of communicative innovation as self-interested moves by market-led strategists is an exercise in cynicism. Personalization can be valued when it opens up perspectives: but if, as the next chapter discusses, it turns into privatized self-absorption, it can also lead us into the trap of navel-gazing narcissism.

# Chapter Four

# PUBLICIZING THE 'PRIVATE' ☐

Jon Dovey, writing about the rise of first-person television, comments 'we are all learning to live in the freakshow, it is our new public space' (2000: 4). Something strange is indeed going on in constructions of the public and the private within the media, and most especially within television. In television's beginnings, social boundaries were clearly marked: ordinary life was 'gritty', usually northern and working class, whereas stars were 'glamorous' and floated in a Hollywood-inspired fantasy world; 'public' life was metropolitan, urbane and masculine, whereas 'private' life happened indoors, often in the imaginative space of drama, feminized and derogated simultaneously as 'kitchen sink' performances. Now, public figures receive training in how to appear personable on television, and ordinary members of the public compete for stardom and celebrity across a range of programming. In the process, notions of 'the public' and 'the private', 'stardom' and 'ordinary life' often appear to have crossed the dividing lines that used to separate them. In investigating these apparent shifts in media discourse, this chapter questions how far this destabilizing of previous norms has achieved a restructuring of the relationship between 'public' and 'private'.

Our conceptions of the 'public' and 'private' spheres have historically been differentiated both in spatial and gendered terms. The 'public' is 'out there' in the world beyond the home, whereas the 'private' occupies internal space and takes us within ourselves. Implicit in these constructed binaries is another set of oppositions: 'performance' versus 'authenticity'. 'Out there' performance and expectations of performance abound, whereas gossip magazines and fan sites feed off a continuing fantasy that, by probing 'behind the scenes', into an interior, 'private' space, we can uncover the 'authentic' person currently masquerading as a 'celebrity' in the public sphere. Yet, none of these oppositions is currently secure. Within the world of media representations, women seem to have taken occupation of public space, men are allowed to cry in public, actors pose as 'real' guests on talk shows and 'real' people become overnight celebrities on shows that we curiously describe as 'reality TV'. In critical discussions of what is going on in this wobbling of once secure goalposts, analysis has tended to centre on the impact on the 'public sphere'. Viewed either as harmful, by followers of the German thinker, Jürgen Habermas, or as potentially hopeful by feminists and others who challenge the exclusivity of the Habermasian model, a movement of the once 'private' into the public arena becomes the focus of attention. This chapter reviews these arguments, but considers also what is happening to 'the private' as the boundaries shift. Questions of the significance of 'performance' emerge as a recurring refrain in the investigation of three areas of apparent change in media practice:

- an opening up of the 'public sphere' of the media to a wider range of voices
- increasing freedom of expression about the private lives of public figures
- a growing presence of 'ordinary' people as celebrities and performers within the public spaces of television.

## HABERMAS'S 'PUBLIC SPHERE' AND THE MEDIA

Debates around Habermas's work have become pivotal in assessing general reorientations in the 'public' and 'private' spheres. Habermas developed his thinking about the 'public sphere' in *The Structural Transformation of the Public Sphere*, published in German in 1962 but not translated into English until 1989. This idealized the liberal bourgeois public sphere as a place where citizens could come together to engage in rational discussion on issues of common concern, and where differences of identity would be put on hold ('bracketed') so that true equality might prevail in reaching a consensus. Far from being an offshoot of the power of the state (what Habermas later (1987) referred to as 'systems'), the Habermasian public sphere envisages citizens actively questioning state authority. Habermas links the operation of the public sphere to what he refers to (in opposition to 'systems') as the 'lifeworld': the realm of personal relationships and communicative action. He sees this as having a public as well as a private dimension, with political debate depending on skills of empathetic exchange developed in the private world of the family (1989: 50–1).

Feminist cultural theorists welcomed Habermas's attempt to rethink the crudity of the public/private dichotomy, but attacked his definition of the public sphere for being based on a number of exclusions. As the title of Habermas's study acknowledged, he was referring to a liberal bourgeois model that ignored the question of differential access, whether of class, ethnic diversity, sexual orientation or gender. Nancy Fraser is especially critical of Habermas's conception of the ideal democratic space as singular, arguing that this makes little sense in an era of fragmentation in people's sense of identity, social belonging and discursive allegiances. She contends instead that democracy depends on challenges from a variety of different perspectives, forming what she calls 'subaltern counterpublics' (1992: 123). Current examples might include anti-globalization protesters, gay rights activists, neo-fascists, environmental or anti-abortion campaigners (although, as Lisa McLaughlin points out (1993: 609), Nancy Fraser's own conceptualization of 'subaltern counterpublics' sanitizes these to exclude groups, such as neo-fascists, who are opposed to egalitarian models of human rights). As a number of feminist critics have stressed, widening diversity in the public sphere requires changing the rules of participation and engagement, and involves more than merely opening the gates to include a broader range of views (see, for example, Benhabib, 1992: 13). Responding to these criticisms, Habermas later admitted that 'the exclusion of women had structuring significance' (1992: 428) in the formation of the idealized bourgeois public sphere, but argued that this posed no fundamental challenge to his model since the bourgeois public sphere has the capacity to transform itself from within (1992: 430).

Despite their limitations, Habermas's ideas have been an attractive reference point for critics anxious to shore up the democratic operation of the media. A vision (however idealized) of the media as offering opportunities for citizens to participate more widely in the construction of civil society has been a touchstone in debates about the televisual 'public sphere' in particular, although its relevance to radio has recently been given increasing attention (see, for example, Peer, 2000). Habermas himself, by contrast, regarded the media as a major force in stifling the kind of debate that he envisaged, accusing them of operating according to commercial rather than civil values to produce a 'refeudalization' of the public sphere (1989: 195). Both in their ownership structures and in their failure to enable the public to engage in any meaningful way in the formation of opinion, they have replaced 'critical publicity' with 'manipulative publicity' (1989: 177–8). The notion that publicity (dissemination of publicly formed opinions through non-state-controlled means) can be 'critical' has, indeed, been virtually eroded from current usages of the term. In later re-evaluation of his ideas, Habermas modifies this position somewhat to acknowledge the resistive power of the consuming public (1992: 438), but still presents that power as marginal compared with the authority of media owners and producers.

Habermas's pessimism about the media has been contested by a number of critics who argue that his model of conducting public discussion is unduly restrictive and denies the validity within that public debate of aspects of lifeworld experience that are normally marginalized as part of a secluded 'private sphere'. Instead, the media are, it is argued, actively engaged in reconstituting the boundaries between 'public' and 'private' spheres, and in unsettling the discursive barriers that have traditionally been erected between them (see, for example, Bondebjerg, 1996). Much of this discussion has focused on the transformation of public discourse by a more open acknowledgement of subjectivity and emotion (as in reactions to deaths of celebrities, for example). As Dovey argues, 'the former distinction between the public and the private is now challenged in very different areas of cultural activity' (2000: 22). The television talk show has especially been singled out as allowing possible redefinitions of the boundaries. Yet television can never merely open up access to the private. It requires of all its participants a measure of performance, and it is the differing inflections of what this means that impact on the construction of public/private relations.

## REVIEWING PERFORMANCE

Even in everyday life it is impossible to offer a neat definition of what 'performance' means. How we perform depends on the context we are in, our aims in 'putting on a performance', the nature of our audience, as well as on our temperamental capacities for expressiveness or exhibitionism. Encompassing everything from a deliberately theatrical display to a reading of our personal behaviour by others, performance's fluidity in everyday situations undergoes transformation when we think about 'performing' on television. Erving Goffman, in his celebrated early accounts of the presentation of self in everyday life, refers metaphorically to a theatrical scenario, with a backstage area serving as a preparation zone for the engagement of the individual in social encounters in which s/he participates 'not . . . as a total person but rather . . . in terms of a special self' (1972: 52). When the notion of everyday performance as a practice of finely honed skills is transferred to the public arena of television, more explicitly performative abilities come into play. As we saw in the previous chapter, even ordinary interviewees become 'social actors' in this process.

In early representations of 'ordinary life' within documentary film, the cumbersome immobility of the camera conspired with the subjects' lack of familiarity with the medium to produce performances that appeared highly stilted. A man on *Housing Problems* (dir. Anstey and Elton, 1935) narrates the death of a child in a matter-of-fact, apparently recited way. Looking at this now, it appears rehearsed, wooden and unnatural. Yet, as John Corner observes, this 'very awkwardness of non-professional performance . . . can be seen as a guarantee of communicative honesty' (1996: 68). At the start of the twenty-first century, this kind of 'performance' would be impossible, partly because technology enables, and then seems to require, intimacy, and partly because we have all seen enough televisual performances to have learned the rules. Increasingly, performance on television becomes a game of emulation or imitation of the professionals. In addition, what is being performed may be governed by the unspoken 'public' conventions of how to appear 'personable' or 'sociable' rather than the 'private' ambition of 'being oneself'. Television, as Paddy Scannell and others have commented, is a medium that trades to a considerable extent on its sociability. In the process, performers on television are constrained within rituals of exchange that delimit the kind of experimentation of the self and exploration of possibilities that Judith Butler (1990) discusses.

In contrast to Goffman, Butler adopts a poststructuralist model of selfhood that sets contingency and impermanence at the heart of our constructions of self-identity, and refuses an ontological 'prior' state of being. Performance, in Butler's thinking, is not a special projection of a predetermined self in public places, but an intrinsic ingredient in the constitution of self and identity. Far from looking at how we can conform to social expectations (the emphasis in much of Goffman's writing), she presents the rigidity with which discourse has constructed oppositional options (especially of gendered and sexual identifications) as inhibiting performativity in the construction of our own identities. Instead of thinking of a duality (masculine/feminine, heterosexual/homosexual), she argues for a more diverse exploration of possibilities that would replace a binary model with a spectrum of opportunities. Butler indeed denies a clear distinction between 'drag' (normally thought of as deliberate theatricality) and our everyday performance of gender, arguing that 'drag' merely points to the lack of essential or necessary fit between our sex and our gender. The performative space of television could ideally, according to this way of thinking, enable a reconfiguring of relationships between personal experience and public discourse that might unsettle conventions and dualistic thinking. By denying the possibility of individuals merely taking their prepackaged, supposedly 'authentic' selves for an outing on television, this mode of thinking further debunks the validity of a performance/ authenticity duality.

Yet the search for an elusive authenticity haunts discussions of even the celebrity performer. When Madonna made a documentary about her own life (entitled *Truth or Dare* in the USA and *In Bed with Madonna* in Britain), it stimulated considerable interest in the degree of 'truthfulness' in its portrayal of the star. Yet, as Deirdre Pribram (1993) points out, its characteristics invalidate the very terms of this debate. Arguing that there is no 'real' Madonna available to the public in any of her performances (including the documentary), but only Baudrillard-style simulations (performances without originals), the question of authenticity becomes pointless. Yet the continuing fascination of this search is sustained by the commodification of television performers-cum-celebrities' supposedly 'private' lives in the extra-textual publicity of the gossip magazines and popular press. Reiterated to excess, it forms the backdrop for the pleasures achieved by any appearance of slippage out of the performance mode. As we will see, this applies especially to those performers whom we believe to occupy positions of influence or wealth. In talk shows, the slippage is both rarer and less fun.

## ALL TALK AND NO SAY?

Especially since the 1990s, the daytime talk show has fragmented into a variety of sub-genres distinguished by subject matter, modes of address, structure and position in the schedules. At least three varieties co-exist: those that focus on studio audience discussion (such as the British programme *Kilroy* on BBC1); those that concentrate on narrative exposure of individual problems (such as *The Jerry Springer Show*); and those that primarily claim therapeutic intentions (such as *Oprah* or the British programme *Trisha*). These categories are by no means fixed, with a constantly evolving pattern of differentiation and overlap between them. Despite generic similarities, these shows vary in their approaches to the expressing of emotion; their privileging of 'lay' or 'professional' discourses; and their attribution of responsibility for the problems they outline. By examining these aspects, it should become possible to analyse how far they can justifiably be claimed to 'confound the distinction between the public and the private' (Shattuc, 1997: 93).

In the audience discussion programmes, the expression of emotion takes the form of narrated experiences of the topic being considered. These vary from themes with evident social ramifications (such as debt or bullying) to personal or sexual anxieties about relationships. The main focus is on individuals who can relate directly to the issue and who are willing to tell their own stories (this usually includes individuals with past as well as current experience of the problem). The confrontational exposure shows use emotion principally for conflict generation, while in the therapeutic shows expressions of feeling form the basis for counselling advice. None of these sub-genres offers sufficient space or time for personal emotions to be fully developed in the speakers' own terms, and at their own pace, although the audience discussion show provides more opportunity for extended narration than the others. Even here, however, the presenter/host intervenes to monitor and manage the unfolding narratives.

Sonia Livingstone and Peter Lunt argue that the audience discussion programme has the ability to challenge established forms of 'public' discourse. Writing about examples from the early 1990s, they claim that this type of talk show contests the Enlightenment premise that knowledge and insight reside in the superior understanding of the expert. Instead, expert discourse is continually undermined by the voice of experience and 'common sense'. Ordinary people's contributions are validated as authentic, relevant and practical, as against the alienated, cold, artificial forms of knowledge generated by specialists (Livingstone and Lunt, 1994: 102). Where conflict develops between the expert and the studio guests, the host will often side with lay opinion (1994: 103). Couched in Foucauldian terms, a discourse associated with the 'private' sphere contests the discourse of the 'public' sphere without any certainty of outcome. On this reading, those disenfranchised within the Habermasian idealization of the public sphere are not merely allowed into the public arena: they are also granted an authoritative voice. Although Livingstone and Lunt's analysis aptly defines the degree of attention that these shows pay to ordinary people's accounts of their own experience, they underplay the role of the host in guiding the discussion and exerting control. In *Kilroy*, for example, Robert Kilroy-Silk does more than manage the discussion: he directs, cajoles, re-interprets what participants have said in order to heighten controversy, and provides a moralizing touchstone for the opinions being articulated. The participants' experiences rarely, within this regime, succeed in being given sufficient autonomous space or time to develop into testimony as I defined it in the previous chapter. Towards the end of their analysis Livingstone and Lunt themselves suggest a different reading of the studio audience's ability to control the agenda: 'participants may act and feel involved, but only as consumers in a managed show rather than as authenticated through processes in the life-world' (1994: 175).

In the conflict-driven shows such as *Jerry Springer*, private narratives are ritualistically accusatory and non-reflective. Instead of an open and exploratory analysis of personal feeling, emotion is orchestrated through a variety of predictable moves. What makes this watchable, and even addictive, is the viewer's sense that what is being staged is a performance of 'cooked' rather than 'raw' emotion, however dependent that performance is on authentic feeling. The sense of theatricality is produced by the set design, the apparently detached, 'observer' behaviour of the host, and the role of the studio audience as a pantomime chorus, alternately booing or cheering the action unfolding on stage. In these shows, the verbal emphasis of the discussion programme is replaced by visual drama, with the articulation in words often being reduced to a string of bleeped invectives. What Laura Grindstaff refers to as the pornography-style 'money shot' (1997: 169) is a moment of visual climax, as verbal insult explodes into physical attack.

The therapy-style shows give more attention to the unfolding of the personal narrative, but this is framed within an insistent discourse of self-help and self-improvement. Following the example of leading hosts such as Oprah Winfrey, presenters often refer to their own past problems of addiction, abuse or depression, using these as exemplary or empathetic endorsements of various forms of treatment. Within this therapeutic discourse, participants are frequently congratulated for being brave enough to venture into the public space of the studio in the search for help. The mode of discourse here is closer to the Foucauldian 'confession' that always grants power to the receiver of the confession over the confessor (Foucault, 1981: 59–63). 'Lay' discourse is presented as incapable of solving its own problems and, within the show, is subject to the counselling advice of the host or expert guest. Longer-term solutions, it is suggested, lie with self-help and self-management regimes, rather than with professional help (Squire, 1997: 108). This recurrent aspect of therapy-show discourse ensures that personal dilemmas are afforded psychological analysis only, and questions of structural power are avoided in the emphatic endorsement of individual agency and control. Elaine Rapping contrasts this approach with feminism's advocacy of consciousness-raising as a means of heightening women's awareness of the radical change needed in institutional and social processes. Talk shows focusing, for example, on addictive behaviour 'interweave feminist analyses with recovery solutions in a way that . . . reduces them to a common, apolitical level of "addictive disorders" with no political component at all' (Rapping, 2000: 237).

Although this discourse of individual agency and responsibility is most strongly articulated in the therapy show, it underpins the other sub-genres also. In the audience discussion show, for example, topics that might raise significant issues about the interaction between individual agency and structural factors are reduced to exhortations to participants to improve their performance. In an edition of *Kilroy* based on a report that one in ten patients in the UK admitted to hospital were likely to leave in a worse state than when they went in, a number of personal accounts of mistreatment constructed a general picture of negligence and lack of accountability. Far from pursuing structural analysis of this problem, Kilroy aimed for an emotional jugular that allowed simple moral judgements to emerge in stark profile: mistreatment of patients is wrong; doctors who refuse responsibility are blameworthy. When the chair of the NHS consultants' association admits that 'the profession' has not responded adequately as yet, Kilroy rounds on him in terms of his own personal responsibility: 'Hang on, when you say the profession you mean you . . . people like you, you, have – 'cos it's no good, there isn't anybody else, it comes down to us.' Failing is individualized and a logic constructed that pushes structural conditions and collective, interactive responsibilities out of the frame.

In the conflict shows, the moralizing voice is stronger, both within the programme and in the coda-style 'Final Thought' that has become a hallmark of *The Jerry Springer Show*. With the studio audience booing the 'baddies' and cheering the 'goodies', these shows resort to a pantomime-style simplicity in separating moral from immoral behaviour. The 'Final Thought' adds gravitas to the spectacle of emotions. While this helps to cement the foundations of what 'normal' relationships and 'decent' behaviour ought to be like, it also underlines the 'freakshow' aspects of what we have been spectating. The pattern is one that is familiar from the oldest print forms of popular culture. The most popular British Sunday newspaper, the *News of the World*, from its mid-nineteenth-century beginnings, claimed moral education as its primary objective, while revelling in stories of debauchery and perversion.

The talk show in its various manifestations claims authenticity and access to private experience in its 'raw' state. Even Jerry Springer maintains that his show is the last reserve of authenticity on television: 'the rawness of the exchange may be the only spontaneous reality left on television today. Everything else – news, sitcoms, soap operas, prime-time drama series – everything else is scripted, orchestrated, excessively edited, performed by good-looking professional actors with great lighting, top-notch photography, background music – it's all canned' (in the UK version of his show, ITV, 20 September 1999). The seriousness of this contention is undermined by his description of his show, only six months earlier, as 'the silliest show on TV' (in a speech to the Oxford Union on 2 March 1999, BBC News Online, news.bbc.co.uk/hi/english/entertainment/newsid_289000/289484.stm). The argument that talk shows grant audience to voices not usually heard on television has, nevertheless, some plausibility. It is only the audience discussion show, however, that grants a modicum of opportunity for the ordinary participants to engage in debate with each other. Despite the constant managing of the discussion by the host, and the inhibition produced by the tiered structure of the studio set, audience members do sometimes become sufficiently engaged in, or angered by, the debate to respond spontaneously and vociferously to each other's points of view. In the other types of show, the studio audience has a much less integrated role, acting mainly as spectators, despite the semblance of 'live' audience reaction now being structured into these shows in the form of camcorder clips of their responses.

In the early years of the talk show's popularity, private revelations were assumed to be authentic, if extraordinary. Since then, questions of authenticity have increasingly been raised by revelations that actors have been posing as 'ordinary people' on a variety of shows (including *Oprah*, *Jerry Springer* and the now discontinued *Vanessa*) and by behind-the-scenes investigations confirming that even ordinary people are capable of 'performing' within the terms the shows' formula requires. As suggested above, claims of 'authenticity' for any television performance need to be approached with caution. Talk shows are as carefully and formulaically constructed as any other popular genre. Exposure shows set narrative expectations that adhere to strictly modulated acts of exposition, conflict generation and freshly calibrated equilibrium, placing the participants immediately within a pre-scripted and routine structure, however individualized their stories. The set design connotes theatricality, with its setting of participants on a stage, and its establishment of a 'backstage' area and 'wings'. Pre-production planning, together with participants' likely familiarity with these shows, ensures that few enter innocently into the arena. Laura Grindstaff, who spent a year as a fieldworker on two US shows, which she labels *Diana* and *Randy*, comments on the contradictory criteria operating in the selection of guests:

> Although producers desire real guests with real problems – people who are not slick or practiced, who express genuine emotion, are not 'media savvy', and have never been on a talk show before – these are the guests who, in some ways, pose the greatest challenge to producers because the very

qualities that make them 'real' make them more difficult to manage in
routine ways.

(1997: 189)

In response to claims that the exposure shows in particular demean those who appear on
them, Grindstaff cites the presenter of one of the shows: 'unlike the news, nobody gets on
a talkshow by accident' (1997: 193). Some degree of personal desire governs participants'
decisions to appear. Despite commenting negatively on the shortage of time to tell their
stories (1997: 187–8), those who take part also appreciate the degree of control the talk
show offers. As one of them commented, 'on a news story, oftentimes, you get edited, and
on a talk show, you don't' (cited in Priest, 1995: 102).

When Patricia Priest interviewed participants on *Donahue*, she discovered a variety of
motivations for taking part: remedying misleading stereotypes and correcting the stigma
attached to marginalized groups; achieving the legendary '15 minutes of fame'; taking
revenge; and seeking promotion for some achievement that they wanted to sell (1995: 45–6).
Even allowing for the possible self-selection of the sample (Priest comments on the difficulties
of finding willing informants), this contests the perspective that participants are passive
victims, or that their primary motivation is to unburden their innermost 'authentic' selves.
Jane Shattuc goes so far as to suggest that the exposure shows demonstrate a 'camp aesthetic',
sending up the earnest, victim-filled discourse of the audience discussion programmes, and
celebrating irony and excess. The camp aesthetic, often attributed to gay culture, involves
exaggerated play on the sensibilities that are deemed 'perverse' or 'abnormal' by the
mainstream (for a fuller discussion of 'camp' see Cleto, 1999). Camp is potentially liberating
in its parodying of dominant culture's anxieties, but it is also, Shattuc claims, ultimately
conservative: 'if nothing is to be taken seriously, then nothing needs to change' (1997: 166).
Thinking of participants' self-revelations as 'camp' or 'play' nevertheless challenges their
characterization as victims, allowing them to be seen as exerting a measure of control, and
launching a potential assault on white, middle-class conservatism.

Shattuc's perspective suggests a much more knowing and self-aware form of
'performance' than that produced by 'authentic' self-revelation. It helps to explain why
there is a ready supply of participants for even the most spectacle-driven exposure shows,
despite the mounting evidence that some individuals do suffer harm from their
appearances. Camp performance, however, does not always dominate, and moments of
rawness and pain can still occur. When this happens, the conflict-driven structure allows
no space for therapeutic intervention, and the temporary rupturing of the masquerade of
emotions has to be dismissed as unfinished business. An episode of *Ricki Lake*, entitled
'Back off! He's mine', broadcast in Britain on Channel 5 on 18 July 2001, illustrates this
dilemma. Based around the complaints of three women that their partners are sleeping
with their ex-girlfriends, it presents the cases in a manner that sympathizes with the women
and, with the corroborative use of the supposedly impartial lie-detector test, establishes the

male partners as dishonourable cheats. In one case, however, the plight of the woman shifts from appearing as a camp form of playful excess to connoting the rawness of discovery-in-process. A veteran of the show (she had already featured at least three times previously, on each occasion in relation to the same partner's cheating), this woman is at first surrounded with the full paraphernalia of camp: bedecked in wedding gown, she makes her entrance (serenaded by the Wedding March) into a set draped in pink and white flowers and featuring a mock wedding cake. She tells Ricki Lake that she is planning to propose to her partner, who is also the father of her children, but will finally reject him if she discovers he is still betraying her trust.

The camp mood turns to despair after her partner turns down her proposal and queries her claim that the child she is carrying is his. The intrusion of apparently non-synthetic distress into the normal narrative trajectory of harmony → exposure → climax → post-climactic quiescence leaves Ricki Lake struggling for a way to recover the ritual form of closure. Suggesting that the latest revelations may be 'the wake-up call' that the wronged woman needs to be able to move on, Lake is instantly rebuffed by the woman's anguished assertion that this is impossible because her partner continually hounds her. There is a sense at this moment that the woman's story has deviated from the script to a different territory of freshly discovered depths of personal misery that the programme has neither the time nor the interest to pursue. As the woman sobs uncontrollably, and now presents herself as a victim of more than a cheating partner, the framework of the show temporarily buckles, and closure has to be achieved by merely abandoning her narrative.

Therapy shows may appear to exhibit fewer camp tendencies, but use of camcorder footage has recently introduced two levels to the participants' performance: the pre-recorded account of their situation and the unfolding of this within the studio. Interestingly, it is often in the pre-recorded format, without the intervention of the therapist, that exaggerated poses are struck, exceeding those subsequently manifest within the recorded talk show itself. This gap provides a measure of the modulations between overtly theatrical performance, geared towards a predetermined relationship with an imagined audience, and the form of performance that is constrained by the interactive requirements of sociability in the studio. The first is playful and self-conscious, the second apparently more reactive, but the difference between apparent masquerade and 'natural' performance provides a further challenge to assumptions that ceding control to participants, within this genre, necessarily decreases the desire to perform.

In the talk show, it is only the residual audience discussion programme that can meaningfully be discussed in relation to a Habermasian-style public sphere. Even here, the lack of control granted to participants, the conventional structure of the programme, and the authoritative or manipulative role of the host reduce their capacity to function as a democratic forum with equal speaking rights. The therapy show replaces the social space of the public arena with a communal version of the therapist's consulting room, enabling psychological investigation and solution-seeking to usurp the challenge to existing power relations envisaged by Habermas. The private, in the exposure show, becomes a commodity offered for entertainment from show producers to audience, but also a form of performance for the participants. In the process, participants achieve not merely their 15 minutes of fame, but the kudos of exerting a measure of power within the televisual mediation of contemporary life. How this relates to the presentation of those at the other end of the social and publicity scale will be examined next.

## POLITICIANS, MEDIA PERFORMANCE AND PRIVACY

Obsession with celebrities dominates the popular media. The popular press, the gossip magazine and the celebrity chat show all feed off and encourage public fascination with their lives. In recent years, this interest has spilled over even into the broadsheet newspapers, despite an often hypocritical distancing of themselves from the popular press's voyeurism. Many of the discourses employed in discussing celebrities reinforce their commodity value, featuring their glamorous lifestyles, speculating about their relationships with other celebrities, or allowing us a supposedly 'behind the scenes' (but highly regulated) glimpse into their private worlds of family and leisure activities. As John B. Thompson indicates, public figures now operate under a spotlight of 'mediated visibility' (2000: 6).

The careful orchestration of most of these private insights by agents and publicists or by the celebrities themselves constructs a commodified 'third space' between the public and the private realms that offers an illusion of revelation to the consuming publics while ensuring protection of a concealed private life for the celebrity. This process entices readers and viewers with promises of disclosure that are rarely realized. Gossip magazine coverlines regularly arouse expectations that the inside pages fail to fulfil. Acting ostensibly against the interests of the celebrity, the media often construct their versions of private lives with celebrity collusion. Even the unflattering paparazzi photograph or gossip column coverage can result from the celebrity's own consent to, or even inviting of, media interest. Princess Diana was only one of many celebrities skilled in luring media attention for her own purposes, despite her antipathy to press intrusions into those areas of her life she wished to keep private. Politicians, and especially prominent politicians, are particularly alert to the value of 'symbolic power' (Thompson, 2000: 98). Under increasing influence from their image-makers, they grant managed access to their 'private' lives. This is intended to humanize them, or even to masquerade as 'insight' into their 'true' personalities.

When breaches occur in the system of control that turns private lives into carefully performed and managed objects of consumption, these consequently generate particular excitement. As the carefully manicured image slips, authenticity, we may feel, has been glimpsed. When, for example, David Beckham put his sick child before his footballing duties, missing an important training session in February 2000, the carefully groomed image of the adoring father was challenged by behaviour deemed to be in excess of an acceptable masculine discourse. 'The private' in such circumstances is glimpsed in what Lévi-Strauss might have called 'raw' rather than 'cooked' form. Against the synthetic,

89

'cooked' construction of private lives, scandal (and especially the sexual scandal) offers especially alluring glimpses of the politician out of the control of the image-makers. The performance that is normally finely honed and professionally attuned to audience and policy-making requirements, slips into 'corpsing' mode (Lury, 1995/6). Even the 'spin doctor', intent on controlling the politician's image, becomes potentially vulnerable to this process (Thompson, 2000: 109, 174–5).

Sexual behaviour has long been seen as the most private aspect of our personal conduct, and, in the reporting of public figures, remained largely hidden from view until the middle of the twentieth century. Court cases, such as that accusing Charles Parnell, the leader of the Irish parliamentary party, of adultery in 1890, were the only means of enabling public discussion without any intrusion into a protected 'privacy'. As Joan Smith (2000) observes, aristocratic divorce cases, with their frequently lurid accounts of sexual excesses, supplied ready copy for scandal sheets as far back as the eighteenth century. Had sexual propriety been a requirement for public office in earlier times, many prominent politicians, including Lloyd George, Palmerston and Franklin D. Roosevelt, would have been decreed unsuitable. Rumours of their sexual infidelities failed to reach a wider public, despite legislation and dominant ideologies of the time being opposed to any form of sexual relationship other than marriage. For politicians especially, seen as quintessential figures of the public sphere, boundaries between public and private behaviour were rigidly observed. Paradoxically, as legislation and social attitudes became more liberal in the 1960s, anxieties about the sexual mores of public figures grew. Yet, as the coverage of the Profumo affair in the British media of the early 1960s demonstrates, titillating personal detail still had to be justified by assertion of a public motive. John Profumo, the secretary of state for war, was discovered to be having an affair with a well-known London society prostitute, Christine Keeler. Profumo initially denied this relationship in the House of Commons, but resigned following the establishment of an official inquiry into his conduct. It was only at this point that the press gave the affair blanket coverage.

In Britain, this was the decade that saw the arrival of the iconoclastic magazine *Private Eye* (1961), the launch of the satiric weekly BBC television show *That Was The Week That Was* (1962), and that witnessed eager coverage of the collapse of the increasingly farcical trial of D.H. Lawrence's *Lady Chatterley's Lover* for obscenity. Although such public displays of libertarian attitudes suggested that the British public would not be unduly shocked by the revelations of the Profumo scandal, the pre-Murdoch British newspapers were initially restrained in covering its sexual details. Daunted by the libel laws, they waited for Profumo's admission of his affair before unleashing lurid personal revelations. The *News of the World*, already well known for its prurient coverage of court cases involving sexual crimes, had bought Christine Keeler's personal story for £23,000, setting in train the process of commodification of the political scandal that was recognized in Lord Denning's report: 'scandalous information about well-known people has become a marketable commodity. True or false, actual or invented, it can be sold' (cited in Williams, 1969: 281).

Media and public censure ensured that Profumo subsequently disappeared from public view. The handling of his case by the media contrasts with many of the political scandals of the 1990s. If the Profumo affair and changing ideologies of sexuality led to greater interest in private peccadilloes, they also spawned a rapid expansion in image merchants vying for control over media discourses. If, as Thompson points out, all scandals require transgression of some established code, they also shore up a sense of what that code might be (1997: 39–41). In an era of strong moral consensus (such as Victorian Britain) this can be relatively simple, but by the late twentieth century transgression was both a more contested and complex concept. In 1990s Britain and the United States, a sequence of political scandals erupted (partly, of course, constructed through media interest) that took the unmasking of public image as their starting point. Despite Stephen Hinerman's reiteration of the search for authenticity as public image and private persona collide (1997: 147), by this point in time authenticity was less at issue than the politician's performance in managing the crisis. The pleasure for viewers and readers lay in watching the emperor parade without his clothes, in a performance abruptly stripped of cue lines, choreography and stage management.

When David Mellor, the British heritage secretary, was discovered to be having an affair with an actress who had starred in porn movies, the codes being transgressed were those of taste and dignity rather than any consensual moral code. The original revelations were published in the popular Sunday paper, the *People*, on 19 July 1992. David Mellor was a particularly appealing target, since in his role as what the *Sun* newspaper dubbed 'minister of fun' he had been waging a campaign for tightening controls on the excessive invasion of privacy by the tabloid press. In the search for titillation, pictures of the 'lovenest' were published, and allegations of Mellor's toe-sucking proclivities and his liking for making love dressed in his Chelsea football strip dominated the tabloid headlines. Even so, these claims were not sufficient to unseat Mellor, as amusement and frivolity predominated over moral censure. As Elizabeth Bird points out, jokes, not moral indignation, have become a key response to the celebrity scandal (1997: 116). While the tabloid press published ever more extravagant claims about Mellor's sexual habits, the gap between Mellor's public image, as the campaigner intent on rescuing the popular press from sleaze, and his private performance, became an object of ridicule. This was not just a case of the emperor without his clothes, but the anti-nudist campaigner stripped of his underpants. Instead of shame, Mellor's reaction was to counter tasteless imagery of his private life with set-piece family photographs that sought to re-establish his credentials as a conscientious, doting father and dutiful son-in-law. Even when he was finally obliged to resign, following further allegations, this time of financial impropriety, his response was not to confess his wrongdoing but to blame the press for its tawdry revelations of his private conduct. His resignation letter avoided any admission of shame, referring instead to 'my folly in becoming *embroiled in revelations of* an affair [my italics]' (widely cited in the press on 25 September 1992). After only a short pause, the 'disgraced' David Mellor reappeared as a broadcasting personality, and in 1997 was appointed to head the government's task force on sport.

What had been played out through the media was not a serious debate about the standards expected of a holder of public office, but a contest for image control that Mellor temporarily lost. His attempts at reconstituting his private persona cut little ice against the entertaining offerings of a tabloid press accusing their moral master of humbug. But, unlike Profumo, who retired to a life of good works carefully concealed from the cameras (Humphrys, 2000: 30), Mellor was able to re-enter public life in a high-profile capacity, with remarkably little damage. Even if this might be explained by the greater seriousness of the case against Profumo (including his misleading of Parliament and the potential blackmail charge), the modest damage done to Mellor's career was replicated in the case of Bill Clinton at the end of the decade.

Revelations of Clinton's private sexual desires and habits, and his laboured defensiveness about his own behaviour, also afforded both irresistible copy and humiliating spectacle. As in the Mellor case, photographic evidence acquired totemic status with widely reproduced images of Monica Lewinsky's stained blue dress, and grainy print images of Clinton giving videotaped evidence to the grand jury in 1998. What was striking about media coverage of Clinton's affair with Monica Lewinsky was how detached the private saga became from the questions of public responsibility or even from the battle for political power that was being waged by independent counsel Kenneth Starr. If 'the private' eclipsed interest in public aspects of the president's conduct, it also took on the aura of a different kind of public performance: a major spectacular that existed on a different and parallel plane, allowing the public role to remain remarkably detached.

The power of performing 'the private' had already been especially apparent when the media focused their attention on Hillary Clinton's carefully cultivated appearance on NBC's breakfast-time *Today* show in January 1998 to defend her husband. This eclipsed coverage of Bill Clinton's annual state of the union address on the same day. The private was gripping not because it was private (Hillary Clinton made no Diana-style revelations about her marriage) but because it was performance of a highly theatrical kind. As the British broadsheet, the *Independent*, put it in its Editorial on 28 January 1992: 'What a performance, what a lawyer, what a woman. Politics on television not fun, not gripping entertainment after Hillary Clinton's appearance yesterday?'. The theatre of private revelations has indeed often seemed to provide the most gripping drama that television can offer.

The Clinton revealed in the inquisition tapes, released for broadcast, unexpurgated, along with written evidence on 21 September 1998, became a source of fascination not because the watching public was allowed to peep behind the mask and see the 'real' human being, but because this version of one of the world's most powerful men was out of the reach of his publicity merchants and spin doctors. Whatever advice they may have given on his unique definition of 'sexual relations', Clinton was on his own defending his conduct in the face of charges that he had lied about his relationship with Monica Lewinsky in his deposition to the Paula Jones hearing earlier that year (Paula Jones had alleged sexual harassment by Clinton). The evidence of the videotapes was all the more compelling for being unintended for public consumption. What the media remarked on was not Clinton the private man, but Clinton the performer; reproducing series of images highlighting the gamut of emotions being played out, and also deploying a theatre critic (*Daily Telegraph*) and popular psychologist (*Daily Mail*) to examine the President's body language (22 September 1998). Within this discursive approach, questions regarding Clinton's fitness for high office disappeared behind curiosity about a performance that inverted normal power relations. As the *Daily Mail* in Britain put it: 'perhaps more than any predecessor, Clinton is renowned for his mastery of television. But now, for the first time, the American public were seeing their President in the raw, without the help of spin doctors, scriptwriters, and skilful editors' (22 September 1998). It was left to the editorial comments to attempt connections between private and public conduct, and to the broadsheet papers to set this story in a political context of Republican intrigue.

The private in this case (as in Mellor's) was being defined as the tawdry sexual antics of the normally highly controlled, and controlling, public figure. It was riveting viewing less because of its titillation ranking than because of its dramatic performance of the flip side of image control. Many of the broadsheet commentaries indeed emphasized the dullness of the tapes' revelations, their failure to clarify or offer new insights into the President's emotional life, and the excessiveness of the warnings that the material screened would be harmful to children. The *Sun*, well known for its love of sexual sensationalism, was reduced to offering its readers hotlines that relayed edited highlights of the 'juicy' bits. For all the so-called revelations about Bill Clinton's sexual proclivities, audiences and readers gained little insight into his psychological make-up, or his views on sexual politics, or the status of his marriage. His wife's supporting role intensified these enigmas. Overtly or tacitly complicit in a performance that was inimical to the very rights of women that she publicly defended elsewhere, Hillary Clinton declared the entire saga to be a right-wing conspiracy against her husband, and deflected attention away from attacks on her husband's cavalier treatment of women, and the issues of sexual politics that it raised. In a media gripped by the performative aspects of the Capitol Hill drama, the political aspects of the President's personal conduct escaped analysis. As his personal discomforts were broadcast on global television, his concurrent delivery of a speech on terrorism to the United Nations General Assembly was similarly eclipsed.

Media discourses emphasizing the performative aspects of the private appear on the one hand to be prioritizing the private over the public, but they also provide a method of distancing the private from the intimate or self-revelatory. Nothing at all is explained about sexuality (in terms of desire and identity) by focusing on details of sexual behaviour that are no more exotic than can now readily be gleaned from many other sources. This is pretend access to the private. While American audiences sat riveted to their President squirming under interrogation, indifference to the implications of this for any judgement about his political capacities remained strong. Public and private appeared to co-exist on separate planes, with little contact between them. The question 'Who believes him?' (see Figure 4.1) was contained within the bubble of his private relations. Far, then, from

Figure 4.1 *Daily Record* front page, 22 September 1998. By kind permission of Mirror Syndication.

unsettling definitions of 'the public' and 'the private' as opposing and separate universes, the construction of the contemporary political scandal has tended to reinforce this duality. If this is the result of delving into the apparently 'private' aspects of icons of the public sphere, the final section of this chapter considers what happens when the pattern is reversed, and the media turn 'ordinary people' into 'celebrities'.

## ORDINARY CELEBRITIES

From programmes celebrating the talent of ordinary people (such as *Pop Idol*) or their attempts to win a contest of meanness (as in *The Weakest Link*), to their survival rating in the hothouse of *Big Brother*, the performance of ordinary people in popular programming has become a recurring feature of the contemporary media. Indeed, the developments in the talk show, discussed above, track a shift from regarding ordinary people as documentary-style witnesses to recognizing their performance credentials. As Dovey puts it, 'everyday life has become the stage upon which the new rituals of celebrity are performed' (2000: 104). The reasons for this lie partly, of course, in the economics of an increasingly global television industry. The format of these shows is easily exportable, with local adaptations, from one cultural context to another, and ordinary 'stars' are both cheap and expendable.

On most shows individuals pit their own performance in one-off contests against each other, and gain their star rating from demonstrating that they are both 'good sports' and able to engage with (or, better still, emulate) the repartee of the presenter. Competitors on *The Weakest Link* vie less for the prize money than for prestige in rivalling presenter Anne Robinson's acidic put-downs. On those shows that have been dubbed 'reality TV', on the other hand, the performance guidelines are less clear-cut, and the individual participants or contestants embark on collective participation in a mode of living that promises exposure of intimacy to the audience. The extent to which this occurs will be examined by considering constructions of public and private space, and patterns of mediated behaviour or performance.

## PUBLIC AND PRIVATE SPACE

Despite being labelled 'reality TV', programmes such as *Big Brother* and *Survivor* occupy fantasy spaces. In each case, the location (elaborate studio set in *Big Brother* or uninhabited landscape in *Survivor*) embodies qualities of the mythic archetype despite the minutiae of naturalistic detail. We are neither fully in the world of the everyday, nor in the stylized or symbolic landscapes of the film set. The *Big Brother* house has standard features of designer living reminiscent of the style magazine, but it exists in a vacuum in terms of both geographical and social location. In Britain, extra-textual sources inform us that the house is situated in the East End of London (for the first two series, and Elstree television studios in Hertfordshire for the third), but it is totally deracinated from the detailed constructions of locatedness that characterize realist drama. The lack of geographical cues dislocates this environment socially, too, from any markers of class or socio-economic distinctiveness. In combining a millennial-style interior (complete with IKEA kitchen) with an apparently rural garden, equipped with chicken run, it additionally breaches one of the key dichotomies (country/city) embedded in our thinking about realist representations. Similarly, *Survivor*'s flora and fauna may situate its locations in real space, but its landscapes primarily signify the archetypal setting where myths of the struggle of humanity against the elements predominate.

The character of these locations tells us much about the type of public space being created in these shows. The set designer on the first series of the British *Big Brother* claims that he was asked to produce a set that would look good but also 'slightly deprivational' (what was dubbed 'prison chic'). In a formulation reminiscent of the Foucauldian 'panopticon' (see Chapter 1), the team's brief was to produce a 'film set that masqueraded as a trendy prison while also being a 24-hour goldfish bowl' (cited on *Inside Big Brother*, Channel 4, 16 September 2000). *Survivor* also provides an environment with panopticon opportunities, even if the absence of surveillance cameras prevents an equivalent intensity of atmosphere. Despite being marooned from the outside world, these constructions of space also differ from the penal establishment in ensuring maximum interaction and refusing individual isolation. In terms of privacy, there is scant refuge. Even if this is easier to secure in a landscape setting with roving camera crews than within the bounds of a house constructed for maximum observational opportunities, the duration of *Survivor* over several weeks nevertheless limits the contestants' chances of avoiding being overheard or overseen. The innovation of running *Big Brother* unedited on the Internet and on the digital/cable channel E4, as edited highlights were being shown to the terrestrial audience, ensured that the goldfish bowl remained open to scrutiny around the clock. Normally 'private' zones within a house, such as the shower room or the night-time bedroom, were both recorded on camera and accessible to viewers (with only the toilet being regarded as out of bounds).

The one space within the *Big Brother* house that promises revelations of the 'private' is the 'diary room'. Diary-writing, as an articulation of private thoughts, has tended to epitomize 'private sphere' discourse: subjective, uninhibited in emotional expression and potentially self-reflective. In television, a variety of precedents, starting with the BBC's *Video Diaries* and *Video Nation* project in the 1990s, aimed to establish a visual equivalent to the Mass Observation experiment of the 1930s. This had the ambition to produce a cross-sectional insight into non-publicized aspects of national culture through an accumulation of accounts of ordinary lives. Enabled by the accessibility of the camcorder, the 1990s' programmes similarly offered ordinary people the possibility of telling their own stories in their own terms, this time on video (for further discussion, see Keighron, 1993; Corner, 1996: 185–6; Dovey, 2000). Inserting the visual into the diary format, however, increasingly turned private narration into a form of public performance that mimicked professional style.

The televisual diary room, despite its confessional appearance, is situated at best ambiguously between public and private discourse. Instead of presenting an alternative to, or an escape from, public performance, it merely offers a differently inflected version. As

Dovey warns, we need to be cautious about applying the concept of confession indiscriminately to all modalities of subjective speech. Instead, he argues for a varied taxonomy, including 'exhibitionism, willing "confessors" in light entertainment, therapeutic "case study" confession, witnessing, testifying, disclosing and coming out' (2000: 111). *Big Brother*'s diary room is principally a location for negotiation with 'Big Brother' (the anonymous voice – actually *voices* – of control) and, through 'him', with the audience. Far from being a disempowering confessional space, it is part of the participants' weaponry in manoeuvring for favours, whether of special treats from the production team or to win audience support for themselves as players in what is ultimately a game-show contest. Even when Nick Bateman was discovered to have been breaking the rules in the first British series, his visit to the diary room was less spontaneous confession than self-justification (a modality that might usefully be added to Dovey's list), and a means of exploring with the rule-enforcer how he could minimize damage to his reputation. Participants are mainly summoned to the diary room by Big Brother, and only infrequently seek it out voluntarily. When they do, their performance rarely manifests any disjuncture in style or posture from their social performance elsewhere in the house.

## INTERACTION, PERFORMANCE AND MODES OF SOCIABILITY

The issues around performing ordinariness, already raised by the talk show, become more pronounced in genres that have winning as one of their objectives. The importance of image in this process cuts across early aspirations that ordinary people, allowed access to the screen, would subvert televisual hegemony not just in content but also in style of presentation. What John Corner graphically dubs 'punk television' (1996: 186) would, it was hoped, play with the established codes of the medium, including conventions of polished performance, in the search for new forms of relating private to public concerns. The *Video Diary* phenomenon appeared initially to offer such an opportunity. Individuals' amateurish efforts to film their own lives frequently manifested awkwardness with the technology as well as with self-presentation in front of the camera. This may have exhibited little of the stylish panache of 'punk' but it certainly presented an affront to professional conventions of televisual performance. Indeed, Peter Keighron suggests that the diaries' amateur character 'cut through the layers of scepticism and cynicism with which we have learned to protect ourselves from the professional media' (1993: 24). Yet in a short space of time, professional techniques were being co-opted by the amateur, in an evident attempt to present individual stories within, not against, the conventional rhetoric of television. There were two likely reasons for this. First, members of the public were becoming increasingly familiar with seeing themselves on camcorder footage, and correspondingly alert to the demands of the medium. Second, the diarists, unlike many of the 'ordinary' people interviewed on current affairs or documentary programmes, were enthusiastic volunteers, eager to communicate directly with an audience, and even, in some cases, to explore the exhibitionist opportunities of a television appearance. If documentary sought out 'social actors', capable of providing interesting performances of their social roles on television (see Chapter 3), the video diary encouraged private actors, anxious to experiment with modes of casting themselves as players in their own mini-narratives. Unlike their counterparts on the talk show, they retained considerable control over how their self-image would be constructed.

The British docu-soap, developed in the second half of the 1990s, adopted a more commercialized approach to a theatre of the ordinary. Based around leisure or entertainment organizations, or around jobs involving considerable interaction with the public, such as vets or traffic wardens, docu-soaps aimed to popularize the documentary genre. Their segmented narrative structure and their dependence on a set of characters carefully selected for their charisma on screen and the diversity of their personality types, emulated the appeal of soap opera. Real people became established performers, interacting less with each other than in complicity with the camera. Stella Bruzzi interprets this positively as debunking the illusion of a purely observational style of filming (2000: 76), but participants' awareness of the demands of the medium inflected their performance. As Trude Mostue, the central character in the long-running BBC series *Vets in Practice* puts it, 'You start to think a bit in the same way as the people we work with' (BBC2, 7 December 1998). Asides to the camera, often displaying humour or wit, increased the sense of a willing engagement in a performance that was, in addition, most often that of the characters' working, rather than 'private', lives. In the wake of the first generation of docu-soaps, the opportunities for key characters to gain stardom beyond the series, as celebrity hosts or performers in other areas of television, fed back into the nature of their performance. Instead of playing themselves, the incentive to play to a persona attractive to the medium intensified. Chris Terrill, director of the BBC's popular *The Cruise* (1998), notable for enabling the emergence of Jane McDonald as a singer-celebrity, explains how this dimension skewed access to ordinary life: 'It's a very adjusted sense of reality because you know that the person I'm shooting has got a different agenda and isn't perhaps letting me in to the central truth of their life' (BBC2, 7 December 1998). Although Dovey contends that 'in its concentration on a popular ethnography of the everyday [the docu-soap] occupies exactly the shifting terrains of private and public' (2000: 138), he also admits that characterization remains very two-dimensional and intimacy is mainly denied (2000: 149–50).

If docu-soaps ultimately encouraged a public performance of something that could only masquerade as 'private life', this was likely to be an even stronger feature in the forms of 'reality TV' that purported to reveal 'ordinary life' in all its rawness, but that were, at the same time, elaborate game shows. Multiplying cameras and microphones, and organizing round-the-clock surveillance of the participants stimulated audience expectations of intimate revelations and liaisons in *Big Brother*, but rarely provided close identification with, or insights into, the construction of the characters' private identities. Performance, in this sense, matched Goffman's notion of the game-playing condition of the presentation of self in everyday life more than it echoed Butler's performativity. Indeed, by extricating the participants from their private network of relationships and their normal habitat, and immuring them in a zoo-like environment, these shows blocked the very connections that might have allowed the contingency of private and public lives to be examined. If this could be defined in any sense as a 'theatre of intimacy' (Dovey, 2000: 104), it was a 'virtual' intimacy only, and arose merely from being granted viewing rights to the normally unseen.

In a variety of countries this included grainy infra-red images of couples engaged in sexual activity, leading to claims that the key pleasure on offer to audiences was that of voyeurism or at least a rarely satisfied anticipation of voyeuristic opportunities. Yet, as the previous chapter indicated, this is voyeurism with a difference. We may be deriving the pleasure of looking at normally unavailable images from a position of safety, but the objects of our gaze *know* that they are being filmed and to that extent are participating in a display of their own behaviour. This changes the relationship that typically prevails between voyeurs and the object of their gaze, introducing the ambiguous condition of *permitted* voyeurism. In addition, in the *Big Brother* or *Survivor* shows, the object of our gaze is not only aware of, but vying for, our attention. The condition of voyeurism is, however, fulfilled (especially in *Big Brother*) in terms of the maintenance of distance between viewer and viewed, and the refusal of intimacy in the camerawork. The repeated deferment of the gratification of the 'money shot' also characterizes the pace and rhythm of these shows, where anticipation that something interesting might happen sustains viewing through long periods of banality. By underlining the ordinariness of what we are watching, the *Big Brother* producers cleverly entice viewers into endless (because unsolvable) speculation about the participants' 'real' personalities and their 'actual' personal qualities. This both encourages conversational exchange and fuels extra-textual hype in the gossip magazines. Quests for authenticity are, however, particularly pointless in a show that has been established on artificial fabrications of the ordinary. Whether the characters are primarily performing themselves, or the version that they think the public will vote for, or versions of themselves constructed with an eye to future celebrity roles, is an unanswerable question. Even the notion of 'performing oneself' is, as both the Foucauldian concept of discourse and Judith Butler's concept of performance make clear, no simple or singular process. If the multi-layering of types of performance in these shows invites a guessing game about authenticity, the excitement of this game depends on a refusal of closure.

As well as a performance geared towards impressing the audience, the participants on these shows also perform sociability in their interactions with each other. In contrast to the individualized video diary or the fragmented docu-soap, the 'reality-TV-cum-game-show' offers a *Friends*-style vision of ordinary people in everyday contact with each other. Sociability is, as Paddy Scannell points out, a key discourse within the broadcast media (1996: 22–57). His focus is on the techniques involved in contriving a sociable relationship between broadcaster and audience, a means of talking to them in terms that 'they would wish to be spoken to' (1996: 24). Taking his cue from Georg Simmel's definition of sociability as the only world 'in which a democracy of equals is possible without friction' and where 'talking is an end in itself' (1950: 130, 136, cited in Scannell, 1996: 22, 23), Scannell identifies the self-sufficient pleasure of sociability as a central achievement of the successful broadcaster.

99

The *Big Brother* format places interaction and sociability at its centre, this time within the screen space rather than between show and audience. Despite their intrinsic awareness of the actuality of being on television and their desire to win, participants need to demonstrate their likeability. At the same time, their role as competitors within a game show provides an added edge to that performance, eliciting forms of behaviour and self-presentation that modulate Simmel's model of sociability as 'lacking all the burdens, the agitations, the inequalities with which real life disturbs the purity of our picture' (Simmel, 1950: 130, cited in Scannell, 1996: 23). Simmel's utopian and static vision of sociability is unquestioned by Scannell, but requires revision in any case in the light of evolving modes of social interaction. For many people, sociability in the early twenty-first century emanates as much from work relationships as from conversing with family or non-work-related friends. 'Talk for talk's sake' in this context is rarely 'pure' or uninfluenced by considerations of Goffman's 'impression management'. Feminist work on gender and discourse also emphasizes the structural and cultural influences on differential patterns of male and female friendship and sociability. The co-existence of competition and comradeship in the sociability of the *Big Brother* house or the *Survivor* island may, therefore, be typical of the tensions and multi-layering of much sociability in the late modern age.

If this is the case, these shows provide vicarious snapshots of how we 'perform' sociability in everyday life without allowing real tensions between private and public discourses and forms of identity formation to intrude. When Nick Bateman's cheating was uncovered in the first series of the British *Big Brother*, his housemates conducted their questioning of him in the style more of a management meeting than of a betrayed set of friends. Personal bonding, formed as a by-product of their cocooned relationship rather than from personal choice, prompted resort to unspoken rules of civility and sociable conduct that contained private emotions. The participants stopped short of humiliating Nick, and grouped together to wish him well on his departure from the house. In the second series of the British *Survivor*, one of the weekly 'immunity challenges' brought private emotion into collision with the sociable interaction that generally characterizes the group's filmed performances. Close relatives or partners were shipped to the island to take part in a contest that required their loved ones to see them, without touching them or even speaking to them. From being a collective group of sociable friends, they were quickly overwhelmed by the strength of their private emotions, fragmenting into solitary postures of intense longing. While humour and camaraderie quickly served to mute the impact of this experience, a rare gap became visible between the continuing constraints on the expression of private emotion in a public space and the conventions of a comfortably performed sociability.

In all of these programmes, the performed sociability is, of course, only partly under the control of the participants. Filming and editing conventions still ensure that, at least for the television audience, modes of interaction can still be manoeuvred in the interests of dramatic development. In addition, the involvement of the audience in the voting procedure, and in tracking the extra-textual careers of those removed each week, encourages a sense of fabricated, 'virtual' intimacy with the performers. But, as with the docu-soap, there is little revelation in these shows of the interface between public and private, and little reflection on social contingencies in the construction of identities. Especially in *Big Brother*, the emphasis on sociability homogenizes the group and reduces difference as a centre of interest. The focus on youth intensifies this process of convergence, and eliminates the intergenerational distinctions that characterized the BBC's experiment in televised living, *Castaway 2000*. That programme dispatched a motley group, accustomed to a cosseted lifestyle, to wrestle with the elements on a remote Scottish island and discover their capacities for self-sufficiency. The mixed nature of the group, together with the roughness of their living conditions, quickly led to rifts in attitudes to work and to the rules that should govern the formation of community. In *Big Brother*, the gulf between performing ordinariness and exposure of private thoughts and experiences was summed up by Bart Spring, the winner of the originating Dutch series: 'I am private in my head. As long as they don't know what you think, you give them nothing' (Persaud, 2000).

## CONCLUSION

The evidence that media discourses are redrafting our concepts of public and private is, at best, mixed. Despite the inclusion of ordinary people in the public space of the television screen, and the exposure of intimate details about politicians or celebrities, the hierarchical supremacy and power of the public world remains remarkably untouched. Whatever conclusions can be reached about the Clinton saga, a feminizing of politics is not one of them. The increasingly mediated visibility of public life has intensified its construction as a performative space where authority and power cannot be assumed but need to be constantly played for by a growing cast of image-makers. It is, indeed, the media's own role in choreographing these performances that allows them to revel in the moments when the theatrical management fails. Whatever the carnivalesque quality of these moments, they have no power to sustain a challenge to the continuing exclusions of the private realm from the construction of politics.

Media incorporations of private emotion or ordinary life into its public domain have also wrought remarkably little change in constructions of the everyday. Its performability has undergone revolution, but without unsettling the boundaries between public and private to any substantial extent. Where feminist theory had envisioned a challenge from 'the personal' to 'the political', leading to a redefinition of conceptualizations of the public sphere, televisual performances of the private neutralize its political effect and absorb it into the growing culture of celebrity.

Section

# A case of 'risk'

# INTRODUCTION ☐

Risk is scarcely a novel concept but as a discourse demanding attention it has been moving quickly up the agenda. A brief keyword search of an Australian daily newspaper confirmed Deborah Lupton's hunch that 'risk' was a term becoming more widely deployed by journalists during the 1990s (1999b: 9–10). Thought by some to be a sign of passing millennial angst, social theorists, on the other hand, argue that late twentieth-century preoccupations with risk marked the arrival of a 'world risk society' (Beck, 1999). Contrary to popular anxieties, they perceived signs of optimism in this process, arguing that it 'demands an opening up of the decision-making process' and a re-inspection of taken-for-granted sources of power and authority (Beck, 1999: 5). Media discourses of risk might equally have the potential to pit 'popular knowledge' against expert analysis, but their role in accentuating ill-focused alarm, and masking the specific operation of power in differing contexts, needs also to be explored. Discourses of risk are capable of endless re-invention, since any phenomenon or situation can be presented as risky given appropriate circumstances; assertions of an absence of risk, accordingly, can only ever be provisional. As a result, the media possess considerable power in helping to structure perceptions of where risk lies. How some phenomena come to be highlighted as risks, and what this tells us about our obsessions and constructions of our own identities forms the inquiry of the following chapters.

## 'WHAT IS RISK?' OR 'WHAT DO WE MEAN BY RISK?'

The questions 'What is risk?' and 'What do we mean by risk?' may sound identical, but they are predicated on different assumptions. The first assumes that risk is an ontological reality – a phenomenon that exists in the real world and is quantifiable, given the appropriate method of scientific analysis. The second regards risk as an epistemological concept, constructed primarily through discourse. Theorists of risk have debated which of these makes better sense. Ulrich Beck, one of the leading thinkers about risk in the contemporary world, argues that risk is both 'real' (i.e. grounded in material reality) *and* constructed through discourse: 'risks are at the same time "real" *and* constituted by social perception and construction' (Beck, 1999: 143). Responding to a distinction made by some writers between hazards (as real problems) and risks (as the social construction of these), Nick Fox adopts what he calls a postmodern position to argue that this distinction is untenable. Both hazards and risks come into being, he suggests, only when we label them as such (Fox, 1999: 16–22). Inert objects remain neutral until we regard them as hazardous, and this can occur only once we have defined them as risky. At the other extreme, what Deborah Lupton calls the 'techno-scientific' approach treats risk 'as a taken-for-granted objective phenomenon' (1999a: 1–2). This position is adopted especially within the science-based disciplines, whereas the social sciences and cultural studies favour a social constructionist perspective.

Within a Foucauldian framework, risk operates as a discursive construction, lacking an ontological status. If, as Foucault suggests, all knowledge is provisional and open to challenge, a conception of 'risk' is merely a discursive freezing of a range of perceptions of anxiety into a singular frame. While, in contrast to Fox's arguments, it is relatively easy to find examples of ontologically risky *behaviour* (deep-sea diving without suitable equipment, or throwing fat on to a fire, for example), definitions of risks themselves can never be so closed to dispute. In line with Foucault's rejection of any equivalence between scientific knowledge and 'the truth', expert analyses of risk are, in this way of thinking, 'regarded as being equally as constructed through implicit social and cultural processes as are lay people's judgements' (Lupton, 1999b: 29). In the chapters that follow, my emphasis will be on the discourses that shape our culture's epistemology of risk. What risk *means* at the start of the new millennium is a more significant question for the analyst of the media than what it might *be*. Discourses of risk may, for example, reveal more about our own perceptions and frameworks of thinking than about external ontological hazards. Why risk has become such a predominant concept in our thinking at this point in history has been the object of extensive discussion.

## WHERE HAS A DISCOURSE OF RISK COME FROM?

Ulrich Beck relates the dominance of the concept of 'risk' in contemporary thinking to the phase of our cultural history variously referred to as 'late modernity', 'postmodernity' or 'second modernity'. Preferring the last of these terms, Beck (1992; 1999) argues that we are now in a phase of 'reflexive modernization' (1999: 73). This is characterized by awareness of the problematic consequences of modernity, accompanied by uncertainty about how to deal with these. 'Reflexivity' comes from grappling with the extent of our 'unawareness', as one body of 'expert' knowledge is constantly countered by another. Beck refers to this as a new state of 'manufactured uncertainty', which he sees as a global phenomenon, however locally and variously it may be articulated in different cultures: 'the main question is how to take decisions under conditions of manufactured uncertainty, where not only is the knowledge-base incomplete, but more and better knowledge often means more uncertainty' (1999: 6). His contention that we now live in a 'world risk society' is based on the prevalence with which events and developments are spinning out of the control of our ability to deal with them (an acid test of this, as he points out, is the growth in the number of risks that insurance companies refuse to cover).

Yet Beck is insistent that this provides grounds for optimism, not postmodern angst or despair. Opportunities for forming new coalitions and modes of response, on a global basis, are a key part of the scenario he outlines. This outlook is shared by Anthony Giddens, who attributes the development of 'risk society' to two phenomena, which he calls 'the end of nature' and 'the end of tradition' (1998: 26). These mark stages in our development where we move away from thinking of ourselves as the victims of what nature does to us, and see our own behaviour as having an impact on what we are doing to the planet. The development of a 'risk society' is not a sign that life has become more dangerous, but that we have heightened expectations of being able to intervene to prevent or deal with hazards. Like Beck, Giddens also differentiates between 'reflexive modernization' and postmodern abandonment of political action. Giddens does acknowledge that this optimism has a class bias, but it is an issue he touches on very lightly, merely acknowledging in passing that choice is differentially distributed (1998: 30). As Deborah Lupton observes, however, 'the self-reflexive individual, as presented by Beck and Giddens, is a socially and economically privileged person who has the cultural and material resources to engage in self-inspection' (1999b: 114).

Critics who have based their thinking more directly on Foucault's ideas of governmentality and regimes of self-discipline, emphasize the role of discourses of risk in encouraging individuals to take personal responsibility for managing risk and fending off its negative impact. This accords with strategies for regulating and monitoring behaviour that are part of a surveillance and self-help culture. The self-reflexive individual, on this reading, becomes less the enabler of networks of resistance to globalization trends than the regimented subject of governmentality who is nevertheless addressed not as a victim but as an 'autonomous, self-regulated individual' (Lupton, 1999b: 88). Which type of subject is constructed by media discourses of risk will be explored in the course of discussing the specific categories considered in the remaining chapters.

## MORAL PANICS, RISK ANXIETIES AND PLEASURES

Definitions of 'risk' may seem merely to be latter-day re-inventions of the earlier concept of 'moral panic', common in sociological criticism of the media in the 1970s (see, for example, Cohen, 1972; Cohen and Young, 1973). Differences between these frameworks of thinking are nevertheless significant. Stirred by the need to explain the media's exaggerated attention to youth subcultural phenomena such as the Mods and Rockers or the use of drugs, 'moral panic' theorists argued that the media were reinforcing an artificial moral consensus by demonizing particular groups or activities, 'amplifying' their negative consequences and identifying them as a justifiable focus for a witch-hunt. This approach was founded on the belief in a moral consensus that allowed 'deviance' both to be clearly defined and to be seen as capable of being dealt with. In this sense, the 'moral panic' was more limited and localized than the later constructions of risk. By knowing no national or cultural limits, a discourse of risk creates monsters that are more amorphous and less identifiable than those of the 'moral panic'. 'Moral panics' at least generate a sense that once the source of deviance is dealt with, tranquillity and order can resume. 'Risk' is much less tractable precisely because no promise of a 'risk free' society or world can carry any persuasion.

Critical attention to 'moral panics' was later criticized by cultural theorists for isolating particular phenomena from the *general* tendency of the media to adopt strongly moralistic positions on a range of issues, and to use these to obscure the contested nature of all representation. As Simon Watney observes, 'moral panics seem to appear and disappear, as if representation were not the site of *permanent* ideological struggle over the meaning of signs. A particular "moral panic" merely marks the site of the current frontline in such struggles' (1987: 41–2). In addition, the growing fragmentation of any sense of a moral consensus meant that deviance was harder to identify and, at least in its subcultural varieties, had even become trendy and commodifiable. The source of the 'moral panic' could therefore be incorporated within the production and consumption values of the mainstream media. As Angela McRobbie and Sarah Thornton point out, any association with a 'moral panic' produces extensive publicity, making the media product 'attractive to a contingent of consumers who see themselves as alternative, avant-garde, rebellious, or simply young' (1995: 572). Discourses of risk lack this subcultural *frisson*, although recognizing the types of pleasure they, too, offer is an important element in understanding their incorporation within the media.

While risk is primarily associated with anxiety, it injects an element of unpredictability into the routines of the everyday. Indeed, as Deborah Lupton (1999b) reminds us, people often choose sporting and leisure activities precisely because they present the thrill of risk. To the extent that it removes us from the mundane, risk provides excitement, operating through the fascination of the unknown and engaging us in the construction of narratives of collective speculation that tame our fears while simultaneously maintaining their power to alarm (much as 'urban myths' combine domestic, homely detail with bizarre or gruesome fantasy). One of the tricks that we use to contain the threat of risks while enjoying their capacity to thrill is the construction of 'the Other' as a projection of our fears. In the horror movie, the construction of risks that demonstrate the illusory nature of our protective boundaries taps into anxieties that are also deeply pleasurable. Even although, in fiction, the terror is containable, strategies for ensuring pleasure in discourse of risk narratives in the media nevertheless require attention. The four chapters that follow explore three specific and distinctive frameworks of thinking about risk that have been intensifying since the late twentieth century: the risk of harm to children from abusers and paedophiles; the lack of safety in our food; and the risk from Islam. These are not, of course, the only constructions of risk in contemporary society (environmental threats, nuclear power, the spread of untreatable diseases or computer viruses are obvious further examples), but they have operated as particularly insistent media refrains.

# Chapter Five

# CHILDREN 'AT RISK' ☐

The refrain that children are 'at risk' in contemporary society has been intensifying in the media since the 1980s. While adults have always classified children among 'the vulnerable' in society, contemporary discourses suggest that risk to children is evolving into new, less manageable and more alarming forms. This chapter argues that these developments tell us at least as much about adult ideologies of childhood and adult anxieties as they do about risks to children. As Patricia Holland puts it, childhood (like femininity) often becomes 'a depository for many precious qualities adulthood needs but cannot tolerate as part of itself' (1992: 14). In constructing 'childhood' as a singular state, constituted in distinction to 'adulthood', adult ideologies also underplay the differentiated threats to children's welfare from variations in socio-cultural position. Children from wealthy, highly educated, non-abusive homes are unlikely to experience 'risk' in the same way, for example, as children who are subject to abuse, or who live in relative poverty, with few life choices. Much, indeed, of our western discursive construction of 'childhood' is based on white, middle-class perspectives, and is less recognizable to other groups. Although rethinking 'the family' is under way, following recognition of differences in structure and ambition between differing socio-economic groups or ethnic communities, constructions of 'childhood' have been more resistant to challenge.

## IDEOLOGIES OF CHILDHOOD

From the Romantic period onwards, western cultures have produced a roseate ideology of childhood as an idyllic state of innocence; a temporary phase of potential bliss before the realities of the adult world crash in to destroy the illusion. The Romantic view was merely an extrapolation from earlier thinking, including Christian metaphors idealizing the child's simplicity and pre-corrupt state as a precondition for entering the kingdom of heaven. Yet within Calvinist strands of Christianity, another version of childhood paradoxically emerged, taking its cue from St Augustine's concept of 'original sin'. By claiming sinfulness to be the essential human condition, this dogma cast children as in the grip of natural evil, and in need of salvation and redemption. It was only through nurturing and divine teaching that they could be transformed from 'little devils' into 'little angels'. As Marina Warner observes, this duality in thinking about childhood informs dominant representations of children:

> . . . for every dozen wonderful innocents in literature or popular culture,
> there are unsettling figures of youthful untruth and perversity: children
> today, far from holding up the lit lamp of hope like the little girl in Picasso's

'Guernica', have become the focus of even greater anxiety and horror than their mothers, than even their single mothers.

(1994: 43)

An ideology of childhood innocence has been progressively eroded by fears about the corruption of childhood, although, as Patricia Holland observes, it still appears in 'decadent forms' such as Christmas card imagery, and lingers as an enduring fantasy, intensifying current anxieties that innocence can now be read only as 'an open invitation to corruption' (1997b: 51). Ideologies of childhood impact discursively on responses and reactions to real children, and inform policy decisions relating to their welfare.

All ideologies of childhood are predicated on the assumption that the state of being a child is separate and separable from the state of being an adult. Childhood is ring-fenced despite the difficulty that surrounds any attempt to define when this 'state' ends. As child psychologists have repeatedly pointed out, children do not develop at the same pace, and any firm attribution of capabilities to age brackets is misleading. The imaginary state of childhood relates ambiguously not just to 'adulthood', but also to other constructions of the non-adult, such as 'the teenager' and 'the adolescent', which have their own discursive histories. From the 1950s' discovery of 'the teenager' as a consumer phenomenon, associated with sex, drugs, and rock'n'roll, the discourse of teen years has been one of rebellion and resistance to adult norms. This implies that 'childhood' is, by contrast, a period of relative quiescence and passivity. 'Childhood' and 'children' are, however, terms that often include the teenage years, especially in discussions of risk. The confusions in our use of terminology reveal a number of instabilities in our thinking about what it means to be a child, but do little to dent adult confidence about understanding 'childhood'.

Part of the authority with which adults speak about 'childhood' comes from what we consider to be our direct knowledge of this state. Unlike other human conditions, every adult has passed through childhood. Psychoanalysis casts doubt, however, on the clarity with which we can perceive our own pasts, suggesting instead that unresolved childhood conflicts contribute to psychic disturbances and disorders in later life. It was indeed the development of psychoanalysis in the early twentieth century, and its subsequent co-option into popular discourse, that fuelled fears about the vulnerability of children and the variety of psychological risks to which they were exposed, even in apparently 'safe' and 'normal' domestic contexts. Advertising's investment in increasing maternal anxieties in the inter-war years led to graphic accounts of potential harm to children deprived of nourishment or sufficient attention to cleanliness. Heart-rending tales of boys left on the sidelines because they were too skinny or unfit to play for the school team underlined the link between physical, mental and psychological damage (Macdonald, 1995: 81). With the post-war emphasis on the importance of women's return to the home and child-rearing duties, bringing up children was turned into a 'science' and spawned a plethora of often conflicting professional advice (Macdonald, 1995: 133–5).

Whilst these developments retained the boundaries between the adult and the child, the rapid expansion of consumerism aimed directly at children in the second half of the twentieth century raised concerns that the boundary between adulthood and childhood was at risk. As long as children's consumption was primarily of toys, these anxieties were contained and articulated mainly by liberal parents worried about the dangers of gender stereotyping or the promotion of violence in their offspring. Even though many of the toys manufactured throughout the century (from dolls' prams to guns) were intended to imitate adult realities, their distinctiveness from the real thing was clearly signified, either in their miniature form or their plastic camouflage. By the 1980s, however, worries grew that children (and especially girls) were not merely being encouraged to play with adult-like goods in a pretend capacity; they were being invited to *become* miniature adults, or at least to *perform* adulthood prematurely. Predictably, these anxieties surfaced especially around what was referred to as the 'sexualization' of girls. Girls' clothing, the kinds of music addressed to them, and the consumer advice of girls' magazines on beauty and fashion, were increasingly viewed as taking girls too quickly out of girlhood into adulthood. This inflection of a general discourse of risk by variables of class and gender was rarely acknowledged.

The Freudian view that children are sexual beings challenged the discourse of childhood's innocence, especially in the West. Indeed, as a number of commentators have observed, sexuality has acted as the most powerful marker of the supposed boundary between childhood and adulthood (Gittins, 1998: 9; Jackson and Scott, 1999: 100). Sexuality, like the knowledge that came from eating the apple in the garden of Eden, was generally seen as a secret of the adult world from which children needed to be protected. In his attack on 'the disappearance of childhood', Neil Postman (1983) blames the media for allowing premature access to adult 'secrets', including sexual knowledge. To the extent that Freud's view of children as sexual beings was granted credibility in public discourse, it was used to reinforce the belief that they needed to be protected from the exploitation of their sexuality by others. Children's sexuality, far from being something to nurture and develop, constituted a source of anxiety and danger. Girls' sexual innocence was in special need of protection. Yet, as Patricia Holland makes clear, the morally applauded state of girlhood innocence also serves to trigger male passions: 'it is that very ignorance that makes her the most perfect object of men's desire' (1992: 137). The sexual predator has almost always been imagined as male in cultural representations, and this assumption has fed through also into policy decisions, especially regarding the age of consent in Britain. Young women were presented as needing protection from marauding men, whereas young men were seen as vulnerable only to homosexual predators.

In 1990s Britain, there was especial public anxiety about young women's magazines (concentrated around the fortnightly publication, *More!*, which included features and advice on sexuality and sexual performance). This had some of the appearance of a 'moral panic' as defined in the Introduction to this section of the book. Amplifying the amount of sexual content in these magazines (Stokes, 1999), this panic was whipped up by a mixture of politicians and media commentators, posing as moral guardians. It was, however, only a specific manifestation of pervasive discourses that present the sexually active young woman as a threat to social stability. These had already surfaced sharply in the early 1990s in the treatment by government and the media of young single mothers who were presented as exploiting their sexuality in order to gain advantages from the welfare system (see the discussion of 'Babies on benefit' in Chapter 3). While earlier social indignation around 'fallen women' or 'unmarried mothers' had been accompanied (even as late as the 1960s) by the retreat of the offending young woman from the social gaze and by an appearance at least of contrition and shame, the open display and acknowledgement of young women's sexual subjectivity in *More!* added considerable heat to public concerns. *More!*'s mode of address was predicated on an 'assumed lack of innocence and naivety on the part of the reader' (McRobbie, 1996: 192).

The widespread eroticization of young girls in marketing and advertising imagery around the same time caused fewer worries, playing as it did to male sexual fantasies. Discursive constructions of 'cuteness' encapsulate the ambivalence of a state between seductiveness and innocence that is especially accessible to masculine fantasies of sexual stimulus and control. The relationship between this commercialized construction of childhood sexuality and paedophilia (to be discussed at more length later) is not generally acknowledged. Significantly, representation of the sexualization of girls or young women has caused more unease outside this overtly commercial context. Narrative developments in films such as *Lolita* (dir. Adrian Lyne, 1997) and even private or aesthetic images capable of a potentially sexualized reading, have been constructed as 'risks'. In 1995, photographs taken by a British newsreader of her child in the bath led to her being questioned under the terms of the 1978 Protection of Children Act (this makes the taking of indecent photographs of children a criminal offence). Six years later, the Saatchi gallery was raided for exhibiting allegedly 'obscene' photographs depicting the photographer's own children. Cultural acceptance of the representation of children as sexual beings is limited to commodified forms of young and nubile femininity.

## DISCOURSES ABOUT THE ROLE OF THE MEDIA

In public debates about the undermining of the innocence of childhood, the media routinely appear as the prime suspects. Screen violence and magazine or screen sexuality have attracted especially vitriolic attack. Extensive research by academics in a range of disciplines (especially in sociology and psychology) has produced a series of contested findings around the 'effects' of the media on children, but in popular media discourse the conflicting nature of this evidence is subordinated to an assumption of direct influence (Barker and Petley, 1997). The academic debate about the influence of the media on consumers in general, and children in particular, rests on contrasting paradigms of the text/reader relationship. Some researchers follow Winn (1985) in constituting readers (and particularly 'impressionable' children) as passive dupes, awaiting inoculation by poisonous media; others (most notably, Buckingham 1993) prefer to attend to how children themselves talk about and construct their viewing experiences.

Despite the extensiveness of this body of academic work, the media have used it highly selectively to reinforce accusations about damaging effects, especially on children. In the wake of the murder of the British toddler James Bulger in 1993, as a number of critics have observed (e.g. Barker, 1997; Cumberbatch, 1998: 265–6), a spurious report produced by a retired academic, and based on no new empirical work, was extensively reported, while a newly released study on young offenders that queried any simple link between media viewing and crime was neglected. Evidence of children themselves becoming involved in particularly dramatic crimes, such as the spate of school shootings in the United States in 1998, almost always triggers a new round of intensive discussion about the harmful role of the media, with particular films, videos, computer games or Internet material coming under scrutiny. The sense of a community at risk is often intensified by agitation for direct action. The exhortation to the British public to burn their 'video nasties' in the wake of the murder of James Bulger by two ten-year-old boys made the consumption of videos, rather than their production and promotion, the target of moral indignation. Treating other media texts as scapegoats puts responsibility for restoring moral order on the individual consumer, or on censorship processes, but leaves the producers and promoters out of the frame.

In the appeal to 'common sense', the public being addressed is an adult one. What is missing from the media's discussion of the impact of the media on children is almost always the child's voice. In media studies' research into this area, the most compelling evidence has come from researchers (e.g. Palmer, 1986; Davies, 1989; Buckingham, 1993; 1996) who have investigated what children themselves have to say about the media that form part of their daily experience. This suggests a less predictable range of responses than media commentaries would indicate, and a greater sensitivity to the importance of the conditions of viewing. Watching with older relatives, and being able to talk about what they have seen, is found to be reassuring, even in the case of the most disturbing material, whereas solitary viewing is often described as more frightening. Even more significantly, this research has demonstrated that children often find non-fictional genres more traumatic than fictional ones, because of their stark assault on the comfort of 'make-believe'. Factual programming also lacks the cues that alert the audience to the imminence of horrifying sequences. One of Buckingham's 15-year-old interviewees, for example, reports that an absence of warning musical cues means that *Crimewatch*'s reconstructions of real-life crimes are 'more scary than a really violent film', even although its visual depiction of violence is much less graphic (1996: 234). Listening to children's accounts of their own responses leads Buckingham to question whether *all* feelings of fear, horror or disgust generated by television programmes should necessarily be described as 'negative' experiences. Arguing that these emotions are often inflected with pleasure, for children as for adults, he regards them as potentially offering ways 'to understand and deal with real-life anxieties and concerns' (1996: 3). Since childhood is characterized by insecurity, stories that enable children to confront their worries in fictionalized form may be especially valuable.

None of this academic attention to children's perspectives has found its way into popular media discourse. Because of their inexperience, children are universally deemed to be 'vulnerable' to media influence and in need of protection from adult intervention. Children are not the only group to be so described (others include the mentally ill and those with a track record of criminal behaviour), but the idealization of childhood means that the urge to protect them is particularly strong. Although, as Buckingham (1996) advocates, adults need to take responsibility for young children's viewing, this requires a close consideration of the varied sources of trauma that affect individual children and of the children's own capacities as decoders of texts. Blanket condemnation of violent or sexually explicit material may be an ineffective response to children's anxieties, but speaks volubly about adult obsessions. If this has been the case in relation to the traditional media, the arrival of the Internet and the World Wide Web has exacerbated adult concerns. Unlike the older media, these are potentially interactive, confuse boundaries between consumers and producers, and are more quickly mastered by children than by adults. Adult bewilderment and a sense of loss of control intensify the sense of risk. Horror stories of children pursuing information on topics that lead them straight to pornographic websites, or of children being stalked by paedophiles masquerading as friends on chatroom sites, suggest a postmodern nightmare where no category or boundary is secure. When this is added to the growing social awareness of child abuse, even in 'respectable' society, the escalation in risks to children appear indisputable.

## RISKS FROM SEXUAL ABUSE IN THE HOME

During the past few decades one of the media's most insistent discourses of 'children at risk' relates to the threat from sexual abuse. This has grown from a concern about the individual child sex offender, to anxieties about a much less containable threat from paedophilia, amplified through the Internet into a globalized phenomenon. Awareness of the extent of child abuse (sexual, physical or emotional) within the family has also intruded awkwardly into a simpler history of 'stranger danger'. Discursive constructions of place and space as 'dangerous' or 'safe' in relation to children have played a central part in this evolving history. Perceptions of the space within the home as providing sanctuary and the safest place for children came under especial strain with the uncovering of the extent of child abuse within families.

In media coverage, early accounts of the risk to children from sexual abuse stressed that the offender was inevitably male, usually a loner and a stranger to the child, and lurking in the ill-defined 'out there' of public space. In the popular press's vitriolic attack on those who defiled the sanctity of childhood, the child abuser was characterized as a 'monster', or a 'fiend', operating beyond the pale of civilized society. As the 1980s progressed, the location of the most damaging risk to children moved, in recurring shock waves, from the public world of streets and parks to the private space of the home. The romantic belief that the home, as a microcosm of the caring adult community, formed a bulwark against threats to children was publicly ruptured. Esther Rantzen launched the campaigning charity *Childline* in 1986, following a massive response to an appeal by the BBC consumer programme *That's Life* for help in conducting an investigation into child abuse. A MORI opinion poll in 1984 had already indicated that as many as 10 per cent of the adult population had been sexually abused in childhood, the vast majority of whom had been abused by members of their immediate families (Evans, 1993: 236). This was a highly uncomfortable revelation for media more attuned to demonizing the outsider and idealizing the family. Yet, at the same time, there was titillating mileage to be had from focusing on *sexual* abuse, rather than on the wider variety of forms of abuse to which children were exposed.

Within these representations of sexual abuse in the home, the perpetrators were almost exclusively depicted by the media as fathers or other older male relatives, and the victims/survivors almost always as daughters or girls. Despite the challenge presented to a discourse of 'stranger danger', the gendered script familiar from media coverage of violence within the home was maintained. Well-worn binaries of predatory males attacking vulnerable and virginal young women, familiar from the time of the silent cinema, could readily be replayed. The media were reluctant to contemplate other possibilities, including sibling abuse or the sexual abuse of boys by men or women. The media were not alone in their reticence. Even feminist theory was often wary about engaging with the ways in which these forms of abuse complicated a simple patriarchal model of power. This left a dangerous gap for conservative forces to colonize, allowing a moralizing rhetoric of degradation and evil to take the place of a probing analysis of the complexity of power relations within a variety of domestic contexts.

When the media did occasionally venture into territory that required them to confront the diversity of forms of child abuse (and even sexual abuse) within the home, they did so only when the circumstances appeared exceptional enough to defy any reaction other than exclamatory moralizing. When Fred and Rosemary West were charged in July 1994 with the torture and murder of a number of family members and acquaintances, media outrage at the involvement of a mother was predictable, enabling a case that raised broader social issues to be individualized (Wykes, 1998). A depiction of an incestuous relationship between siblings on the Channel 4 soap opera *Brookside*, in 1996, was accused both of glamorizing the issue and of exceeding the bounds of good taste, even though the brother and sister themselves were narratively presented as agonizing over their passion for each other, and as acknowledging that what they were doing was 'wrong'. This moralizing framework was not sufficient to deter a large volume of complaints about the broadcasting of this type of material before the 'watershed' (9 pm), and the regulatory body, the ITC (Independent Television Commission), insisted that Channel 4 broadcast an apology to its viewers. A public by now inured to child sexual abuse stories in the press was still not ready for the dramatization of a story about incest that asked too many questions about hidden power structures and sexual desires within the family. Although Bel Simpson, the mother character, asserted that 'ordinary families' are not 'like this', the soap had hitherto presented them as a shining model of the middle-class nuclear family. In her search for an answer as to what had 'gone wrong', the stable structure of the family edifice began to collapse as she accused her husband of abusing his daughter when she was a young child. Even the broadsheet press and current affairs programmes on television shied away from engaging with the taut relations between sexual desire and power within the family structure. Certainties about the boundaries between adulthood and childhood, between sibling relations and sexual desire, or even between gender and sexual power, might have been shaken in the process.

In addition, the media began to grasp eagerly at suggestions that allegations of the extent of child sexual abuse within the family might have been exaggerated. A framework had already been established as far back as the 1970s for blaming the deaths of children in the care of social services departments on the inadequacies of the professionals charged with looking after them. The popular press countered evidence of multiple forms of deprivation in vulnerable children's lives with the utopian vision of a care service capable of mounting flawless rescues and restoring, without fail, the enchanted garden of childhood. The deaths of children in care, from Maria Colwell in 1973 onwards, led to blame being attributed almost as much to social workers as to those who abused and killed the children. Sometimes accused of lethargy and inaction, sometimes of being interfering busybodies, care professionals were ascribed the qualities discursively attached, more broadly, to 'the allegedly inefficient, but overly interventionist social democratic state; ineffectiveness and authoritarianism' (Franklin and Parton, 1991: 10). These dual and contradictory accusations were predicated on an ideological need to retain belief in family life as the key provider of security for children. When this was dented by evidence of child abuse and child murder within the family, it was more comfortable to locate blame on those outside who failed to prevent harm to children, than to re-evaluate risk *within* the confines of the home itself. In the emergence of clusters of child sexual abuse cases, the popular media had a ready-made template for dealing with an otherwise intractable challenge to ideologies of the family as a safe haven for children.

In what became known as the Cleveland 'scandal', retrenchment from the evidence of the scale of child sexual abuse in the home was achieved through a vilification of the care professionals involved. In the intemperate words of the *Daily Mail*, they were typified as 'abusers of authority, hysterical and malignant, callow, youngsters who absorb moral-free marxoid sociological theories' (*Daily Mail*, 7 July 1988, cited in Franklin and Parton, 1991: 15). Following the appointment of a number of key child-care personnel in Cleveland County Council in England, 121 children had been taken into care in 1987 on suspicion of sexual abuse. The professionals involved in making the diagnosis were vilified, while the parents were treated as innocent victims of a misguided campaign. Special spleen was vented on two women (one a paediatrician, the other a sexual abuse consultant) without regard to their incorporation within a wider team. The ready availability of powerfully sceptical male voices reinforced press hostility. The local MP, Stuart Bell, became a tireless campaigner against the allegations, supporting the innocence of the parents and relentlessly attacking the care professionals. An internal dispute between the police surgeons and the hospital paediatricians over the boundaries of their respective responsibilities also provided a voluble police source eager to pour scorn on the diagnostic methodology being used.

The media neglected to mention that many of the families investigated had a history of suspected abuse of their children (although that abuse was not necessarily sexual in nature), and that in a number of cases the children themselves had disclosed the abuse. The 'immense verbosity' on Cleveland in the media disguised the degree of silencing within the dominant discourse. The police point of view was presented as authoritative and reliable, with no attempt to contextualize it as a strategic move in an internal professional dispute. The two women professionals who bore the brunt of media ire were unable to continue working in Cleveland, and even ten years later Dr Higgs, the paediatrician at the heart of the dispute, was unable to participate in a 1997 Channel 4 documentary on Cleveland because the health authority in which she was then working banned her from appearing. Sue Richardson, the sexual abuse consultant, resigned from her job with a children's charity after being told that she would face the sack for taking part. In the Foucauldian-style contest between differing perspectives on this affair, key voices were missing. While Foucault would have perceived Cleveland as a contest for power between competing discourses, his model of power being wielded *through* discourse leaves an awkward question. In the contest for power, certain groups or individuals find themselves outside discourse, whether temporarily or permanently. In the Cleveland case, power produced uniformity of perspective where there should have been contest, and resistance to this hegemonic view, where it arose, was contained in pockets of the less popular media or in academic investigation. Cleveland's suggestion that child sexual abuse could be happening in any home throughout the country posed too uncomfortable a challenge.

A major study of the reporting of child sexual abuse cases concentrating on the period between 1986 and 1991, conducted by the Glasgow University Media Group, confirmed that the media preferred to focus on specific cases of abuse and neglected analysis of the overall problem. Stories that would generate sensation and drama were given priority, with the popular press in particular showing little interest in discussing contributory factors. As Soothill and Walby indicate, the statistics from bodies such as the NSPCC (National Society for the Prevention of Cruelty to Children) were eagerly reproduced, especially in the period before Cleveland, to intensify the sense of risk to children, while these bodies' analysis of the reasons underlying the increase in the number of cases was ignored by all except the more liberal broadsheet papers (1991: 113–15). From Cleveland onwards, as the Glasgow researchers point out, the media began to exhibit 'child-abuse fatigue' (Skidmore, 1998: 212), requiring 'new angles' to revive interest. These included the claims of ritual and Satanic abuse (the two were often conflated in media accounts), and the allegations of what became labelled 'false memory syndrome' (Skidmore, 1998: 210). Both reinforced, rather than challenged, the already-established discourse of over-zealous intervention by care professionals.

Anxiety about what became known as 'false memory syndrome' quickly spread from the United States to Britain in the 1990s, providing sustenance to fathers whose daughters had accused them of abuse through the recovery of memories during psychoanalytic therapy. As Jenny Kitzinger indicates, the media sided with the articulate pressure group, the British False Memory Society, who claimed that memories could not be resurrected in this way but were instead being falsely implanted in impressionable young women. The daughters' voices were rarely heard in the coverage that followed, while their allegedly abusive fathers gained ready access to columnists and the airwaves: 'accused parents were seven times more likely to be quoted than the person recalling the abuse' (Kitzinger, 1998: 190). Hegemony about the integrity of the family, and of patriarchy in particular, was being reasserted. The allegations of both ritual abuse and false memory syndrome were presented in a manner that validated the responsible behaviour of parents as against the dubious antics of care professionals, whether therapists or social workers. The media appeared happy to believe that parents were 'naturally' protective of their children, whereas workers in the caring professions were irresponsibly amplifying and exaggerating risk.

After a period of emphasizing the possibility of sexual, physical and emotional risks to children, the media retracted their concerns as the threat to 'family values' became too strong. Instead of looking inwards, to the strains within what was seen as the microcosm of social order, the media found new targets lurking outside, which were especially threatening by virtue of being invisible to caring parents. Whereas one, the threat of the paedophile in our midst, was intensely localized, the other, the threat of Internet pornography and paedophilia, appeared terrifying precisely because of its capacity to cross known boundaries and to resist, like a virus, any attempt to confine it within a particular territory.

## THE PAEDOPHILE IN OUR MIDST

The term 'paedophilia' has now passed into standard use, at least in Britain and Europe, as a pejorative and emotive evocation of the dominant contemporary threat to childhood innocence. Literally translated as 'love of children', 'paedophilia' has a complex and contradictory discursive history. Its adoption by a group of men who were campaigning in Britain in the 1970s for the rights to express their sexual feelings for children without censure, first brought it to public attention. Claiming that they were misrepresented by a repressive culture that both overestimated childhood innocence and was hypocritical about respect for children's rights, this group, known as the PIE (Paedophile Information Exchange), sought to validate paedophilia as part of the spectrum of varied forms of sexual expression that any liberal society ought to accept. Endorsing the Freudian view of children as intrinsically sexual beings, the PIE claimed that children were capable of deriving pleasure from sexual contact with adults. On the tricky question of the power differential between adults and children, and the difficulty of establishing a child's 'consent' to sexual relations, the PIE pointed to the degree of coercion in many adult/child relationships. Within dominant discourse, this either went unnoticed, or was claimed to be beneficial to the child. Much of the basis for the PIE's arguments lay in arguing that a taboo about children's sexuality was obscuring the hypocrisy of a society that deplored paedophile longings while happily abusing children's rights in non-sexual respects, and eagerly commodifying the very sexuality that it denied (see Evans, 1993: 228–39 for a fuller discussion of the PIE and the debates it stimulated).

The arguments advanced by this lobby were manifestly antithetical to dominant discourses of childhood and sexual morality, but the media and public response ignored the challenge that they presented to unacknowledged inconsistencies in prevailing ideologies of childhood. Child (almost always girl) beauty contests, children's clothing manufacturers, Barbie doll producers and advertisers all promote children as sexual beings (and especially legitimate the availability of little girls for an adult sexual gaze). The sexualization of young girls, latently acceptable in the commercial sphere, becomes shocking and disturbing when articulated as an explicit claim. The alleged hypocrisy of those who attacked paedophiles for abusing children's rights while themselves failing to promote these in any other sphere also merited debate. But any opportunity for a frank discussion that would have exposed difficulties and inconsistencies in the paedophiles' own arguments (especially around the issues of coercion and consent) was demolished by increasingly hostile media demonization of the paedophile.

The transition in media discourse from labels such as 'sex fiend' or 'monster' to 'paedophile' indicated a shift in the allocating of blame. While aberrant individuals operating beyond the pale of acceptable behaviour were deemed to be solely culpable for their own actions (although inadequate mothers were often held partly to blame), 'paedophiles' implicated the state in the failure of control. By introducing a quasi-scientific categorization, the monster rampaging out of control was transformed into a devious manipulator capable of duping state and legislative authorities. When 'paedophiles' are identified, more is suggested to be at stake than an individual attack on the sanctity of childhood. The failure of government, legal or care authorities to control the problem and protect those seen as the most vulnerable in society is also suggested. As one of the consequences of this, passions inflamed by media discourse prompted vigilante action against paedophiles (real or imagined) amongst communities who felt particularly abandoned by an uncaring state. British media commentary on the release from prison of a number of convicted paedophiles in the 1990s, together with the revelations of child murders by paedophiles in Belgium, helped to reinforce this way of thinking. High-profile coverage of the murder of Megan Kanka in the United States in 1994 and of Sarah Payne in Britain in 2000 strengthened the perception that the source of risk was now omnipresent and transnational. In the process, paedophilia came to imply more than an illicit sexual lust for children and appeared as a synonym for child murder. Whereas the child molester had been characterized as a loner, operating in the vague 'out there', the paedophile connoted a manipulator, often integrated into a wider network, who was, with state connivance, being allowed to live in streets and areas populated by children. The threat had moved from an indefinite, abstract location to the local neighbourhood. In the process, the local park, the local school playground, the local funfair and even the street or the child's own backyard were all transformed from child-friendly and safe places to play into sites of possible danger.

In 1995, the kidnap and death of four girls and teenagers in Belgium (some of whom had been imprisoned in a cage, starved and raped) led to suspicions of a paedophile network that operated with the collusion of members of the government and judiciary. Although Marc Dutroux was eventually arrested for the murders in 1996, police incompetence in the period immediately following the kidnaps was so dramatic as to raise suspicions of a cover-up at a high level. Allegations that Dutroux was merely working as a go-between, providing young girls and women for a client who was well connected within the upper échelons of Belgian society were not proved, despite substantial evidence from witnesses. Investigators found that their inquiries were blocked, and key potential witnesses died, often in mysterious circumstances, before they could offer testimony. When the investigating magistrate responsible for the arrest of Dutroux was removed from the case in 1996, Belgians took to the streets of Brussels in a massive protest demonstration, known as the 'White March' because of its symbolic use of white doves, balloons, flowers and clothing. At the time of writing, this case remains unresolved and Dutroux has never been brought to trial, although investigative journalists both in Belgium and elsewhere have disclosed substantial evidence of his link to other paedophiles and of an extensive cover-up (Bulte *et al.*, 1999; BBC2 *Correspondent* investigation by Olenka Frenkiel, 5 May 2002).

The international publicity around this case encouraged widespread fears about the extensiveness of paedophile networks, and the deviousness of those involved. It also generated acute anxieties about the failure of the authorities to protect children at risk. Despite the possible uniqueness of the Belgian circumstances, they resonated with alarm bells ringing elsewhere that even a 'nanny state' could not be relied upon to ensure child safety. In Britain, worries intensified around the release into the community in the late 1990s of high-profile sex offenders who had served their sentences for child murder. Vigilante protest in any area thought likely to house these people amplified the hostile discourse of the tabloid press. By the time of their release, changes in the legislation affecting sex offenders were either under way or had already been introduced, making it necessary for sex offenders' names to be placed on a register, and ensuring that they were subject to continuing monitoring by the police and prohibited from places such as playgrounds where children might congregate. Although these measures were non-retrospective, and could not be applied to the key figures being released in 1998 and 1999, these changes were rarely recognized in the media alarm surrounding these cases.

A *Panorama* programme on BBC1 (11 May 1998), 'Defend the children', focused on the crimes committed by a ring of paedophiles who had conspired to sexually abuse and kill teenage boys. Timed to be broadcast in the midst of media hostility to the release into the community of Sidney Cooke (the alleged leader of the group) in April 1998, it focused on the trauma of the victims' families and the impossibility of finding suitable accommodation for such men. It paid only lip-service to the ongoing legislative changes and ignored the lack of proportion in highlighting these cases. It was only in the final ten minutes of the 40-minute programme that a senior adviser to the Prison Sex Offender Treatment Programme pointed out that forcing sex offenders into hiding could increase rather than diminish risk, and distract attention away from more pervasive sources:

> This attention to convicted sex offenders is actually more dangerous to public safety. We know that children are much more at risk from being abused by people in their families, by people in clubs that they might be going to, if they're in institutions, within those institutions and it's there that we need to be doing things to protect children. Simply focusing on one individual and somehow thinking if we could cleanse society of him our children are safe I think is a dangerous solution.

The concentration on the risk from paedophiles released back into the community received a further boost in the late 1990s from the murders, in the United States and Britain, of two young girls, and the ensuing campaigns initiated by the girls' parents for improved government intervention to protect children. The killing of seven-year-old Megan Kanka in the United States in 1994 and of eight-year-old Sarah Payne in Britain in July 2000 crystallized discourses around the brutal destruction of childhood innocence by paedophiles. In both cases, the children came from caring families, and the abductions took place in locations assumed to be safe (Megan Kanka was lured into a house on her own suburban street; Sarah Payne was abducted while playing near her grandparents' home). By the time Sarah Payne met her death, Megan's killer had been established to be a paedophile, but in Britain the popular media immediately made this assumption. The parallels the media drew between the two cases grew with the campaign of Sarah's parents for the introduction of legislation in Britain equivalent to the new Sex Offender Registration Act 1996 in the United States (popularly referred to as 'Megan's Law') that requires every state to hold a register of convicted sex offenders and to provide details to local people when sex offenders are released into their community. Responding to populist demand, a number of states have even yielded to the temptation of publishing the identities of sex offenders on the Internet. In Britain, the popular Sunday tabloid, the *News of the World*, ran a 'name and shame' campaign in the summer of 2000, in support of Sarah Payne's family, until hostility from even police authorities arguing that it was driving paedophiles underground, forced it to change its mind. Civil liberties groups had also protested that this campaign was provoking vigilante attacks on innocent people, mistakenly identified as paedophiles. This 'name and shame' campaign was, in any case, in excess of Sarah Payne's parents' request for controlled right of access to the names of the most dangerous paedophiles living in an area.

While 'Megan's Law' preoccupied the popular media as the answer to the risk of paedophiles to children, a number of difficulties were given little attention (although these did receive some attention from the broadsheet newspapers). The possibilities that such legislative measures would encourage paedophiles to go into hiding, or might even make it easier for them to establish contact with other paedophiles, were ignored, as was the injustice of implying that all sex offenders continued to pose equivalent risks to children. In addition, the emphasis on 'stranger-paedophiles' drew attention away from other sources of equally serious harm to children. Compared to abuse and murder by non-strangers, the threat from unknown paedophiles lurking outside the home has been both relatively static and statistically modest. A Home Office report published in February 1999 showed that 'over 80 per cent of abuse is by those well known to their victims' (Birkett, 1999). Studies of public perception suggest a widespread belief that children are much more at risk from strangers now than previously. In terms of child murder, however, the statistics (at least in Britain) indicate this not to be the case. Between five and ten children a year are murdered by strangers, figures that have remained unchanged for at least 30 years, while annual child homicides by friends or family members average around 80. In addition, clear-up rates for the latter are substantially lower (27 per cent as against 90 per cent for strangers according to one estimate) since a loophole in English law enables parents to escape prosecution (where there is no independent evidence) if they blame each other for the killing (Hall, 2002). At the same time as the discovery of Sarah Payne's body was preoccupying the media, the brutal murder of another two young children passed relatively unnoticed. This murder was by a father, and took place within the family home. A correspondent writing in a broadsheet newspaper sums up this disparity: 'it seems we're enthralled by the murder of a child if it's by a stranger, a bogeyman, a devil among us. But if it might be by daddy, we don't really care' (Birkett, 2000).

Within the media's 'immense verbosity' about paedophiles and paedophilia, the voice of the paedophile was almost entirely absent. Even in the less public medium of the written word, society has carefully monitored whose sexual stories can be voiced, and the reflections even of the non-offending paedophile remain little heard (Plummer, 1995: 116–19). When the media venture into this territory, they face hostility and censure. In addition, popular discourses linking 'manipulativeness' and 'deviousness' especially strongly with the paedophile put presenters and listeners particularly on their guard on the rare occasions that interviews are printed or broadcast. A Channel 4 documentary, 'The devil amongst us' (8 January 1998), presented by Dea Birkett, was sharply attacked for its approach, despite appearing on a minority channel. This programme defied unitary stereotyping of the paedophile by talking to five men, each with differing stories to tell about their own behaviour and desires. None of them, significantly, had ever previously been interviewed by any journalist (Birkett, 1997). Of the five, only two had been convicted of a recent offence (although a third had been convicted as a teenager). Some of the witnesses were particularly articulate about current ideological constructions that demonize sexual desire for children. They argued instead for a more measured approach that would regard paedophilia as one of a spectrum of sexual desires, open to abuse as much as, but not more than, sexual practices that are deemed perfectly 'normal' or 'respectable' (abuse within heterosexual marriage, for example). The variety of contributors to this programme also insisted that paedophilia does not necessarily result in sexual intercourse with children. Desire for children can be pursued through what they described as consensual touching or through the viewing of material on the Internet. The erroneousness of assuming that every paedophile is a practising *abuser* was repeatedly emphasized.

The programme did, however, skirt around the difficult issue of the differential power between adults and children, and the potential abuse of trust involved in inviting children to 'consent' to particular kinds of sexual practice. At only one point does this emerge as a clear issue. The presenter asks Paul, who was a leading member of the PIE, whether a four-year-old can consent to sexual activities. The evasiveness of his answer suggests the need for a debate that would centre on this issue of pressure and the abuse of trust, and the problematic entanglements of sexual desires with power relations. As complex and contentious issues, even in relation to adult sexuality, these cannot be tackled or illuminated either by a discursive silence around childhood sexuality or by a demonizing of the paedophile.

Despite opening up a rare space for paedophiles' own voices to be aired, this programme's own discourse defensively anticipates hostility. Emphasizing the tone of disapproval signified in the programme's title, Dea Birkett explains her mission at the start of the programme as being 'to meet *and confront*' (my italics) her interviewees. By the end, she acknowledges the difficulty of reducing the variety and complexity of the paedophiles she has met to a single pattern, but, by stressing that there is no 'simple neat solution', she concedes to the dominant construction of paedophiles as a problem. She uses an 'us/them' formulation to distance herself (and the viewer) from claims made by paedophiles in the programme that sexual desire between adults and children is no more unnatural than other forms of sexual desire: 'we know that sex between adults and children is wrong. We cannot allow them to realize their desires'. At the same time she argues for dealing with them in a way that avoids 'violence or fear'. This sets her position (and the programme's) apart from the vigilantes seen towards the end, advocating, minimally, exclusion and, at worst, torture of any paedophile in their area. Attacks on the programme were swift to follow. The popular newspapers, the NSPCC, NACRO (National Association for the Care and Resettlement of Offenders), the children's charity Childline and some Channel 4 viewers all objected, with varying degrees of vituperation, that the programme gave a platform to shameless offenders without any regard to the children they had abused. In her own defence, Dea Birkett (1998) argued that television had previously ignored the lack of shame expressed by many paedophiles, and misrepresented them as typically repentant, shadowy figures whose blanked-out faces and wringing hands reinforced their characterization as pathetic loners.

In one respect, 'The devil amongst us' reinforced popular conceptions of paedophile risk. In a society that wants to construct 'safe' spaces for children, one of the most frightening forms of visualizing the paedophile is to emphasize his wily success in invading, *incognito*, supposedly protected and fun-filled spaces. By affronting powerful constructions of nostalgia for a golden time when children played safely on urban streets or explored the rural wilds without adult supervision, these images are particularly provocative. In the collapse of this mythology, the paedophile is more easily constructed as the enemy than the combustion engine, computer games or the changing structures of family and community life. When vigilante groups protest about the presence of paedophiles in 'our street', 'our neighbourhood', near 'our school' or 'playground', they evoke an imaginary child-friendly space that can be ring-fenced from hostile outsiders. Spatially configured, the risks acknowledged to be a part of modern life can be conceptually removed by being physically distanced. It is the invasion into our proximate space of enemy/outsiders that has the power to stimulate fiercely territorial protest (much the same rhetoric has attended public hostility to the 'invasion' of other people characterized as 'outsiders', such as refugees and asylum-seekers). As we have already seen, the murders of Megan Kanka and Sarah Payne were particularly emotive for violating neighbourhood space; ironically, the invisible home of parental murder remains, on the other hand, private and outside the responsibility of the community. In 'The devil amongst us', paedophiles are shown invading the supposedly safe and carefree environments of the beach, the home backyard and the garden tent, defiling the spaces associated in representational terms with happiness, security and childhood freedom. If this breaking of established and normative boundaries is guaranteed to instil fear in the viewer, the potential of the Internet to make a mockery of all boundaries (invading even the supposed 'sanctuary' of the home) raises the sense of risk to a new level of intensity.

## THE INTERNET AND PAEDOPHILIA

Every 'new' communications technology has been accompanied by contradictory discourses of utopian promise or dire foreboding. Just as the arrival of radio in Britain produced discourses of global harmony ('nation shall speak peace unto nation') and, at the same time, predictions of the demise of literacy, so the rapid development of the Internet and the World Wide Web divided commentators sharply into optimists or pessimists. To some these developments heralded a new democratic public sphere, globalized and accessible to all; to others, a dangerous space where cultural values and freedoms could easily be eroded by dark and satanic forces (McNair, 1998: 181–4). If adults were thought to be 'at risk' from this new development, children were more particularly so: their 'natural' vulnerability was accentuated by their facility in manipulating this new technology. While parents welcomed the Internet as an educational tool, the dangers lurking in this new uncontrollable and unbounded transnational space raised especially strong anxieties among those parents with little knowledge of the Internet themselves. As a Pew Internet survey of over 2000 American adults during February 2001 revealed, child pornography dominated concerns about Internet crime (80 per cent of those surveyed claimed to be 'very concerned' about this, with women particularly so) (Pew Internet and American Life Project, 2001). In addition to the risk of encountering pornographic material on the web, the ability of those communicating through chatrooms to adopt false personae raised new forms and levels of fear. While liberating for the participants (especially for those who feel their 'given' identity to be restricting or oppressive), this posed fresh dangers for children perceived to be naturally trusting and innocent about adult wiles. The image of the lone paedophile cultivating friendship with children became additionally alarming when perceived to be potentially occurring in the child's own bedroom and in the guise of someone pretending to be the same age, and even the same sex, as the online child.

The conventional media have demonstrated customary alacrity in fuelling fears about their 'new' competitors. By focusing on sexual risks, to the exclusion of perils such as neo-Nazi propaganda or information on how to make bombs, adults' own unresolved anxieties around sexuality are again revealed and accentuated. In addition, the risks at stake here are mainly those of fantasy or image consumption rather than direct contact. The *Oprah Winfrey Show*, in devoting an edition to the dangers of children encountering unsolicited pornography on the Internet, or being lured to expose personal details to paedophiles (Channel 5, 16 March 2001, first broadcast in 1999), repeatedly stressed adult bemusement and shock at its revelations. Oprah herself talked about being nauseated by the evidence that children could stumble upon types of pornography that would be out of reach of adults even in specialist outlets. Cutaway shots emphasized the disbelief and horror of parents in the audience, as the universality of the problem was underlined: 'if you don't think this is happening to your children, you are so wrong'. The 'expert' brought in to offer advice, Donna Rice Hughes (once famous for an affair with Gary Hart, but now presented as a campaigner for child safety on the net), accentuated the level of threat. Much less time, however, was spent on indicating how protection against this might be achieved (despite the programme's admission that children encounter computers not only in their own homes but in friends' houses, as well as in the more monitored confines of the school or library).

Exposure to pornographic material, or to sexual predators in chatrooms was automatically assumed to be harmful, without any querying or modulating of this assumption by listening carefully to what children themselves had to say. While the voices of a number of children, aged 10 to 15, were included in brief interview clips, what the audience was cued to hear differed from the children's own accounts. Despite Oprah's introductory assertion that 'we were blown away' by their revelations, the youngsters themselves appeared more concerned to withhold information from their parents on the types of material they were encountering online. Although pornography was included in their list of experiences, it sat alongside anarchist material, terrorist information and ready access to means of purchasing drugs, handguns and alcohol. None of the young people appeared to be particularly disturbed by the pornography they had seen, although they were clearly aware of its unacceptability to the adults in their lives. The mismatch between Oprah's introduction and the matter-of-fact delivery of the youngsters themselves suggests that tuning in more acutely to how young people themselves perceive the Internet might question the universal appropriateness of the adult discourse of alarm, and of its exclusive emphasis on *sexual* dangers.

Media discourses about risks to children from cyberporn are echoed in political discourses also. The notion that America can be made 'safe for children' underpinned Attorney General Ashcroft's comments to a news conference on 8 August 2001. Describing a number of initiatives that will 'help make the Internet a safe place for children to play and learn', he used a common metaphor for the Internet as a place also of danger – that of 'back alleys and dark corners' where evil can lurk:

> ... the work of the Department of Justice to provide a safe America for
> children now extends well beyond the physical world into the electronic
> universe of cyberspace. Few would disagree that the World Wide Web offers
> unparalleled educational and recreational opportunities for our young
> people, but there are back alleys and dark corners of the Internet where our
> children can be exposed to inappropriate material or even become
> susceptible to offenders who view them as sexual objects.

(Ashcroft, 2001)

The dark, labyrinthine space of the Internet is, like the wilderness, ultimately untamable, but the menace this poses to our protective attitude to childhood is built upon the paradoxical presupposition that a 'safe America' or a 'safe childhood' is still a possibility. By suggesting that safety can be achieved through external controls, political discourse perpetuates a myth of childhood as a state that can be ring-fenced from danger, and obviates the need for approaches that will enable children themselves to negotiate their relationship to an inevitably risky world with confidence.

## CONCLUSION

The abuse of power over children rightly evokes strong antipathy and condemnation, but this chapter has suggested that the discursive emphasis on *sexual* risks to children, whether directly or through the mediation of the Internet, tells us more about adult anxieties and aspirations than it does about the relative threats to children's welfare. Based on an unrealizable dream of a childhood utopia where innocence can be sustained until the child is 'ready' for adulthood, and where protected spaces for children can be guaranteed, this discursive construction both promises what no policy, or even dedicated parent, can deliver, and distracts attention away from measures that might enable children who are subject to abuse to have access to less prejudiced adult ears. The popular media's preoccupation with sexual risk from adult predators skews our sense of where risk is most to be found. Even although statistics are dubious reporters of actuality, evidence from the British NSPCC indicates that the number of children on child protection registers in England in 2001 for 'sexual abuse alone' amounted to only two-thirds of those suffering 'emotional abuse alone' and to only one-third of those suffering from 'neglect alone' (NSPCC, 2001). A survey conducted for the same organization in 2000 discovered that the biggest category of sexual abuser of children was not the adult male but brothers and stepbrothers (43 per cent) – other children, in other words (Carvel, 2000). The top modern killers of children, according to official statistics, are 'car accidents; congenital malformations; cancer; sudden infant death syndrome and leukaemia' (Travis, 1999). Such statistics get at best modest attention from media obsessed with sexual risks from paedophiles.

The depth of public and media hostility to any attempt to re-evaluate risks to children was sharply pronounced in reactions to an edition of the Channel 4 spoof documentary series *Brass Eye*, which parodied the excesses of current preoccupations with paedophilia (26 July 2001). According to an interview published in the *Guardian*, the intention of the producer, Chris Morris, was 'to make us think not about the media, but our own laughably confused attitude to children' (5 August 2001). A number of vignettes made biting attacks on the double-standard of expressions of outrage about paedophilia being combined with public complacency about the commodification of children's (and especially girls') sexuality. The beauty contest's construction of ever younger girls for sexual display was the butt of a scenario in which 'tarted-up tots', including a small child with fake breasts, paraded for the pleasure of the spectator. Young girls were also shown defying hegemonic expectations by expressing adoration for a rap artist despite his paedophile status. If these images were disturbing, they merely exaggerated constructions of childhood sexuality that have been widely accepted within consumerist discourse.

As well as inviting us to laugh uneasily at the elusive dividing line between acceptable and unacceptable forms of commodifying children's sexuality, *Brass Eye* also made fun of the adult exaggerations of the risks of online sex offences. Authoritative celebrities, some of whom were conned into appearing on the programme, earnestly informed viewers of the devious strategies typically used by paedophiles within online games to enable them to touch and molest children. The ludicrousness of their assertions revealed the depth of adult ignorance about the very technology they claimed to find so threatening. The programme provoked a large number of complaints from the public, but also a substantial degree of support. The popular media overlooked the extent of approval, amplifying the concerns expressed, and giving full voice to the chorus of disapproval from government ministers (some of whom had not even seen the programme). The *News of the World* called for 'Channel Filth' to be 'kicked off air' (29 July 2001) and the *Daily Mail*, voraciously continuing its long campaign against Channel 4, declared the programme to be 'unspeakably sick', indeed 'the sickest TV programme ever shown' (30 July 2001). Even some of the broadsheets sounded a note of caution about taking too liberal a view on its approach. The *Guardian*, despite its liberal leanings, asserted in an Editorial that '*Brass Eye* was a deeply unpleasant piece of television that degraded children much more than it satirised either the media or celebrities or politicians' (31 July 2001). It also published what it described as 'two opposing views on the row', neither of which endorsed the programme itself. While a sketch featuring paedophile Sidney Cooke being exiled into space, with an eight-year-old boy mistakenly immured along with him, may have been offensive to surviving relatives of Cooke's victims, the general accusation that the programme was harmful to survivors of abuse was based on supposition rather than evidence (some survivors of abuse indeed claimed in letters to the broadsheet press that the programme was helpful in giving voice to their concerns about media sensationalism).

Only shortly before this furore, the popular ITV soap opera *Coronation Street* had run a storyline involving the abduction of a teenage girl by a man whom she met via an online chatroom, imagining him to be someone of her own age. Depicted as a devious and desperate middle-aged man, confused about his own sexual impulses and desires, this fictional paedophile conformed to the general media script. Although some viewers complained about the intrusion of social-issue storylines into the lighthearted *Coronation Street*, and others found the dramatic portrayal too stereotyped and badly acted to be convincing, there was general support for the educational intention behind the idea. Warning teenage girls and their parents about the risk of paedophiles on the Internet was an acceptable project whereas asking people to laugh at the assumptions built into their own constructions of paedophilia and childhood sexuality was too discomfiting.

Adult discourses of risk to children focus on those that echo most strongly with adult hang-ups. Although all discourses elide alternative ways of constructing 'reality', discourses of risk are particularly potent in this respect because of their play on deep-seated and often unconscious fears and emotions. The desire to protect children evokes especially powerful passions and any discursive construction capable of claiming this intent has a persuasive advantage. By focusing on adult concerns, however, the voice of the child, and children's capacity for being as variegated in their reading of images and fantasies as adults, is suppressed. A climate of hysteria never provides the best environment for allowing children the space to articulate their own worries, confusions and concerns.

# Chapter Six

# 'UNSAFE' FOOD

When a British newspaper editor reported that the inspiration for the play he had just co-written came from reading *The Day of the Triffids* to his daughter, his desire to escape from the maelstrom of world events into fantasy might have been presumed. But this was a play about genetically modified (GM) crops and the dilemmas their unknown future poses for humanity. The spark for this creative journey tells us much about the interweaving of information, memory, nostalgia and fantasy in many of our contemporary constructions of risk. Food is at once mundane, but also deeply written into our psychic and imaginative narratives. Fears about food safety are, however, a relatively recent phenomenon. In the pre-1970s universe, where memories of wartime food rationing survived, the correlation between eating and health was inscribed in public discourse. Advertising slogans as late as the 1960s cajoled us to 'Go to work on an egg', 'Drink a pint of milk a day' or even to believe that 'A Mars a day helps you work, rest and play', echoing popular beliefs that fish was good for the brain or that eating greens was beneficial to more than Popeye. The obsession that has since developed in public discourses about the risks lying latent in our food is both a relatively recent phenomenon and one whose origins and breeding conditions need to be explained. This chapter considers how discourses about food safety have become ways of talking about concerns that extend far beyond food itself. From initial worries about how the individual can control risks from unsafe food, concerns have escalated into deeper anxieties about failures in good governance and in scientific access to knowledge.

Current levels of concern are almost certainly disproportionate to any risk inherent in specific foods, and indicative of more profound changes in our thinking about a controllable universe. Whereas food in films has been used metaphorically in recent decades to articulate the nature of desire, and in particular sexual desire, in other areas of the media food's perceived riskiness has triggered disquiet about the interface between personal freedoms, and has increasingly questioned processes of governance in a globalized world. Through a discussion of a number of food 'scares' and worries about genetically modified organisms (GMOs), this chapter argues that the initial assumption that food risk could be allayed through scientific and governmental intervention has given way to more fundamental doubts about the credibility of a range of official discourses. In Britain, this trajectory can be seen in the chronology of concerns aroused first by bacteria such as salmonella, listeria and E. coli, then by BSE/CJD links, and latterly by the development of GM foods. Yet, despite these shifts, the frame of media thinking has remained attuned almost entirely to western perspectives. Although food is globalized in its production and distribution, a diversity of international perspectives is absent from most of the scripts the western media deploy in talking about it.

# RISKS INVADE EVERYDAY LIFE

The earliest worries about government failures to protect consumer safety arose in relation not to food, but to medicines. Initially contained and localized, these began to acquire cumulative resonance in the 1970s. A typhoid epidemic in Aberdeen (Scotland) in 1964 had produced consternation in the media about the violation of an everyday food product (imported corned beef), but media discourses attributed the outbreak to specific hygiene lapses, and emphasized the need for personal and institutional vigilance in the handling of food. Individual lack of care, rather than any intrinsic doubts about food safety, was underlined by the tracing of the outbreak to a hitherto well-regarded store in a city admired for its granite sparkle and cleanliness. Since the contamination had spread from the originating source to other products in this retail outlet, the local media stressed the need for intensive hygienic precautions in food preparation both in shops and in the home. The successful containment of this epidemic reinforced the official discourse that problems of food safety could be allayed by responsible individual adherence to public guidelines. The consumer was to become the self-policing and self-regulating subject of the Foucauldian concept of regulation (Lupton, 1999b: 86–8).

Worries about the safety of medicines, on the other hand, began to escalate in the 1970s, when the repercussions of what had become known as the 'thalidomide scandal' spilled over into revelations about risks associated with the contraceptive pill. As with later claims about the risks of food, these anxieties were particularly sharpened by the contrast between the utopian view of drug intervention (fostered ever since the invention of penicillin) and the new realization that apparently beneficent medicines could also have harmful consequences. The thalidomide exposure especially increased public awareness about the power of the pharmaceutical companies and the inadequate testing of new drugs before they were released and marketed. Babies of women who had taken this drug in order to alleviate nausea and insomnia during pregnancy in the late 1950s and early 1960s were born with highly visible physical defects. The sense of alarm generated by the initial discoveries was revived when *The Sunday Times* published in 1972 the first of an intended series of revelations about the drug's history. Despite the distance in time, Distillers, the company responsible for marketing and distributing the drug in the UK, was still in dispute with the parents of many of the children over the payment of compensation, and contempt of court legislation was used to prevent further publication of evidence against its interests. The thalidomide case became as a result the first stimulus for a discourse of risk that acknowledged the power of the vested interests at stake. Risk was in this instance attributable not to an individual who could be demonized, but to the faceless and elusive corporations of capitalism and their ability to defy democratic accountability while preying on society's search for panaceas.

Given the specific circumstances of this case, the risks might have seemed as evanescent as those surrounding the typhoid epidemic in Aberdeen. But in the 1970s, considerably later than the harm accomplished by thalidomide (the offending drug was withdrawn from the market in the early 1960s), a number of 'scare stories' emerged about the contraceptive pill that gained resonance from *The Sunday Times'* exposure. Since only a limited number of women had taken the thalidomide drug, it could still appear a contained and one-off risk, but the same could not be argued about suggestions that the side-effects of long-term use of the contraceptive pill might be deleterious to women's health. As Germaine Greer remarked in a *Sunday Times* review (2001) of Lara Marks' history of the contraceptive pill, those who used this form of contraception were too preoccupied with the difficulties in getting hold of it at that time to contemplate its possibly adverse effects on their eventual physical well-being. In the 1960s, the liberating potential of the pill predominated in most users' thinking, and the assumption that medicines available in reputable chemists had been fully tested remained strong despite the thalidomide scandal. The alacrity with which the medical profession rushed to defend the safety of the contraceptive pill in the wake of each new allegation of risk suggested a closing of the ranks between pharmaceutical giants and doctors (doctors, on the other hand, claimed their motivation was to discourage women from risking unwanted pregnancies by abandoning the pill precipitously). A seed of suspicion, that vested interests rather than patient safety were uppermost in official thinking, had been germinated that would find fruition in the food scares of the 1980s and 1990s.

Despite this initiation in scepticism, scares around medicines could always be contained because of the element of choice in their use, and the availability of alternatives. In both these major alarms, the consumers of the affected drugs were young women, who were unlikely magnets for public sympathy. Indeed, in some quarters of the media, health scares around the contraceptive pill were heralded as a welcome warning against the liberalization of female sexuality. In the case of thalidomide, it was the palpable presence of 'innocent children' affected by the drug that elicited public concern. The revelation of risks associated with sexual activity in the wake of the AIDS developments of the 1980s was the first example of a medical crisis rippling out from what was thought originally to be a circumscribed group (AIDS as a 'gay plague') to include the entire community of sexually active people (by the early 1990s, indeed, figures suggested that the heterosexual population was more at risk from contracting the HIV virus than the homosexual one). Much of the spread of the disease was, however, attributed to casual sexual encounters, especially on holiday, allowing it to be perceived, erroneously, as a problem without implications for everyday sexual relations.

It was the association of risk with the most everyday items of food consumption that broke the charm of believing that risks 'out there' could be avoided through sensible choices and precautions. Salmonella was the first area of risk to be highlighted by the media as a generally applicable source of worry in the late 1980s. Because salmonella affected eggs and chickens, two regular items in most people's diets (numbers of vegetarians in Britain were relatively low at this time), it passed into popular vocabulary and consciousness as a risk that had penetrated the innermost reaches of the home, and lurked also in the canteens, sandwich counters and takeaway outlets that many of the population frequented during the working day. It was soon to be joined by two equally foreign-sounding invaders: listeria and E. coli.

## SALMONELLA, LISTERIA AND E. COLI

The dangers of the salmonella bacterium infecting food were known before the 1980s, but its association with eggs greatly intensified public alarm in the latter part of that decade. Initially, salmonella had been discovered in raw poultry, and public warnings had been issued about cooking chicken carefully. Battery farming methods and the widespread retailing of frozen poultry, both of which transformed chicken from a luxury item to an everyday meat, increased the risk of infection. Although there are over 2000 varieties of the bacterium, it is one variety (*salmonella enteritidis* phage type 4) that has been responsible for the outbreaks that led to media panics. Rare in the early 1980s, it accounted for 45 per cent of salmonella infections by 1994 (Association of Medical Microbiologists, 1995). Although evidence was emerging by the 1980s that this bacterium could appear in raw eggs, official disclosure of this information was slow to appear. What transformed the situation and led to blanket media coverage was the statement by the then Junior Health Minister, Mrs Edwina Currie, on 3 December 1988, that 'most of the egg production in this country, sadly, is infected with salmonella' (cited in Fowler, 1991: 151). This announcement provided the popular media with the basis for a first-class story, both in terms of its implications for everyday life and because of the political storm that accompanied its announcement. In the furore that followed, Mrs Currie was obliged to resign, her later modification of her pronouncement coming too late to save her (Fowler, 1991: 154).

Eggs, from seeming the universally nutritious, health-giving food of Fay Weldon's 'Go to work on an egg' advertising slogan of the 1960s, were now transformed into a potential poison, especially if given raw, or in partly cooked form, to the elderly or to young children. Although in most cases recovery from the symptoms of this infection was speedy and total, rare cases of death as a result of salmonella were exploited to suggest a wider risk. An outbreak of listeriosis (from the listeria bacteria) that claimed some lives early in 1989 added impetus to the panic. This generated widespread alarm, partly because in the case of listeria the specific source of infection was uncertain, and partly because the foods coming under suspicion – cheese, milk and pre-cooked meals – were, like eggs, staple ingredients in the British diet. While eggs could be avoided (sales plummeted following Mrs Currie's warning), the potential for unwitting consumption of infected food was markedly increased by this new scare. If the source of risk could not be specified, risk could be present in any number of foodstuffs regularly purchased by British consumers.

By emphasizing risk to the consumer, rather than the material conditions of production that allowed these bacteria to flourish, popular media discourse successfully obscured the policy implications of these developments and focused instead on regimes of individual consumer responsibility. Advice to consumers was predicated on the notion that 'food safety' was an attainable ideal. As Fowler points out in a perceptive analysis of the salmonella episode, although the roles of politicians, the food industry and its monitoring agencies were discussed, especially in the broadsheet newspapers, the popular press placed the burden of responsibility on the 'housewife' (already by the late 1980s a mythic construction, given that few women of working age were routinely at home during the day). The discursive assumption, most acutely visible in the popular press, that risk could be countered by individual precautions, allowed a number of entrenched interests to escape inquiry.

'The housewife', not for the first time in the twentieth century, was an easier target. As in earlier decades, appeals and tributes to her capabilities were used to win her consent to new regimes of hygiene in the kitchen (despite changing practices, household management remained a feminized concept). Commercial interests, too, were quick to take advantage, bringing out new surface-wiping cleansers guaranteed to 'kill all known bacteria'. In the inter-war period, advertisers in Britain had exploited similar tactics to alarm mothers about germs that could be exterminated only by purchasing the new cleaning agents emanating from the burgeoning chemical industry. Persuasive modes of address mixed flattery about women's nurturing skills with emphasis on the scientific knowledge necessary to be an adequate housewife. Similar strategies reappeared in the 1990s with warnings about food storage, kitchen hygiene and care in food preparation, constructing the housewife as an apparently naive but well-intentioned woman whose devotion to family outstripped any inconvenience to herself. The most popular British tabloid, the *Sun*, went as far as to suggest that shopping daily for fresh foods, rather than relying on convenience products, was the most assured means of lessening risk (see extract from the *Sun*, 13 February 1989, in Fowler, 1991: 198–9). The impracticality of this solution for most of its readers was ignored.

Even in some broadsheet papers, emphasis on domestic hygiene prevailed (Fowler, 1991: 187–202). Here, however, the risks from food did raise a wider number of issues for debate, including the responsibilities of the food industry and the inadequacies of a form of control (the Ministry of Agriculture, Fisheries and Food) that was supposed to negotiate the frequently conflicting interests of food producers and consumers. As yet, however, salmonella and listeria appeared largely controllable, and although the outbreaks raised worries about government efficacy in dealing with them, these accusations were contained, and mainly provided a means of attacking the Conservative government of the time. The discourse of risk established by Mrs Currie's pronouncement was far from being a marker of an intensified public health *danger* (compared with other health risks from food, the danger of undercooked salmonella-infected eggs remained minor). As Roger Fowler puts it, 'the great egg scare was not a medical phenomenon, not an epidemic; it was a construct of discourse' (1991: 148).

The E. coli bacteria, on the other hand, posed more of a threat to public health. Yet, because cases appeared localized and sporadic, they drew less attention from the media in terms of a discourse of universal risk. This in many ways inverted the pattern of the salmonella coverage. Whereas that had inflated a risk that was modest, by attaching it to a common consumer product, the threat of the E. coli bacterium to public health was minimized by localizing it. E. coli 0157, the most deadly strain of the bacterium, is to be found in cow dung, and transfers to human beings through contact with microscopic residues passed on through contact with animals, through the water supply or through eating infected food. Considerably more infectious and life-threatening than the salmonella bacterium, it has produced a growing (or increasingly visible) number of infectious outbreaks since the beginning of 1990 in the UK, Japan, the United States and Canada. While these have dominated media coverage in the West, the more routine million or so deaths each year from this bacterium outside the developed world have gone largely unnoticed.

An outbreak of E. coli 0157 food poisoning in Lanarkshire (Scotland) in 1996 was widely covered by the Scottish media, but gained less publicity nationally than the salmonella and listeria outbreaks despite being responsible for the deaths of 18 elderly people. Coverage concentrated on attacking the source of risk. Because this was readily identified as emanating from a hitherto highly regarded butcher's shop, the more general questions this outbreak raised about abattoirs, animal-rearing methods and even food controls in retail outlets, were muted by the provision of a solution to the immediate narrative enigma. A British current affairs programme, *World in Action*, broadcast almost two years later (ITV, 24 August 1998), did, however, adopt a mode of address that aimed to stimulate a sense of general risk beyond the local circumstances. Announcing its intention to investigate 'the frightening rise of E. coli 0157, the battle to control its spread and find a cure, and the risks of another killer outbreak', the programme's initial focus on the specific Scottish case soon gave way to everyday images of a pork chop being served in a butcher's shop. This transition marked a shift from local to general implications of risk. Later, the commentator emphasized the gravity of the risks by introducing a comparison with salmonella: 'it would take a million microbes of salmonella to make you ill. But E. coli 0157 is so much more dangerous that just ten of these bugs would be enough to strike you down.'

Despite information that 15 per cent of cows tested in Britain were thought to be carrying the disease, and that abattoirs had no means of removing infected animals from the food chain, *World in Action*'s own random tests failed to discover any of the deadliest bacteria in the samples of meat bought from a number of butchers. This apparent absence of risk was, however, translated into proof of risk by an expert, bacteriologist Professor Hugh Pennington, who argued that if E. coli was present at all (and it had been shown to be in the sample) 'well, that could have been E. coli 0157'. Although the modal 'could have been' suggested doubt, the commentator translates this into 'Experts say that proves that we're at risk from the killer strain.' Later, the programme presents undercover footage from three butchers' shops in Lancashire demonstrating the poor hygiene standards in operation. By emphasizing scenes of everyday consumption, filmed and edited, in the undercover manner, to appear distorted and frightening, this programme succeeded in suggesting the universal nature of risk from this bacterium.

The scientists appearing in this programme accentuated the risks of E. coli 0157, but at the same time provided reassurance that this problem could be controlled by the exercise of vigilance. The microbiologist Professor Richard Lacey, who along with Professor Hugh Pennington has been the British media's most frequently represented expert on food safety issues, was filmed in a kitchen cooking frozen lamb burgers to the manufacturers' specifications. While the aim was to demonstrate the inadequacy of the instructions, the choice of a domestic setting indicated that the solution (more thorough cooking) lay with the individual consumer. When the last segment of the programme radically questioned the individual's capacity to make good the failures of public policy, the scientist was on hand to allay concerns. The mother of a boy who died following a local outbreak of the bacterium from an unknown source expressed regret that the authorities seemed less concerned to detect the killer than they would be if her son had been murdered. Responding to the mother's challenge, Professor Pennington reassures the viewer that all these cases were preventable, and could have been avoided with proper investigation and the application of scientific knowledge.

Within the bacteria-based risk narratives, scientists are still presented as friends of the consumer, and as confident of their epistemological grasp of the 'truth' about the phenomenon being discussed. Negligence, where it exists, is attributed to government or 'the authorities'. From the distant guru, speaking in terminological riddles, and remote from everyday realities, the scientist is domesticated to be the ally of consumers against the faceless indifference of governments and public bodies. Professors Lacey and Pennington appeared consumer-friendly, confident in their knowledge base, and critical of the inaction of policy-makers. Good governance was still a possibility, given the political will. In the BSE/CJD crises that became the subject of media discussion in 1990s' Britain, such certainties about scientific knowledge as a potential barrier against risk began to crumble.

## THE UNCERTAIN CASE OF BSE/CJD

Bovine spongiform encephalopathy (BSE) in cattle is a fatal disease, manifest first through serious disturbance of the brain and nervous system functions, and undetectable before these symptoms appear. Thought to develop from an accumulation of abnormal prion proteins in the brain and nervous system, it has similarities to Creutzfeldt-Jakob disease (CJD) among humans, historically a rare disease and one mainly affecting people over the age of 40. Concerns about BSE first surfaced in Britain in the late 1980s when a sharp increase in the number of cases of this disease in cattle was becoming evident. Although the reason for this has never been totally determined, use of the remains of animals in cattle feed emerged as the most accepted explanation. The government was sufficiently worried in 1988 to establish a committee of inquiry that reported in 1989 and stated that it was 'most unlikely that BSE will have implications for human health' (Southwood, 1989). Although this report also added, more cautiously, that, because of the long incubation period, 'it may be a decade before complete reassurances can be given', officials used the lack of evidence to the contrary to emphasize the safety of beef. The widely distributed images of the then agriculture minister, John Gummer, feeding a beefburger to his young daughter in May 1990 became the most memorable symbol of the endorsements of safety given by a range of government ministers.

Advertisements from the Meat and Livestock Commission (established in the 1960s to promote British beef) also appeared in the national press in May 1990 asserting that 'Beef Is Safe' and claiming that this view had been endorsed by 'independent British and European scientists' and by the Department of Health. The small print of these advertisements stated 'Eating British Beef is completely safe. There is no evidence of any threat to human health caused by this animal health problem (BSE).' These two statements, initially presented as synonymous, were later to be driven apart by the revelations during the official inquiry into BSE (Phillips, 2000). This demonstrated how precisely worded scientific assurances that there was *no evidence of* a link were interpreted, wrongly, by government spokespeople to mean that *no link* therefore existed.

In this initial phase of the possibility of risk, the media were largely happy to support the official view. The absence of a strong human element to the story meant that media interest declined rapidly (see Kitzinger and Reilly, 1997: 338–44 on fluctuations in reporting), to be revived only by the government's announcement on 21 March 1996 that the recent deaths of a number of young people from a new variant of CJD (vCJD) suggested that transmission of the disease from cattle to humans was now a possibility. This *volte-face* produced a flurry of activity in the media, but also posed a number of difficulties for news reporting. Unlike the bacteria incidents, this new health danger could not be countered by consumer prudence, since infection from beef, if that were indeed the source, would almost certainly have already occurred (a number of measures, including the banning of feed products made from animal remains, had been introduced from 1988). Exhortations to regimes of good housekeeping and self-help were consequently not an option in this case. Since the disease leads inevitably to harrowing forms of death, even the human-interest story provided grim reading, especially as the vCJD victims (in contrast to those of CJD) were mainly young. Media dedicated to searching out the immediately startling were also ill-tuned to dramatizing risks that would produce no clear evidence until a nebulous point in the future (the incubation period for vCJD remains unclear but spans years rather than weeks or months). Hard information on the specific route of transmission was also lacking because of the limits of scientific and epidemiological knowledge. What made BSE especially anxiety-provoking was the lack of certainty about what 'the event' was. For perhaps the first time, the popular media were reporting a phenomenon as a 'crisis' at the same time as they were reporting on public scepticism about this discursive labelling of the developments.

The media's solution was to divert the sense of risk away from the healthiness or otherwise of beef or beef products (Adam, 2000), and project it on to other targets: on to Europe, for example, for its ban on beef and its endangering of British agriculture and the economy; or, later, on to the British government and official secrecy for concealing early evidence of cross-species transmission and for obscuring the degree to which the precautionary measures instituted at the end of the 1980s were being flouted in practice. By focusing especially on the economic arguments, the media were able to construct a national 'beef crisis', which, as Adam observes, took them 'back on familiar territory: answers to questions about when, where, what, who, why and how could once more be factual, clear and unambiguous' (2000: 128). Differing media outlets' relation to the then Conservative government inflected their reactions. With anti-European sentiments running high in the Murdoch tabloids in particular, their eagerness to criticize European alarmism over British beef was predictable. Even the BBC drew on discourses of Englishness and nationalism in its reporting of the 1996 announcement. 'Saturday,' the report began, 'is usually the day to buy the traditional Sunday roast beef. But today . . . beef is off the national menu.' Later in the same item, dramatic pictures of European road blocks were shown as indices of a crisis of confidence in Europe that 'could devastate the British beef industry' (tx 21 March 1996, BBC News/UK/BSE Timeline, 23 November 1998).

While the popular papers reacted to the government's 1996 announcement with risk-confirming headlines such as 'MAD COW CAN KILL YOU' (*Daily Mirror*, 20 March 1996) and 'COULD IT BE WORSE THAN AIDS?' (*Daily Mail*, 22 March 1996), the provisional 'can' and 'could' were signals that the drama of risk to health was too uncertain to be sustainable. The risks to jobs and to the wider economy were, on the other hand, readily susceptible to graphic treatment. The *Daily Record* (the most popular daily newspaper in Scotland) splashed 'Beef ban will butcher jobs' on its front page. Unable to resist further puns, it headed its page-2 story '200,000 Scots beef workers fear chop over mad cow alert' and captioned photographs of meat workers 'Jobs at steak' (22 March, 1996). In an article headed 'We're in a right stew', the Scottish edition of the Murdoch *Sun* declared that farmers were 'facing ruin as Britain is gripped by mad cow scare' (22 March, 1996). Reporting on the ban on imports of British beef being imposed by European countries, it blames the 'boffins' who linked CJD to BSE for producing 'panic'. Implying an excessive reaction, it invites its readers to vote on the issue, and triumphantly reports the following day that 'Angry *Sun* readers yesterday insisted the mad cow scare would NOT put them off eating British beef. Hundreds of callers jammed our switchboard to blast the new revelations as a "load of bull"' (23 March 1996).

As Brookes and Holbrook observe (1998), these popular papers were promoting a masculine discourse of beef. The *Sun* deployed a photograph of 'sizzling' Ulrika Jonsson (significantly on page 3, regular site of the *Sun*'s pin-up photograph) to urge readers not to 'destroy the great British banger' (22 March 1996). It sustains its tongue-in-cheek, but heavily gendered, approach with a prominently positioned story about a London butcher who displayed a sign outside his shop proclaiming the 'Shock News' that 'Professor Rumpy from Alnight University' had declared that steak would 'beef up your sex life'. 'Steak,' the butcher is quoted as saying 'has lots of testosterone – just what a chap needs to boost his performance' (23 March 1996; see Figure 6.1). Gender discourses were intermingled with nationalistic appeal. Beef's symbolic association with Britishness, together with the *Sun*'s hostility to any closer approximation to Europe, politically or economically, enabled the evoking of nationalist sentiments (Figure 6.1). An Editorial of 27 March 1996 captures the flavour of this discourse, and demonstrates how a query over food safety is incorporated into a frame of reference that was already familiar from other attempts to preserve British consumer symbols from European erosion:

Figure 6.1    Beef, Britishness and masculinity, the *Sun*, 23 March 1996. © News International Newspapers Limited, London.

> If Brussels has the power to stop Britain from selling a product anywhere in
> the world, then we are no longer an independent sovereign nation with
> control over our own affairs.
> We are just one of the herd.
> John Bull has been neutered.

As Rod Brookes comments, this kind of nationalistic discourse helped to 'avoid a forensic approach which traces the origin and spread of infection in favour of a symbolic regime which tries to draw a cordon sanitaire around the nation' (1999: 260). This discourse was particularly strongly evoked in papers hostile to closer ties with Europe. Even the broadsheet papers joined in the refrain. *The Times* (another Murdoch paper), in a nostalgic Editorial headed 'Poor John Bull', traces the historical associations between beef and Britishness, and its status as national symbol of power and well-being, and ends with the lament: 'After this week any thought of preserving beef as symbol of virility and liberty looks, at best, forlorn. ... Tomorrow's Sunday lunch will be a melancholy mealtime as Britons recognise it will never be glad, confident, carving again' (23 March 1996).

Even though the media, in this initial phase of reporting, were playing down the health risk, they were generating alarm and loss of confidence about governance. A problem that was being described as involving consumers, nationalistic interests and the welfare of Britain's agricultural economy in its ramifications began to undermine confidence in good management by government and its scientific advisers. Although public confidence about eating beef was dented by the perceived 'crisis', this material effect appeared to be less dramatic than the heightening of scepticism about officialdom. Consumption of beef in the UK did not fall as dramatically as elements of the British media were suggesting (between 1994 and 1996, consumption of beef and veal fell by about 22 per cent, but by 1997 it had risen again to almost the 1994 level (figures from BBC/UK/BSE Timeline, 23 November 1998)). A stronger impact could be traced on public opinion. A Gallup poll taken shortly after the 1996 revelations indicated a substantial loss of confidence in the credibility of both the government and other agencies. When asked whether they trusted government announcements on 'mad cow disease' or not, 86 per cent of respondents replied that they were suspicious about the information they were being given, and 90 per cent believed that the Ministry of Agriculture, Fisheries and Food was 'withholding some facts' (report in the *Daily Telegraph*, 5 April 1996). The government was additionally perceived as putting the interests of farmers before those of consumers. The beef saga was not, of course, the sole stimulus to public scepticism at this time. Stories of political 'sleaze', together with an increasingly confident Labour opposition, helped to discredit a Conservative government accused of mismanaging a number of areas of public life.

If rumbling disquiet about governance pursued the government's 1996 announcement of a possible link between BSE and vCJD, the revelations of the official inquiry into BSE, chaired by Lord Phillips and running from March 1998 until October 2000, provided additional ammunition. This allowed the media a straightforward focus for their reporting, but the story that emerged from this investigation was one of obfuscation, protection of the interests of officialdom and oversimplification of the scientific evidence. In terms of discourse, one of the most significant moments in this inquiry arose when Sir Kenneth Calman, chief medical officer of health from 1991 until 1998, defended his assurances that beef could be eaten safely on the grounds that this was not meant to imply that 'safe' was synonymous with 'no risk'. 'Safe', even in common usage, 'does not mean no risk', but implies a high level of confidence in the entity to which it is attached, as in 'safe driver', for instance (cited in the *Guardian*, 13 October 1998). The speciousness of this analogy ignored the specific connotations of a claim of 'safety' when it counters preceding allegations of potential harm. In this context, 'safe' asks to be read as 'lacking risk', even if the provisional state of human knowledge backs a wider scepticism about any such possibility. In addition to increasing public cynicism about official discourse, and the play on words that often accompanies 'spin' or lobbying of any kind, this debate about the meaning of 'safe' set in motion a ripple of doubt about scientific knowledge, and about the good faith of those disseminating it, that would later gather momentum around the issue of genetically modified organisms in food.

From a Foucauldian perspective, Sir Kenneth's suggestion of instability in the concept of 'safety' may have had the merit of appearing to recognize the contingency and contested nature of knowledge, but it also drew attention to the vested interests endeavouring to ensure damage limitation around a basic British commodity. In the process of this inquiry, the link between official discourses and the power of a strong lobby of farmers and meat producers was becoming increasingly visible. The power of such an interest group had already been demonstrated in the United States when Texan cattle ranchers attempted to sue Oprah Winfrey under the terms of food disparagement laws for claiming, in a programme broadcast in April 1996, that anxiety about beef 'has just stopped me cold from eating another burger' (Brookes, 2000: 198–200). Although jurors dismissed the case after a six-week trial early in 1998, the allegation that Oprah's remark had led to collapsing cattle prices was sufficiently serious to induce her to offer a substantial out-of-court settlement before the trial began. The ranchers refused to abandon the contest, but had their claim for damages rejected by the US Court of Appeals in February 2000. While in the United States the battle for supremacy was between commercial interests and 'free speech', in Britain commercial and political interests intertwined to produce a more formidable opponent. In addition, promises of greater public access to information and more open government, made by the new Labour administration before it came to office in 1997, were being belied by its own failures to deal candidly with the ongoing anxieties around beef and meat. This accentuated perceptions that no government in Britain was able to deal adequately with risk to human health and well-being.

The broadsheet papers responded to the Phillips Inquiry (2000) with analyses of the growing distrust of the public in political or official pronouncements, and (in the more liberal papers) with renewed recommendations for freedom of information legislation. Lord Phillips' report was declared to be an attack on a 'culture of secrecy and complacency' (headline from *The Times*, 27 October 2000) and 'a damning indictment of the system of government that kept the public in the dark about the country's worst human and animal health crisis' (introduction to an article by David Brown and George Jones in the *Daily Telegraph*, 27 October 2000). The sense of public disquiet at the mismanagement of this 'crisis' had already been visible in the derision with which the media greeted the Labour administration's introduction of a ban on 'beef on the bone' (T-bone steaks, oxtail and beef ribs) in December 1997. The government was responding to advice from the Spongiform Encephalopathy Advisory Committee (SEAC) that a slight risk existed of contaminated beef entering the food chain through swellings on nervous tissue near the spinal cord of the animal. Whereas in the early stages of the BSE epidemic, the Conservative government had been attacked by the media for not being sufficiently responsive to the advice of a variety of scientists, the Phillips Inquiry found the Labour administration unduly ready to allow scientists to construct policy when their proper role should have been merely to interpret evidence. This echoed the media's repeated ridiculing of the ban on beef on the bone as the excessive reaction of a 'nanny state'.

Although the Phillips Inquiry brought a measure of closure to the particular worries about beef, it left a lively legacy of heightened awareness of flaws in governance. The establishment of an independent food standards watchdog in Britain in 2000 helped to quell fears about the power of vested interests to direct food policy, but anxieties about official maladministration quickly transferred to other topics. In the foot and mouth outbreaks in Britain during 2001 the spectre of BSE mismanagement was frequently evoked as a means of criticizing the ability of statutory bodies, government and scientific advisers to operate in the interests of citizens rather than commercial interests. A similar frame of reference was repeated in worries about the MMR (measles, mumps and rubella) vaccine later that same year. The unsolved conundrum of the likely extent of the spread of vCJD and the possible appearance of BSE in sheep also led to fresh flurries of alarm around BSE itself. In 2001, for example, a report on the deaths from vCJD of five young people, who all had a connection with the same Leicestershire village, claimed that a variety of factors conspired to produce this cluster, including traditional abattoir and butchery practices. Coverage of this discovery revived earlier fears that traditional butchers, thought to be selling high-quality meat, might be as risky a source of BSE infection as hot dog stands or cheap beef burgers. The *Sun*, despite its scorn in 1996 for the exaggeration of risk around beef, extravagantly headed its report 'The Village Under Sentence of Death' (22 March 2001). In October 2001 earlier accusations of Machiavellian government tactics gave way to ridicule in media discourse, when scientists working on a four-year research study into the possibility of British sheep being infected with BSE were discovered to have been investigating cow rather than sheep brains by mistake.

The BSE/CJD 'crisis' was, then, much more volatile than the other food scare stories considered earlier. From authoritative declarations in 1990 that British beef was 'safe' to eat, to the banning of beef on the bone in December 1997; from reluctant hints that cheaper cuts and processed beef products might pose a higher risk than select and expensive ones, to the disclosure in 2001 that traditional village butchery methods may have been a liability, there was little sense of stability in the emerging account. The pattern was one of growing confusion rather than increased enlightenment. The news media's general difficulties in dealing adequately with scientific analyses compounded the tendency to construct stories about mismanagement, obfuscation and official bad faith. As investigations of other areas of science reporting have discovered, the dearth of reporters (other than special correspondents) with an adequate scientific background is compounded by the increasing tendency of journalists to rely on secondary sources (including other media) instead of on direct contact with scientists (see, for example, Wilson's study of climate change, 2000: 215). The provisional and contested nature of scientific knowledge itself (a live issue in establishing the causes and epidemiology of BSE/vCJD) was acknowledged in the broadsheet papers but never became a dominant discourse. In relation to genetically modified food, this was to acquire greater emphasis. In addition, BSE had been very much a British story, despite manifestations of the disease in other European countries and occasional flurries of anxiety in the US media. Worries about GMOs were set to amplify a number of these concerns and project them on to a global screen.

## FROM GENETICALLY MODIFIED ORGANISMS TO 'FRANKENFOODS'

With the beginnings of the genetic modification of food, risk shifted from being visible to being theoretical. Whereas the manifestations of salmonella poisoning or an unusually high number of deaths from new-variant CJD were indisputable, the intangible and hypothetical risks attaching to genetically modified (GM) organisms were much more contentious. Genetically modified food involves the deliberate modification in a laboratory of the original genes of a plant or animal providing a food source. It is a biotechnology intended to transfer the benefits of a single gene from one organism to another, often across species. This process can, for example, extend the shelf life of fruit or vegetables by inserting a gene that 'switches off' the chemical reaction that produces decay. If discourses around the BSE issue were inflected by concerns about poor governance, proposals to modify food genetically raised broader concerns about the instability of scientific 'knowledge', and anxieties about the exploitative nature of capitalism and the risk to the well-being of the planet.

Why these concerns appeared especially strongly in Britain owed a great deal to the earlier food scares. The media's preference for stories with immediacy and strong visual appeal made them even less likely to be drawn to genetic modification than to BSE. With GMOs, the temporal remoteness of risk was compounded by a lack of proof of harmfulness. But the suspicions about governance generated around BSE were eminently adaptable as a discursive framework for this new phenomenon. As with BSE, also, powerful commercial lobbyists struggled for control of media discourse against consumer groups and campaigning activists, especially in Britain and Europe. Significantly, however, scientific discourse, in this confrontation, became less the means to settle the dispute through appeals to empirical and verifiable evidence, and more the site of bitter contention in itself. Within the unfolding play for power, a discourse of risk, as in the case of BSE, became detached from its original stimulus and was appropriated variously by different interest groups.

Ulrich Beck, writing in 1992, commented that 'the focus is more and more on hazards which are neither visible nor perceptible to the victims; hazards that in some cases may not even take effect within the lifespans of those affected; . . . hazards in any case that require the "sensory organs" of science – *theories, experiments, measuring instruments – in order to become visible or interpretable as hazards at all*' (1992: 27). As Beck later acknowledges (1999: 105–6), this prefigures accurately the nature of hazard that surrounds genetically modified organisms and their entry into the food chain. But, in this case, the 'sensory organs' of science were themselves constructed as inadequate interpreters. Both scientists proclaiming the safety of GMOs and their professional opponents were suspect: the first because of the legacy of distrust generated by BSE, and the second because definitive proof of harm was lacking. With most scientific funding coming from large corporations, including those with vested interests in biotechnology, the power of the pro-GM lobby could easily be disparaged through the David-versus-Goliath narrative that had worked in favour of Greenpeace during the *Brent Spar* incident (see Chapter 2). As Jonathan Freedland commented in the *Guardian* (17 February 1999), the big biotechnology companies suffered the disadvantage of combining the negative representational baggage of both the 'mad scientist' and the 'evil corporation bent on profits'.

Scientific uncertainty over GMOs and other forms of genetic intervention had been established in the 1970s, with American scientists at a conference in California in 1975 agreeing to halt this kind of work because of its potential risks (Beck, 1999: 106). In Foucauldian terms, uncertainty and inconclusiveness are intrinsic to knowledge formation (including in the sciences), but this is neither the popular expectation of science nor, as Beck points out, one tolerated by 'globalized business, genetic advertisers and their fellow-travelling philosophers, stock market speculators and governments under the threat of unemployment' (1999: 105). Accordingly, by 1983 the first transgenic plant had been created experimentally in the USA and by 1993 commercialization of a tomato resistant to decay had occurred. In 1996 the first genetically modified food product, tomato paste, was being sold in British supermarkets. In the same year, the EU approved the importing and use in animal and human food of soya beans produced by one of the major biotechnology companies, Monsanto, to withstand its own Roundup weedkiller. By the end of the decade, GM crops were being grown commercially in eight countries, with the USA the biggest producer. Over half the soya beans being produced in the USA were genetically modified and GM soya was entering the food chain in a number of everyday food products, from packets of crisps to an array of 'convenience' foods. In Britain, the government gave the go-ahead at this time to farm trials of genetically modified crops, but no commercial development was permitted.

Public concern over genetically modified food was growing in Britain in the course of

1998, across different social classes. By the summer of 1998, the rumblings of opposition were strong enough to persuade Monsanto to spend £1 million on an advertising campaign targeted at the British middle classes. This claimed environmental and global benefits from genetically modified foods, while appearing to acknowledge a diversity of perspectives on this issue. The advertisements even included the contact numbers for organizations, such as Friends of the Earth, who were directly opposed to GM. As well as being visually discreet, the verbal style was far from declamatory, preferring instead a tactical reliance on apparently factual statements about the extensive testing and regulation of the products. The mode of address invited trust in a responsible conglomerate that was also open and accountable, and willing to engage in debate with its opponents. Despite this strategy, the Advertising Standards Authority (ASA) upheld four complaints from a number of bodies that the advertisements' claims could not be authenticated (*Guardian*, 11 August 1999). Monsanto's openness to discussion with its opponents was also belied by the widespread fear amongst media companies that it would willingly sue anyone who challenged its integrity. Evidence of censorship, direct or indirect, of those publicly daring to criticize Monsanto was growing. In 1997, Fox TV had fired two Florida television producers for refusing to broadcast misleading reports about Monsanto's controversial Bovine Growth Hormone. Shortly after Monsanto's advertising campaign, fears of being sued prompted the long-established printers of *The Ecologist* magazine in Britain to pulp an edition devoted to criticism of the company, and even after a new printer had been found, leading distributors refused to handle it.

Monsanto's ambition to be well regarded by the influential classes was, however, underlined by a leaked document from the company published in the *Guardian* in November 1998. This expressed concern about the growing hostility to GM food in Britain over the previous year. Its author, Stanley Greenberg (1998), blamed reporters and especially 'the media élite' for misleading the public. It was especially scathing about the lack of support for GM amongst the 'super socio-economic AB segment' in Britain, despite the enthusiasm for biotechnology among the equivalent groups in the USA. The contest not only for the hearts and minds of the wealthy and powerful but also for the confidence of the everyday consumer would increase sharply in the following year. This dramatic rise in media interest is evident from a list of UK and world news stories, which notes a total of only 14 stories on genetically modified food between the end of May 1992 and the end of 1998, but around 400 items during 1999 (see www.connectotel.com/gmfood).

The visibility of commercial pressure from the biotechnology companies increased perceptions that science, far from allowing access to neutral knowledge, was both intrinsically discursive and discursively fought over. Controversy over a *World in Action* programme (10 August 1998) sharpened this awareness. *World in Action* reported the findings of research by Dr Arpad Pusztai indicating that the organs and immune systems of rats had been adversely affected by eating genetically modified potatoes. The subsequent attempts by fellow scientists to discredit Dr Pusztai's results drew accusations of political pressure, adding to perceptions that scientific discourse was itself tainted by competing interests. In the battle that followed between Dr Pusztai, his employers at the Rowett Research Institute (who announced four days after the programme was broadcast that his contract would not be renewed), the Royal Society (the leading scientific body, which condemned his findings), sympathetic colleagues and Greenpeace, any sense that science could deliver 'the truth' about GMO risks was effectively destroyed. Although *World in Action* would not have attracted a mass audience, Pusztai's allegations of possible harm resulting from the genetic modification of food immediately attracted the attention of a much wider range of media outlets, including the popular press. When the medical journal, *The Lancet*, finally agreed to publish Dr Pusztai's findings in March 1999, in order to allow his data to be subject to peer review, and to allay concerns about a 'cover-up', several newspapers claimed that Dr Pusztai's fears about the safety of genetic modification had been vindicated.

While Pusztai was caricatured by many in his own profession as a self-publicizing pariah who was getting mileage out of a shoddily conducted experiment, he was cast as a justified Cassandra figure by the popular media. His opponents had a harder task in getting a favourable press against a tide of consumer demands for precautionary action, not least because, in the wake of the BSE saga, it was impossible for them to declare GM foods to be 'safe'. The Royal Society, in a departure from normal practice, appointed its own reviewers of Dr Pusztai's work, but, as one of them indicated in what he wished to be a confidential observation, disapproval of Pusztai's conclusions did not amount to a declaration of non-risk: 'it would be of the greatest importance to avoid the error made by others over BSE – that no evidence of effect is the same as evidence of no effect' and 'it is not possible to conclude that Professor Pusztai's work can be taken to indicate that there is no possible cause for concern' (from correspondence between Dr Pusztai and the Royal Society on Dr Pusztai's website, www.freenetpages.co.uk/hp/A.Pusztai/correspondence.htm). The unfolding of claim and counter-claim heightened public suspicion of science and introduced fresh cynicism about the independence of the scientific advice that was helping to shape government policy.

Pusztai's contestable scientific evidence acquired the discursive authority of 'proof' for a media now sceptical about claims of lack of risk, and a public campaign to require food manufacturers to label food and to persuade supermarkets to withdraw GM products from sale quickly gathered pace. The popular media had already seized on the label of 'Frankenstein foods' (sometimes shortened to 'Frankenfoods') that had been attached to GM produce by the head of the Iceland frozen-food chain (Iceland was the first British store to ban GM ingredients from its own-brand products in May 1998). This metaphor, accentuating accusations about the incompetence of scientific 'boffins', together with the spectre of 'mutant crops', posed an artificial antithesis between 'natural' foods and GM foods, and also fuelled fears that science was spinning out of control.

This discourse was not confined to the popular media. In May 1999 a *Panorama* programme entitled 'Frankenstein foods' set out to investigate public concerns about the safety of GM foods: 'Tonight on *Panorama* the inside story of the battle to put Frankenstein

145

food on our plates.' By aligning itself with the consumer as potential victim, and taking us frequently within the visual space of the supermarket, it established scepticism about the array of official committees, peopled by scientists and government appointees, acting as a supposedly protective barrier against unsafe foods. The commentary constructed binary oppositions between the 'traditional British countryside' and its invasion by 'something a little less traditional', and between 'natural' food and 'Frankenstein food': 'the latest quest is checking whether food is natural or whether it's GM – now being called "Frankenstein food"'. Throughout the programme, the message of loss of trust in those who set themselves up as social protectors is strong: as the commentator asserts, 'Few people now trust the government – and its array of committees – to do what's best for them.' Although we are told that most scientists and the government believe that GM foods pose no hazard to human health, a repeated discourse of suspicion undermines these pronouncements. Ordinary knowledge and ordinary fears are given primary status through *vox pops*, everyday supermarket scenes and the supportive role of the commentary. This emphasis on the welfare of the consumer, combined with an opportunity to attack the Labour government, encouraged an anti-GM discourse in other unlikely places. The conservative and middle-market *Daily Mail*, not normally associated with any form of social protest, stimulated anxiety by publishing ten questions about GMOs raised by the Prince of Wales, which reverberated through much of the press's subsequent coverage (*Daily Mail*, 1 June 1999).

Whatever public assurances were still being enunciated about the safety of GMOs, official practices and behaviours were articulating a different narrative. Early in 1999, the Local Government Association ordered the withdrawal of GM foods from the menus of schools, old people's homes and town halls, and by March 1999 most of the major supermarkets in Britain, led by the Iceland chain, had agreed to prevent GM products reaching their shelves, leading to extensive comment and some humorous treatment in the press (see Figure 6.2). The government (hitherto supportive of GM technologies) found itself trapped between discourses of technological optimism (New Labour wanted to project itself as a modern party for a modern, hi-tech age) and populist discourses of ensuring consumer safety. A public opinion poll conducted in early June 1999 discovered that scientists were now trusted 'a lot' by only 35 per cent of those questioned, and 'not at all' by 12 per cent, while the comparable figures for politicians were 10 per cent and 25 per cent respectively (*Guardian*, 8 June 1999). Not all of this was attributable, of course, to discourses around BSE/GMOs. The finding that journalists were trusted 'a lot' by only 4 per cent and 'not at all' by 48 per cent of respondents demolished any notion that credibility might be accruing to the profession helping to fuel suspicions about scientists and politicians.

In addition to the fears about the unknown, and unknowable, health risks of eating GM food, an environmentalist discourse of risk was also developing around GMOs. As crop trials got under way on British soil, so did the protest movement intent on stopping them. While the protesters of Greenham Common and other movements designed to force a

**Figure 6.2** Cartoon by Kipper Williams, the *Guardian*, 24 March 1999. Reprinted by kind permission of the cartoonist and the *Guardian*.

rethink about Britain's commitment to nuclear weapons had been derided by the popular media in the 1980s and before (see, for example, Hollingsworth, 1986), and while anti-capitalist demonstrators received little sympathy from most of the media when they challenged the World Trade Organization at the start of the twenty-first century, anti-GM activists attracted a more sympathetic press. Tactically sophisticated, and alert to the need to provide evocative pictures as well as good copy, they were able to pose as the righteous Davids taking on the mighty Goliaths of the multinational agro-chemical industry. Photographs or film of them wearing white protective clothing and masks became important symbols of the purity of their crusade *and* powerful indices of the risks that GM crops might pose to health as well as the environment. In Radio 4's long-running agricultural soap opera *The Archers*, the trashing of a genetically modified oil-seed rape crop by a youthful member of the Archer clan and his friends in 1999 engaged positively with his publicly spirited motives within a narrative trajectory that refused a punitive resolution.

Whereas in Britain the association of GM innovation with transatlantic corporations exacerbated opposition, in the United States, the media initially mocked the risk of GM as a peculiar manifestation of European angst. John Micklethwait, bureau chief of *The Economist*, wrote an opinion piece in the *New York Times* (14 June 1999) in which he marvelled at the fervour of the British reaction, and underlined the alienation it would provoke in a country where GM stands more self-evidently for General Motors and where 'it is hard to imagine the home of the microwave dinner and the Big Mac banning new sorts of food'. Yet Micklethwait did warn that this period of quiescence might not last and that agitation for clear labelling of GM products might ensue. While the environmental discourse found little support in a country where agricultural land is invisible to the mass of the population, and where issues of cross-contamination or damage to the ecological system seem remote, worries about food safety took firmer root. By early 2000, a number of protests had taken place in American cities against GM, and anti-GM activists had participated in the Seattle demonstrations against the World Trade Organization conference in 1999. These were spurred in part by anger at the multinational corporations' ability to impose their will on the rest of the world, and the failure of national governments to impede this; but participants were also responding to the consumer anxieties echoing from the other side of the Atlantic. One protester demonstrating in Boston at the time of a major biotechnology conference in that city in March 2000 compared the promotion of GMOs to the thalidomide scandal (cited in *New York Times*, 27 March 2000).

Despite the growing recognition of genetic engineering as a problem that cannot be contained within spatial boundaries, popular media discourses in the West have paid scant attention to the risks extending beyond western borders. With issues of risk relentlessly domesticated, the major biotechnology companies' claims to be providing solutions to world hunger have escaped investigation by the popular media. Even in the more overtly analytical media, sporadic insights into the limitations of western perspectives have led to undue readiness to endorse alternative discourses, without due questioning of their ideological complexion. A programme in the science series, *Equinox*, on Channel 4 (March 2000), for example, established a discursive contrast between ill-informed western liberals and science-based evaluation of the benefits of genetically engineered food for developing world economies. This inverts the domestic discourse of reliable popular opinion versus untrustworthy scientific claim. The presenter indeed comments, in emphatic endorsement of the very polarity that Foucault rejected, that 'for many campaigners their opposition to GM is not based on science but rather ideology'.

Instead of positioning the viewer within the familiar space of the supermarket, the programme begins in Cuba with a state event honouring the man credited with 'inventing' genetic modification in plants, Baron van Montagu. The mood is upbeat, as the soundtrack plays lively Cuban music against a vivid landscape. Fears about GM in the developed world are criticized by a series of scientific spokespeople for paying insufficient attention to the needs of developing countries for cheap and plentiful food production. While the programme is not entirely one-sided, permitting access to one scientist who is opposed to GMOs, it loads its dice heavily in favour of the developing world's challenge to the unscientific prejudices of western consumers. In counterpoint to the conventional binary of presuming that discourses of science and rationality dominate in the West, while primitiveness and superstition reign supreme in developing countries, *Equinox* presents a

Kenyan scientist who accuses western opinion of falling prey to irrationality: 'We know that this technology is not dangerous and for forces of superstition and ignorance out there to block this technology is simply catastrophic.' Scenes of four upper-class women from the 'Women Say No To GMO' campaign chatting about the dangers of GMOs over a copious lunch are also ironically positioned against the shrivelled landscape and visible poverty of the developing countries. From a shot of one of these women claiming that peasant farmers have no desire to plant GM crops, the programme cuts to an image of dying plants and an African couple who were so much on the point of starvation that the production team had to take them to a source of food before filming could proceed. The juxtaposition makes the white western women appear cocooned within a privileged perspective, and remote from the daily subsistence problems facing developing countries. Science in this programme, in contrast to *Panorama*, is seen as the only defence against mythology and a return, as Baron van Montagu puts it in the final comment of the programme, to the days of 'the Inquisition'.

*Equinox* is unusual in forcing attention on to the international complexities of the trade in GM seeds and food. At the same time, it privileges a discourse of science as knowledge, and technology as answer to global problems, which ignores that these are also highly contestable positions. When Monsanto and other large biotechnology companies claim they can provide the solution to world hunger, they ride roughshod over arguments from a number of developing countries, NGOs and campaigning groups such as Greenpeace and Friends of the Earth that world hunger is produced by poverty and unequal distribution of food rather than by food shortage. Arguments that genetic engineering will improve food yields disregard the evidence that many of the crops encouraged by the biotechnology giants are being produced for western consumption, not for feeding local populations. They also fail to consider the impact on biodiversity, and on the self-determination of domestic agriculture in these countries resulting from the likely patenting by the big companies of indigenous seed and crops. Campaigning groups also point to the biotechnology companies' opposition to food labelling and their reluctance to abandon completely the controversial 'terminator' technologies that would prevent farmers from reproducing crops from seeds. On the *Equinox* programme, an oppositional scientist is allowed to present her case, but her voice is overruled and undermined by the consensus emerging from most spokespeople in the programme that GMOs have the capacity to solve developing-world problems and that opposition on the basis of risk to health and the environment comes from bad science (Dr Pusztai's work is strongly criticized), or from irrational and self-indulgent campaigners. Despite functioning as a useful corrective to the insularity of most coverage of GMO risks, this programme is limited by its own discursive emphasis on science as saviour.

## CONCLUSION

As debates, supposedly about food safety, have evolved, the risks at stake have grown from a concern with specific products to worries about good governance and the instability of scientific knowledge. A shortage of journalists with scientific backgrounds has made it increasingly difficult for evaluation of scientific arguments to resist the inter-discursive influences of lobbying and campaigning groups or powerful corporations. Scientists themselves, jockeying for influence and funding, are under pressure from a variety of non-scientific interests and discourses. Increasingly, the Internet has become an important site for conducting a discursive battle over GMOs. That this battle is less than open about the identities of key discursive players adds to the ideological confusion. The intrigues of the Pusztai affair appear modest when compared with the chicanery that appeared to pursue the publication in *Nature* (29 November 2001) of research by two Berkeley scientists indicating the contamination, across vast distances, of native maize in Mexico by GM pollen. According to an investigation by environmentalist George Monbiot (published in the *Guardian*, 14 May 2002 and 29 May 2002), fake individuals posted attacks on a website that could be traced back to the lobbying firm employed by Monsanto in order to discredit this work. More surprisingly, the editor of *Nature* took the unprecedented step of publicly recanting the decision to publish the article. In the conflicts of cyberspace it becomes yet more difficult than Schlesinger (1990) suggests to disentangle 'primary definers' and their ideological allegiances. Commercial jitteriness about attacks on GMOs has contaminated the very sites that journalists access for information on their stories.

Particularly in the transition from BSE to GMO coverage, food safety has become only the apparent or surface topic of concern. More significantly, these issues have become a launching pad for a wider range of contemporary anxieties about inadequate governance, the untrustworthiness of official forms of knowledge and the challenges of global ecology. As a consequence, the magnitude of the risk to individuals is depicted as coming not from specific sources, such as eating unsafe food, but from the wider ramifications of living in a world where normal western expectations about being cocooned from major risks have broken down. Nevertheless, the discursive emphasis, especially in the popular media, has still been on western worries, with little regard to the 'polycentric multiculturalism' advocated by Shohat and Stam, where 'no single community or part of the world, whatever its economic or political power, should be epistemologically privileged' (1994: 48).

# Chapter Seven

# DEMONIZING ISLAM

Fuelled by ancient myths and legends, western fears of Islam have been sharply revived by a series of developments since the 1980s. In the process, Islam has been reified into a unitary system of belief, without regard to its internal variations or the variety of contexts in which it is practised. In its binary construction it is set not against a contrasting religious belief but against western civilization itself, appearing as a metonym for barbarism, oppression and a retreat into a medieval 'dark ages'. As the writer Edward Said puts it, 'malicious generalizations about Islam have become the last acceptable form of denigration of foreign culture in the West' (1997: xii). The growth of Islamophobia (irrational fear of Islam) has been aided and inflected historically by racist constructions of the Arab and, more recently in Britain, of the young Asian male. In the western media, reporting of a series of discrete events, including the *fatwa* against Salman Rushdie in Britain in 1989 and the Oklahoma City bombing in 1995, reinforced an association of Islam with pre-modern ruthlessness and aggression. In a western world deprived of communism as a convincing threat since the ending of the Cold War and the collapse of the Berlin wall in 1989, Islam has formed a convenient substitute. Simplified western constructions of Islam's treatment of women have served as evidence of its arrested development and lack of modern enlightenment. This chapter considers how constructions of terrorism, fundamentalism and the oppression of women have been loaded, increasingly exclusively, on to Islam, and how these produce, in the process, their own endorsements of western values. The following chapter will offer some preliminary reflections on the impact of the events of September 11th 2001.

## THE ORIGINS OF WESTERN DISCOURSES OF ISLAM

Edward Said (1991; 1997) has traced the recent discourses of Islam back to constructions of Orientalism in western culture. Whatever the Orient's physical delimitations, its function within discourse has been to establish its inferiority to the West or Occident. By defining 'the Other', we also implicitly define what holds 'us' together as 'non-Other'. As Stuart Hall indicates, in the discursive construction of 'the West and the Rest', 'the Rest was ... essential to the West's formation both of its own sense of itself – a "western identity" – and of western forms of knowledge' (1992: 318). Said is careful to distance himself from a wholly Foucauldian position of believing discourse to be by itself the generator of power relations. The material structures of colonial imperialism both underpinned, and were underpinned by, the discursive formation of Orientalism. Within this context, Said traces the intricate variety of discourses that co-operated to shape a form of binary thinking that also had the consequence of setting Christianity in opposition to

Islam. This was paradoxical, given the closeness of both religions doctrinally. Both are monotheistic, both believe in submission to the will of the divinity (God in Christianity, Allah in Islam), and both value spiritual devotion and selfless commitment to good works. Yet, as Said documents, a plethora of western scholarly texts, travel writing, cultural artefacts and moral commentaries contributed to the establishment of Orientalism as the study of an inferior, if exotic, 'Other' (1991: 12). His own seminal study is limited to 'the Anglo-French-American experience of the Arabs and Islam, which for almost a thousand years together stood for the Orient' (1991: 17). As a child growing up in Palestine and Egypt, Said was both the recipient of a western education, and yet aware of his 'Oriental' belonging. Although not himself a Muslim, he follows, in part, an autobiographical journey 'to inventory the traces upon me, the Oriental subject, of the culture whose domination has been so powerful a factor in the life of all Orientals' (1991: 25).

Islam, as a world religion, has become peculiarly identified in the public consciousness with the Arab world, and especially with those parts of the Arab world thought to be hostile to western interests. Although Islam had its foundations in Arabia in the seventh century, the continuing association between Muslim and Arab ignores the evidence that less than 20 per cent of Muslims are currently Arabs (*New Internationalist*, no. 345, May 2002), and that although the majority of Arab countries have overwhelmingly Muslim populations, a number (including Lebanon, Syria and Egypt) have significant Christian minorities. Many more Muslims now live in South and Southeast Asia than in the Arab world. Even historically, during the rise of the Ottoman Empire from the fourteenth to the sixteenth centuries, the Muslim world was driven by the imperialist ambitions of the Turks, not the Arabs. As Said perceptively remarks, the diverse geographical and historical manifestations of the spread of Islam became less significant in the construction of unified western discourses than an 'imaginative geography' (1991: 54–5) intent on mapping as alien that which was, paradoxically, in many respects familiar to western and Christian thinking: 'Mohammed is always the imposter (familiar, because he pretends to be like the Jesus we know) and always the Oriental (alien, because although he is in some ways "like" Jesus, he is after all not like him)' (Said, 1991: 72). The growth in Islamophobia cannot, then, be explained by simple reference to the global expansion of the Islamic religion. Racist ideology, manifest particularly in constructions of the Arab and (more recently, in Britain) of young Asian masculinity, has contributed powerfully to its formation.

As Stuart Hall reminds us in relation to racism, hatred of 'the Other' is rarely untinged by envy or admiration: 'the play of identity and difference which constructs racism is powered not only by the positioning of blacks as the inferior species but also, and at the same time, by an inexpressible envy and desire' (Hall, 1996: 167). To some extent, this duality in thinking has been gendered in relation to the Arab, and inscribed through a differentiated 'imaginative geography', with the Arab male the object of anxiety, and the sensual and exoticized Oriental woman (now associated less with Arab countries and more with Southeast Asia) the object of sexualized (and predominantly male) longing. Embedded in cultural forms as diverse as children's stories and comics, respected works of western art and film, the derogation of the Arab male as devious, greedy and prone to barbaric forms of violence, and the construction of the Oriental woman as enigmatic and sexually enticing, have been repeated relentlessly. The popular press, too, has perpetuated these stereotypes in particularly graphic form. In response to the expulsion of British nurses from Saudi Arabia for drinking in 1986, the *Sun's* Editorial attacked Arab hypocrisy under the heading 'Ali Baba's desert hypocrites'. Arguing that Arabs in Britain 'soak up booze faster than a sponge' and 'fornicate like stoats', it alleged that 'but for Providence and their oil wells, these arrogant Sheiks of Araby would still be squatting around their camel-dung fires' (4 November 1986). Duplicity, sexual and financial avarice, and primitive barbarity were simultaneously evoked.

Yet any simple gendering of stereotypes ignores the degree to which the lustful and opulent male Arab (personified in the image of the sheik) was also constructed as an object of envy and desire. The lascivious Arab male (like the sexualized construction of black masculinity), was threatening because of his appeal to white women, but simultaneously enviable because he embodied impulses repressed in hegemonic white masculine culture. While the Arab sheik, as depicted in film, was generally the lecherous ravisher of the young white maiden, intent on incorporating her into his harem, Rudolph Valentino's fascination for women (in George Melford's film, *The Sheik*, 1921) was fuelled by his 'ambiguous and deviant identity' (Hansen, 1991: 275). More 'Latin lover' than 'lecherous Arab', his proneness to feminized forms of masochism, and the late revelation that he is the son of Europeans, both modulated the conventional stereotype of Arab masculinity.

In the racism of constructions of the Arab during the heyday of British and European imperialism, Arabs were more regularly despised than seen as a threat. The attribution of positive qualities could be tolerated, provided Arab power was kept at bay. However primitive in western eyes, the Arab could still offer friendship, comradeship and loyalty at least equal to that of the English 'gentleman', enhancing his appeal to women as well as men. In David Lean's film, *Lawrence of Arabia* (1962), set during the campaign against the Turks in the First World War, the loyal Hasimi Bedouin escorting Lawrence of Arabia on his mission to find Prince Feisal is shot dead by a fellow Arab from the rival Harith tribe for drinking from a forbidden well. This sequence constructs the Arab as peace-loving, committed to a code of gentlemanly conduct, and yet at the same time as engaged in barbarous internecine conflict and aggressively contemptuous of human rights. Lawrence's passionate declaration to the killer Sheik Sherif (Omar Sharif) – 'So long as the Arabs fight tribe against tribe, so long will they be a little people, a silly people, greedy, barbarous, and cruel, as you are' – signifies his anger about the shooting of his companion, but also the superiority of the upper-class English officer. This duality continues throughout the film, combining the dignity and heroism of the Arabs when oppressed, alongside their inability to govern or avoid inter-tribal hostility and barbarity once they capture Damascus. However helpful their co-operation against the Turks, their inferiority to Lawrence and the English rulers is underlined.

Links between the negative construction of the Arab and anxieties about Muslim expansionism became embedded in western consciousness at the time of the Crusades in the eleventh to thirteenth centuries. The brutal aggression and acts of infamous cruelty perpetrated by Christian avengers were claimed by the West as just retaliation for the imperialist Islamic conquests in what we now think of as the Middle East, North Africa and Spain. The contrast between (Oriental) 'barbarism' and (Occidental) 'civilization' could hypocritically be maintained, despite the evidence of atrocities on the 'civilized' side, by defining the contest as a 'holy war' waged against 'infidels' and 'Saracens'. This discursive pattern was, of course, to be inverted in later Islamic definitions of 'holy wars' from the twentieth century onwards, justified in turn as being fought not against other religions but against a new brand of 'infidel', committed, this time, to secularism. From the late seventeenth century, however, anxiety about Islam's expansionist aims and the risk these posed to a western way of life lay relatively dormant for almost three centuries. In the age of empire, the West felt invincible. In addition, the political developments of the twentieth century demonstrated that threats to civilization and liberty could come from ideological sources unconnected to Islam. Communist rather than Islamic territorial ambitions dominated mid-twentieth-century political angst. If this pushed fears of Islam into a temporary background, three developments served as potent excuses for reviving its status as arch-enemy in the late twentieth century. The first was the collapse of communist states; the second the growth of international terrorism; and the third the increasing preoccupation with women's rights in the late twentieth-century western world. These magnified earlier fears that Islam could destabilize the security of the capitalist universe. If terrorism suggested a primarily physical source of risk, Islam's attitudes to women and freedom of expression became significant metonyms for its pre-modernist, backward-looking challenge to western ideologies.

## THE GROWTH OF THE TERRORIST THREAT

The collapse of the 'red peril' of communism in the late 1980s left a vacuum in the West's construction of global risk of catastrophe that was to be replaced by terrorism – perceived, just as communism had been, as both localized, yet miasmic in its infectious potential. Risk that was initially safely 'out there' for the West became, again like communism, the 'enemy within'. In the formation of a specifically Islamic source of terror, awareness of the *ummah* (global, if virtual, community of Muslims) strengthened the perception that Islam was capable of replacing communism as the primary challenge to the West. Even aspects of Islamic rhetoric were reminiscent of communist calls for the dismantling of capitalism and justice for the underprivileged and disenfranchised.

The terms 'terrorism' and 'terrorist', as discursively constructed by western media and governments, conjure up unprovoked and irrational acts of barbarity, symptomatic of a lack of civilized values and contempt for democratic means of argument and persuasion. Although they are capable of being impartially deployed, to apply to all acts of terror against a civilian population, from whatever source, the media's operation within constraints of nationalist ideologies makes this improbable in practice. As a consequence, the news agency, Reuters, decided to proscribe the use of the terms 'terrorism' or 'terrorist' by its journalists; a decision that was to become the object of attack in the wake of September 11th, as the next chapter will explain. Terrorism, in media discourse, is readily allied with a manifestation of 'evil', thereby setting it within a purely moral paradigm where easy condemnation forms a ready substitute for analysis of its political formation. The differing stimuli and objectives of actions described as 'terrorist' are edited out, and the awkwardness of investigating relationships between legitimated (state) and outlawed (terrorist) forces in a contest for power is bypassed.

Although the well-worn saying that 'one person's terrorist is another person's freedom-fighter' recognizes the ideological import obscured in the generic label, this challenge to discursive certainties has attracted little more than the occasional genuflection from the popular media. The exclusion of the voice of the 'terrorists' or their sympathizers from the mainstream media re-affirms that any attempt to understand the politics of acts defined as terrorism is tantamount to condoning a moral outrage. When Cherie Blair commented, in an off-the-cuff remark on Palestinian actions against Israel in June 2002, that 'as long as young people feel that they have got no hope but to blow themselves up you are never going to make progress', her remarks were widely interpreted in the media as expressing sympathy for Palestinian bombers. Although this interpretation was compounded by the timing (shortly after a Palestinian attack on a bus in Jerusalem) and by her position as the British Prime Minister's wife, it was also indicative of the media's readiness to present any attempt to understand the concerns that fuel 'terrorist' actions as amounting to approval and support of immoral acts.

Although the United States was protected from terrorism within its own borders until the 1990s, this was not the case in Britain. From the 1970s, 'terrorist' acts connected with the situation in Northern Ireland had been a regular occurrence in that province and a more sporadic, but powerfully felt, form of assault on the English mainland. Several European countries had also experienced the resort to terror tactics of various political groupings, frustrated at the lack of political means to promote their cause. In reporting of the Middle East, 'terrorism' dominated the headlines. Although the shared label brought these differing conflicts into a common rhetoric of image and word (pictures of dazed victims staggering through debris with blood streaming from their wounds; burned-out ruins and glass-strewn pavements; grief-stricken relatives, accompanied by terms such as 'massacre', 'outrage', 'carnage'), an element of diversity prevailed. Divergent dress and architectural styles, coupled with varying positioning on the news pages or within bulletins, signified the difference between 'home' and 'abroad', and intercepted any sense of emerging global threat.

With the rise of what was described as 'Islamic terrorism', however, specific attributes began to give way to a more generalized and universal sense of insecurity. The connotations of 'desiring world domination' already attaching to Islam added considerable *frisson* to acts of terror that were defined as 'Islamic', or the work of 'Islamic fundamentalists'. Terrorism, on the basis of this single descriptor, moved from being

155

localized and containable to being seen as globally dispersed, and supported by the supposed Islamic commitment to *jihad*, most often translated as 'holy war'. *Jihad* is not, however, an aggressive concept within Islam. Literally meaning 'struggle to realize God's will for humanity', in Islamic thought 'the concept is noble and powerful. It is the desire to improve oneself, to attempt betterment and to struggle for the good cause' (Akbar Ahmed, 1992: 42–3). Although it has been interpreted by some of the most conservative factions within Islam as permitting the conduct of a 'holy war' to further this mission, the Qur'an sanctions warfare only on defensive grounds to protect Muslims when they are already under hostile attack (Marty and Appleby, 1991: 422–3). Blowing oneself up while also killing others (variously described as 'suicide bombing' or 'homicide bombing' – again, each has differing connotations) similarly receives no endorsement from the Qur'an, although some Muslim leaders preach this as a route to martyrdom. Karim points out that in the western media's discursive conventions, *jihad* is regularly used to refer to aggressive Muslim action that the West wishes to condemn, whereas the term *mujahidin* has been the favoured term to refer to indigenous fighters for causes supported by western powers (1997: 170). Subtle distinctions of this kind, when insistently repeated, solidify ways of thinking about the opposition between 'terrorism' and 'just wars'.

Anxieties about international links between terrorist groupings did not, of course, emerge with perceptions of Islamic terrorism, but earlier hints of organized activity conjured up sophisticated mafia-style networking, sharing of technological know-how and financial resources that aligned terrorism with the modern world of technical wizardry and corporate planning. 'Islamic terrorism', on the other hand, resurrected nightmare visions of ancient modes of barbarity and ruthlessness that replaced carefully targeted precision and effectiveness with indiscriminate killing and destruction. The variety of stimuli from western actions in the Arab and Middle-Eastern worlds could be ignored within a discourse of the abstract, but intensifying, global risk from 'Islamic fundamentalist terrorism'. At the heart of the unspoken tensions helping to fuel terrorist actions lay western interests in oil, the need to protect lucrative trading partnerships and the protection (especially on the part of the United States) of Israel. The West's demonization of Islam provided a useful symbolic prop for American imperialism in the Arab world, allowing economic and political deals to be done with oil-producing Arab countries while ideologically maintaining a distance from them. America's support for 'friendly' Arab states such as Egypt and Jordan, or even for the ruling royal family in Saudi Arabia, could be justified on the grounds of holding at bay Islamic extremism and maintaining the stability of the region, while masking the impact of selective military and financial aid on internal politics within the area.

The Iranian revolution, which overthrew the Shah in 1979, and the rise of explicitly Islamic opposition to Israel from militant groups such as the Palestinian Hamas and Islamic Jihad or the Lebanese Hezbollah intensified the mutual antipathy between the West and Islam. America's financial and military support for Israel, and the West's lack of support for the claims of Palestinians to their own homeland, had already been nourishing

Arab and Islamic antipathy to the western world. In addition, Arab and Muslim countries accused the United States of exploiting their help to wage western wars (whether against Saddam Hussein or the Soviet Union) and then abandoning them as soon as the immediate crisis was over. The siting, for example, of American troops and military hardware on the Muslim holy ground of Saudi Arabia during the 1991 Gulf War intensified Saudi-born Osama bin Laden's resentment against the West. Little of this context found its way into the mainstream media; in the popular media it was an invisible tale. Also written out of the script was the degree to which the technical know-how, military hardware and expertise of those labelled 'terrorists' were supplied by the training the *mujahidin* received from western sources, or the ability of oil-rich Saudi Arabia, profiting from American revenues, to fund the international development of the most conservative and militant forms of Islam (Al-Azmeh, 1989). The binary oppositions that were producing derogatory versions of the 'terrorist' were simultaneously conspiring with material complaints to produce Islamic constructions of the West (and in particular the United States) as rapacious, mendacious, arrogant and uncaring. The rise of what the media quickly called 'Islamic fundamentalism' was rarely contextualized, but appeared to rise like a sudden excrescence, filled with intemperate bile and venom.

## 'FUNDAMENTALISM' RAMPANT: FROM RUSHDIE TO THE NEW MILLENNIUM

The charge of 'fundamentalism' against Muslims implies both their adherence to pre-modern systems of belief and their unwillingness to make concessions to contemporary westernized culture. The irony of western media associating 'fundamentalism' with a scourge originating in Islam has not been lost. 'Fundamentalism' was a term proudly conjured into existence in the second half of the nineteenth century by American Protestants who were eager to dissociate themselves from the corruption of liberalizing tendencies in their church (Yuval-Davis, 1992: 279; Conway, 1997: 7). In relation to Islam, 'fundamentalism' indicates a similar attempt to reclaim the 'essence' of the faith and adhere strictly to its principles, as a prelude to creating an Islamic state. Modood traces its South Asian birth to the 1940s, and comments on its association not with uneducated primitivism, but with the fervour of those wishing to create 'an authentic Islamic intelligentsia to rival the existing Westernized one' (1992: 267). Supported especially by Saudi Arabia, it owed some of its international spread, ironically, to western oil money. In popular discursive association with Islam, however, 'fundamentalism' translates into 'militancy' and any form of aggressive action.

When the Iranian Ayatollah Khomeini issued the *fatwa* against the author Salman Rushdie for blaspheming against Islam in his novel, *The Satanic Verses*, in 1989, the eagerness of a number of British Muslims to demonstrate their indignation by burning copies of his books on the streets of Bradford led to cries of 'fundamentalist militancy' in the media. While Britain was by this time used to eruptions of racial tension, especially in inner-city areas, this was the first major evidence of dissent based explicitly on religious belief and carried out by a cross-generational group, supported by 'community leaders' more commonly associated with quelling youthful restlessness. The shock these protests provoked was consequently intense, and exacerbated by the evocative associations of images of book-burnings with Nazi persecution of the Jews. The press in particular responded with particular vehemence, characterizing the events as a battle between liberal British values and the intolerance of 'fundamentalists'.

Yet, as Tariq Modood (1992) claims, this was a conflict of religious and cultural values, heavily inflected by social class, which had little connection with any Islamic fundamentalist movement. Most of the Muslims involved were Pakistani Barelvis, who follow traditional cultural values but lack any 'political grand plan' (Modood, 1992: 267). They felt let down by secular Asian intellectuals in Britain, many of whom sided with liberalism and rejected their complaint that *The Satanic Verses* constituted a blasphemous affront against Muslim religious beliefs. Although the street protests were represented in the media as erupting from irrational anger, Muslim organizations had tried, without success, to invoke the Race Relations Act and the Public Order Act as means of banning Rushdie's book (Al-Azmeh, 1989: 17). Because of divisions between the mainly Sunni British Muslims, and the Shi'ite Iranians, the *fatwa* imposed by the Iranian Ayatollah would not automatically have provoked vociferously supportive reactions. But the strong defence of Rushdie by the British political and intellectual establishment stirred passions even before the *fatwa* was announced on 14 February 1989. Media coverage of the Rushdie affair provided the first alert to the presence of Muslim militancy *within* Britain, and amongst groups (British Asians) previously thought to be relatively peaceable and committed to dominant values such as hard work and the nurturing of family life. The role of Islam in dislocating this co-option of the Asian by white society was to have repercussions later in the disturbances in northern British towns in the summer of 2001. In the interim, Islamic fundamentalism became aligned particularly strongly with terrorism.

In the 1980s, Arab Muslims had been blamed for several atrocities against American interests, including a number of attacks in Lebanon and the bombing of Pan Am Flight 103 over Lockerbie in December 1988 (Said, 1997: xii). These strengthened an increasingly routine discursive link between 'terror' and 'Islamic fundamentalism'. At the start of the following decade, the Persian Gulf War was often portrayed as a simple contest between the West and Arabs, despite the support offered to the West by some Arab countries, and especially by Saudi Arabia. The consequences for Arab-Americans of their own country's propagandist exaggeration of Arab brutalities were severe, with violence and death threats against them showing a marked increase (Kellner, 1995: 218). In addition, the bombing of the World Trade Center in 1993 strengthened readiness to equate any act of terrorism directed against US interests with 'Muslim fundamentalism'. The conviction of Sheik Omar Abdel Rahman for this offence reinforced the belief that this was a reasonable assumption, although few accounts drew attention to the less palatable evidence that Rahman was a veteran of the CIA-funded *mujahidin*, trained to fight the Soviet occupation in Afghanistan in the 1980s.

When terrorism invaded America with the bombing in Oklahoma City in April 1995, which killed 168 people, the reflex reaction of blaming Arab Muslim fundamentalists was again instantaneous. Like the monster of the horror movie, the terror was no longer 'out there' in far distant countries, but had penetrated deep within the American psyche. Bewildered American commentators mused that this would be expected 'somewhere else', in 'places far, far away, places with strange-sounding names': it was 'not something that's supposed to happen at home'. On ITN's *News at Ten* on the day of the bombing (19 April 1995), Geoffrey Archer, the diplomatic correspondent, commented that 'the target was probably the US administration itself and the attack may have been sponsored by an Islamic state like Iran'. Archer does refer to the additional possibility of a connection with the FBI storming, exactly two years previously, of the Branch Davidian sect in an attempt to end the Waco siege in Texas, which led to the deaths of 82 people (the bureau investigating the sect had an office in the Oklahoma building). But his overall conclusion is that 'tonight a Middle Eastern connection to the Oklahoma City attack is thought the most likely one'.

In the United States, a number of commentators eagerly jumped to the same conclusion. A terrorist expert from the United States, Jeff Kamen, later explained his assumptions in the following terms:

> ... within moments of my having heard about the bombing in Oklahoma City my mind immediately went to Islamic fundamentalist militant terrorist action because it really is right out of that textbook and if you look at the bombing of the World Trade Center in New York City [1993], this is a piece of that paradigm, that model. So it was reasonable and legitimate and my first response was 'the bastards have hit us again'.

> (Interview with Yasmin Alibhai-Brown on Channel 4 programme *Frontline*, 20 September 1995)

Challenged by Alibhai-Brown to admit that he was wrong, he is reluctantly forced to agree, but insists on 'the reasonableness of my assumption'. Newspapers, too, were swift to print condemnatory headlines such as 'In the name of Islam' over a photograph of a rescue worker carrying a dead one-year-old baby (in the middle-market newspaper *Today* in Britain, 20 April 1995). Bernard Levin (in *The Times*) notoriously envisioned Oklahoma becoming 'Khartoum-on-the-Mississippi' as Muslim rule pervaded American society. The revelation that the chief suspect for this bombing was Timothy McVeigh, a disillusioned veteran of the Gulf War (without any connection to Islam), produced few apologies to a Muslim community terrorized by the hostility they endured in the wake of these allegations.

Although wariness about jumping to similar conclusions about responsibility was to emerge in the immediate aftermath of the September 11th attacks in 2001, no reticence about assigning blame accompanied a variety of assaults on western interests in the intervening period. These included the killing of 19 US soldiers in Saudi Arabia in 1996, the attacks on US embassies in Kenya and Tanzania in 1998, and the assault on the British embassy in the Yemeni capital Sana'a following the suicide attack in 2000 on the destroyer, USS *Cole*. By the late 1990s, terrorism was being routinely and repetitively associated with Islamic fundamentalism, as if no alternative sources existed. In November 1997, the killing of almost 60 tourists near Luxor in Egypt by members of an armed faction opposed to Mubarak's government received extensive coverage in the media, with the specific group responsible (al-Gama's al-Islamiya) variously generalized as 'Islamic/Moslem/Muslim terrorists' (in the popular papers, 18 November 1997), 'Islamic militants' (*The Times* and the *Guardian*, 18 November 1997), or 'Muslim fanatics' (*Daily Telegraph*, 18 November 1997). Only the *Independent*'s Robert Fisk referred to them as 'gunmen' and 'killers' before identifying their political cause as part of a five-year rebellion against Mubarak's regime for being, in their view, 'corrupt and un-Islamic' (18 November 1997). By stressing their political aims, rather than their religious affiliations, Fisk identified a struggle for internal political power as the driving force behind their actions. The *Guardian* reported, with some scepticism, the group's claim to have been seeking hostages to secure the release from custody of Sheik Omar Abdel Rahman.

Other papers, in their repetition of an Islamic-terrorist synergy, masked the specific politics and underlined an association between religion and terrorism that was not applied equally when members of any other religious grouping perpetrated terrorist attacks. The *Daily Record*, for example, emphasized a repressive motive, depicting the gunmen as wanting to 'topple' Mubarak and to bring in strict Islamic rule 'including a ban on alcohol, the veiling of women and a tax on religious minorities' (18 November 1997). The *Daily Telegraph*, despite its attempt to relate this massacre to political support for Saddam Hussein, evoked in its editorial strong religious imagery to cast the group's actions as alien and irrational: 'Now the barbarians have visited the temples'; 'In the shadow of some of the most sublime buildings of human civilization, it is a crime of surpassing dreadfulness, and senselessness', perpetrated by 'the hotheads of the mosque' (*Daily Telegraph*, Editorial, 18 November 1997).

The crash of EgyptAir Flight 990 just off the coast of the United States on 31 October 1999, in which 217 people died, led to extensive speculation in the western media that the co-pilot in control at the time of the disaster was on an Islamic fundamentalist suicide mission. This theory was based on the difficulty of establishing any mechanical source for the loss of the plane, and on the slender evidence from the cockpit transcripts that the co-pilot had been heard to pronounce 'tawakilt ala Allah' ('I put my faith in God's hands') just before the plane dived to its destruction. This phrase could be interpreted as either the natural response of anyone of a religious disposition facing a life-threatening crisis or as the invocation of the deity in whose name an act of missionary zeal was being perpetrated, but the western media largely ignored this ambiguity and pursued the latter assumption. Although the final report by the US National Transportation Safety Board in March 2002 did eventually argue that this was the most plausible explanation, it still remains unproven and contested by the Egyptian government. Whatever the ultimate 'facts' about this incident, the rush to judgement was at least premature. As Faisal Bodi put it in the *Guardian*, 'for many, Islamic expression plus air crash equals terrorism is a conclusion that's just too tempting to resist' (18 November 1999).

Despite distinctive political circumstances, the assumption of an Islamic hue to terrorism was reiterated in September 1999 accounts of bombs exploding in the Russian capital, Moscow. While British media reports exhibited some distance from this stance, the Russian media placed unreserved blame for a series of bomb explosions in Russia and Dagestan in August and September 1999 on Chechen 'rebels' or 'bandits' motivated by revenge for their failure to establish an Islamic state in the Caucasus. With over 300 people killed, assumptions about an Islamic link (including a possible connection with Osama bin Laden as chief financier) quickly replaced early theories that the first of these bombs (in a shopping mall in Moscow) was the work of anti-consumerist groups. Western broadsheet papers commented in the main that there was no conclusive evidence to substantiate the Chechen connection, yet the *Daily Telegraph*'s correspondent, Marcus Warren, profiled the chief suspects (recognized leaders of the ongoing Chechen guerrilla campaign in Dagestan) in terms that reproduced stereotypes of the Islamic threat:

> Both men look the part, sporting bushy beards and with ribbons printed with verses of the Koran draped around their head dress. Khatab, known by only one name, oils his shoulder-length hair. Basayev, whose namesake Imam Shamil defied Russian rule in the Caucasus for decades in the last century, is the leader, quietly spoken and calculating.
>
> Khatab is a professional revolutionary and hothead . . .
>
> (*Daily Telegraph*, 15 September 1999)

Being 'calculating' affords Basayev the sinister credentials of the silent terrorist, relying on cunning instead of passion.

'Islamic fundamentalist terrorists' were, then, repeatedly cast as the arch-enemy in a series of incidents throughout the 1990s. Even when the attribution was justified by the horrific nature of the attacks perpetrated on innocent people, the media made little effort to explain the terrorists' claims of provocation or their perception that they, too, had been victims of terrorist acts, this time by the West or by groups enjoying western support. Profiling the perpetrators as religious 'fanatics', 'extremists' and 'fundamentalists' meant that they appeared as religiously inspired maniacs, driven by irrational fervour rather than by impassioned political intent. By allowing the specific political stimulus to their campaigns to remain at best in the background, their pre-modern religious fanaticism appeared especially inexplicable to the western mind. Sheltering behind this smokescreen, western commentators could avoid confronting comparably damaging and reprehensible actions on the part of western powers or allies.

The maintenance of a righteous 'us' versus a malevolent 'them' was inscribed in discourse through a number of nuances of terminology and sentence ordering that have been especially visible in coverage of the Palestinian/Israeli conflict. Following the resumption of the Palestinian *intifada* in September 2000, for example, Palestinian attacks against Israel were frequently articulated in terms of a hostile and unprovoked assault, whereas Israeli attacks against Palestinians were depicted as 'retaliation' against the action of the aggressor. Labelling of the West Bank also suggests clear frameworks of responsibility for the ongoing struggle. As Robert Fisk, veteran Middle East correspondent, noted: 'Only weeks after United States diplomats were instructed to refer to the Israeli-occupied West Bank as "disputed" – rather than "occupied" – territory, American journalists began using precisely the same word' (1998). A study by the Glasgow University Media Group in 2002 that surveyed the understanding of the conflict by 300 young people (aged 17 to 22) demonstrated that only 9 per cent knew that the occupiers were the Israelis (11 per cent, indeed, thought them to be the Palestinians). An analysis by the same group of television coverage of the *intifada* during the first half of October 2000 discovered that 'Israelis spoke twice as much on television news as Palestinians' (Philo, 2002). This, together with the patterns of images that regularly represent the Palestinians in aggressive pose, may explain why only 30 per cent of the young people surveyed understood that Palestinian deaths outnumbered the Israelis', despite television's accurate verbal accounts of relevant statistics.

The established pattern of reporting in the British media began to falter somewhat around the growing evidence of Israeli atrocities in the spring of 2002, but in the United States the need to appease the power of the Jewish lobby led to swift retractions from any hint of prevarication. In June 2002, reported comments by Ted Turner (founder of CNN) that 'both sides [Palestinians and Israelis] are involved in terrorism' (Burkeman and Beaumont, 2002) sent CNN into public relations overdrive to counter the damage done to its reputation in Israel. Quickly instituting a policy to avoid giving voice to defenders of Palestinian suicide bombers, it also broadcast a special report on 'victims of terror' that commented exclusively on Israeli victims of the ongoing conflict. This discourse of terror ignores the imbalance between the two sides in military hardware and financial strength, remains silent about the role of the United States in providing massive material and ideological support to Israel, and sidesteps the occupation of Palestinian territory that might encourage a very different discourse of colonialism and anti-colonial struggle. By assuming a discourse appropriate to an implicitly pro-Israeli audience, the American media reproduce the power of that lobby. Although there is a rough equivalence in size between America's Muslim and Jewish populations (*New Internationalist*, no. 345, May 2002), this bears little relation to the power differential between them. A key mechanism used to sustain existing discourses is a charge of 'anti-Semitism' against anyone who is publicly critical of Israel (Pilger, 2002). By construing all criticism as necessarily antagonistic, this operates, like 'political correctness', as an emotive inhibitor of debate. Like 'political correctness', too, it turns legitimate arguments about power into an issue of moral authority.

Discourses of Islamic fundamental militancy do not merely denigrate 'the enemy', they also produce influential discourses of how the West sees itself. In news reporting, as in fictional accounts of Islamic terrorism, sanitized (and sometimes saccharine) versions of western virtues and nobility of purpose have often been the unacknowledged flip side of discourses of Islamic terrorism. Hollywood films that confirm the 'Arab Islamic terrorist' as the arch-post-communist villain have been particularly prone to construct idealized versions of the United States through the negative construction of 'the Other'. As Jack Shaheen (2001) points out, negative stereotyping of the Arab in American film is as old as Hollywood itself, but the emphasis on the *Islamic* militant terrorist has become particularly pronounced since the 1980s. In the action thriller genre, the repetitive pattern of agencies of American power (whether the military, the FBI or the CIA) successfully pitting their muscle or wits against the Islamic fanatic has become as standard a narrative formula as the cowboy-and-Indian shoot-outs of the classical Hollywood era. In the 1990s, a series of films, including *True Lies* (James Cameron, 1994), *Executive Decision* (Stuart Baird, 1996) and *The Siege* (Ed Zwick, 1998), attracted criticism from pro-Islamic groups for their replaying of clichéd stereotypes of Arab Muslims. While *True Lies,* as a vehicle for Schwarzenegger excesses, offers a caricatured portrayal of incompetent but fanatical terrorists, their senseless barbarity provides the foil against which the solidity of white American family values and emotions can be celebrated. Since the terrorists lack individuation or voice, their mission (labelled 'Crimson Jihad') has only shadowy political purpose, and their threat to explode nuclear bombs in major American cities lacks narrative credibility. Killing Arabs in this film is presented as sport for the all-white American hero.

In *Executive Decision*, the thriller- rather than action-based structure provides a sharper sense of risk and a more intense battle for control between an élite American task force and the air-borne Arab terrorists intent on destroying the eastern seaboard of the United States with powerful nerve toxins. Played out within the confined space and limited timeframe of an aircraft travelling between Athens and Washington, DC, this film's narrative generates a stronger sense of menace in its creation of a contest that depends less on physical prowess and more on outwitting opponents technologically and electronically. The characterization of the terrorists remains flimsy, but they are no longer presented in opposition to a mythical white American society. By being counterpoised against a multicultural task-force, the Arab Muslim's ostracism beyond the pale of even an ethnically diverse American society is accentuated. Despite the terrorist leader's (David Suchet) archetypal construction of the Muslim motive: 'we are the true soldiers of Islam. Our destiny is to deliver the vengeance of Allah into the belly of the infidel', the film confirms anti-Muslim supremacy by ensuring triumph for 'the infidel' (this time in western guise).

*The Siege* depicts what the other two films present only as foiled plans: successful terrorist strikes at the heart of New York society. This film devotes more attention to both the political backdrop to these events, and the paranoid response of a state that eventually imposes martial law and rounds up all young Arab males residing in Brooklyn (the location of the terrorist cells), herding them into a stadium. Reminiscent of the tactics of

American-supported dictatorships confronting a communist threat, the flouting of constitutional rights that this signifies is set against the moral and liberal vision of FBI agent Anthony Hubbard (Denzel Washington) who strongly disapproves of the law-breaking tactics adopted by General Devereaux (Bruce Willis). An idealized FBI agent becomes the protector of western freedoms. Yet, despite its powerful visual iteration of the alignment of 'terrorist' with 'Islamic extremist' (the terrorist's preparatory moves of washing, praying and setting up of explosives are replayed at key points), this film's script does at least sketch out links between the Arab action and American operations overseas. As agent Elise Kraft/Sharon Bridger (Annette Bening) explains, the CIA trained those now wreaking revenge on the United States as part of the American campaign against Saddam Hussein. The film also allows soundbite news comment on the caricaturing of all Arabs as terrorists, and includes a 'good Arab' in Hubbard's partner Frank Haddad (Tony Shalhoub). Distinguished from the Palestinian terrorist by being a Lebanese Shi'ite Muslim, he remains a secondary character, resigning his FBI role when his son is held in the stadium. His return to aid Hubbard in the defeat of the terrorists also provides a sentimental ending to occasional moments of identification, enabled through Hubbard's disapproving vision, with the Arab-Americans' suffering. Father and son are happily reunited, bringing easy closure to the wider community's intimidation and harassment.

The film's reinforcement of a generalized Arab-Muslim menace is powerfully established in the opening sequence of the film. News footage of an attack on American military barracks in Dhahran, Saudi Arabia, in which 19 servicemen were killed in 1996, is followed by the fictional ambush in the desert of the man thought to be responsible, Sheik Ahmed bin Talal (an obvious surrogate for Osama bin Laden). Shots of him praying, looked down upon by a white, besuited American male (later revealed to be military commander General Devereaux) give way to shots of the Muslim call to prayer in a mosque, situated in the heart of New York. The Arab-Muslim menace has been smoothly transferred from the sand-dunes of the distant desert to the core of the contemporary American metropolis. Attempts, later, to question the appropriateness of the association between (ordinary) Muslims and terrorism lack clarity or emphasis. Although the dialogue acknowledges that eliminating one cell will not stem the terror, the film resorts to traditional Hollywood closure, with the strong moral voice of FBI agent Hubbard once more in control as the defender of American freedoms. While the institutional values of the FBI can be synthesized fictionally with the American dream and embodied in a black hero, 'good' Muslim Arabs remain shadowy and the Palestinian Muslim Arab retains his position as the rank outsider. The only person in the film torn between both worlds, the CIA agent played by Annette Bening, is killed, her dying intonement of the Christian Lord's Prayer significantly ending with the Arabic term 'Inshallah' (if Allah wills).

The Council on American–Islamic Relations (CAIR), a central opponent of the increasing number of Hollywood films derogating the Arab Muslim, succeeded in persuading Warner Brothers to make eight changes to *Executive Decision* before its release on video (Shaheen, 2001: 189). Aware of the likely objections, the makers of *The Siege* invited pre-release comments from CAIR and from specialists, including Jack Shaheen. Their advice that the terrorists' allegiances should be changed, to remove the Arab-Muslim connection, was rejected. The film-makers' defence that they were showing diversity amongst Arabs by depicting Frank Haddad in a positive light reminded Shaheen of the justifications Hollywood once offered for negative portrayal of the Native American Indians: 'in movies displaying scores of savage Indians massacring settlers, moviemakers pointed to the presence of Tonto' (2001: 431). The hostility generated by *Executive Decision* did, however, lead to new sensitivities towards portrayal of the Arabs on the part of Warner Brothers. In 1998, the film company invited Shaheen to advise on the script of a new film, *Three Kings* (David O. Russell, 1999). His criticism resulted in a film that depicted Iraqi Arabs as rounded human beings, sharing more with their American GI counterparts than divided them, despite being set in the wake of the hostilities of the Gulf War. *Three Kings* remains an exception to the rule of Hollywood's portrayal of sinister Arabs, intent on fanatical destinies as martyrs to some shadowy cause.

## EUROPEAN MUSLIMS

If the Arabic Muslim fundamentalist was reducible to a cardboard cut-out figure, events in the former Yugoslavia in the 1990s demanded more complex responses. The conflict between 1992 and 1995 in the former Bosnia-Herzegovina, following the break-up of the Yugoslav federation, produced bitter hostility between the Bosnian Muslims, Orthodox Christian Serbs and Roman Catholic Croats. Despite being ethnically similar, and living for many years in peaceful co-existence (with a degree of inter-marriage, especially in the cosmopolitan cities), historic hostilities were ripe for rekindling as soon as the communist glue holding the Yugoslav federation together gave way. Although religion inspired few passions in what was a secular, westernized society, the weak military position of the Bosnian Muslim population, relative to the Serbs and the Croats, led to concerns in the Arab world that they were being neglected because of their association with Islam. As Norman Fairclough observes, the label of 'Bosnian Muslim' (however inevitable as a marker of position within this conflict) also became 'an identificational logic that is hung up on difference' and that, in this case, 'harmonizes . . . with the political solutions favoured by British and European Union diplomats, the Vance-Owen plan, turning Bosnia into a jigsaw whose pieces are – unequally – labelled "Croat", "Muslim", "Serbian"' (1994: 431).

In this conflict, the 'Bosnian Muslims' were nevertheless represented in the western media more as victims of 'ethnic cleansing' than as perpetrators of nefarious deeds. These were not 'fundamentalists' bent on expansionism and anti-humanitarian destruction, but people caught up in a conflict not of their own making. The media and official discourse engaged in demonization of the Serbs, who were depicted as the clear imperialist aggressors, even to the extent of at times misattributing atrocities to them, and ignoring their subjection also to acts of terror carried out by Bosnians and Croatians. Image was as important in this process as words. The dissemination by ITN and *Guardian* journalists of images of the Serb detention camps at Omarska and Trnopolje in August 1992, with their emaciated, desperate prisoners immured behind barbed-wire fencing, evoked chilling memories of Nazi concentration camps even before these words provided 'anchorage'. In a documentary (*Journalists at War*, Channel 4, 1993), journalist Joan Phillips challenged correspondents (such as the *Guardian*'s Maggie O'Kane), who had explicitly labelled these 'concentration camps', to admit that they were guilty of distorting the evidence. The images themselves, however, would have resonated for many viewers in these terms. Sporadic evidence of 'Bosnian Muslim' violence could, within this paradigm, be depicted as an inevitable consequence of conflict, and as less maliciously inspired than the Serbian or the Croatian atrocities.

Yet, despite this partly sympathetic discourse, the attribution of Islamic identity to the Bosnians appeared to diminish identification and concern. While neither media nor western European governments were willing to mount an open attack on Bosnians, the attributions of Islamic faith meant that politicians were unwilling, equally, to support their political cause. As both 'Muslims' and victims, the Bosnians were disempowered, and their cause came to be defined as one requiring humanitarian assistance, not political or military intervention. The Dayton peace accord, brokered by the United States, may have ended the fighting in 1995 but it left the country divided, and handed on a legacy of inter-ethnic bitterness that the Bosnian authorities had worked strenuously to avoid. This provides a useful reminder of the different tactics of derogation that can occur. While Muslim 'fundamentalists' provoke feelings of violent antagonism, as a hostile 'Other', the Muslim as victim evokes sympathy without the kind of identification that promotes action.

In Britain, in the summer of 2001, an eruption of disturbances in northern towns, once wealthy production centres for wool, cotton and textiles, but now suffering the devastation of post-industrialization, underlined the interweaving between discourses of Islamophobia and racism. As Akbar Ahmed points out (1993: 160), the position of Muslims in Britain, as in much of Europe, emerges out of a colonial past that still informs thinking and encourages an absence of concern about the poverty that characterizes life for many. British Muslims lack the associations with the black power movement, and the positive role models (such as Muhammad Ali or Malcolm X) that enabled at least male American Muslims to assert pride in their identity. When, in Bradford, Oldham and Burnley, white and Asian youths clashed with each other and with the police in street riots, fresh anxieties were especially raised about the disruptive threat of young Asian and Muslim men. The media's readiness to associate the perceived Asian problem specifically with Muslims, despite the presence of Hindus and Sikhs in the Asian communities, was symptomatic of wider Islamophobic discourses and encouraged by the actions of the extreme-right British National Party (BNP). Actively campaigning in these areas for the white working-class vote by provoking anti-Muslim sentiments, the BNP also attempted to forge alliances with Sikhs and Hindus to deny claims that they were driven by racism. Historically, policies of housing and education had fragmented these communities, providing a breeding ground for prejudice and misinformation.

In the discursive association both between Islam and terrorism, and Islam and social unrest, the chief evokers of 'risk' have always been characterized as male. Despite the involvement of women in the Palestinian *intifada*, active and assertive representations of Muslim women do not fit with the western construction of women's position within Islam. While the Bosnian women subjected to degradation and rape could be depicted as 'victims' of fellow Europeans, the oppression of women within Islam has become a key signifier of the religion's backwardness and its passionate antipathy to contemporary liberal thinking. This element in the construction of 'Otherness' particularly emphasizes an assumed egalitarianism towards women in western cultures. The West can emphasize its claim to be secular, modern, liberated, rational and sophisticated against a religiously driven form of fanaticism that is presented as being repressive, led by emotion and regressive. As Shohat and Stam comment about the West's Eurocentrism, it 'sanitizes Western history while patronizing and even demonizing the non-West' (1994: 3).

## WOMEN IN ISLAM

While the barbarity of terrorism has been used to confirm a medieval image of Islam, this discourse gains additional credibility through repeated accounts of Islamic suppression of women's freedoms. In media discourse, these have been accentuated through representation of the veil as a key symbol of the silencing and depersonalizing of women. As Helen Watson comments, 'the image of a veiled Muslim woman seems to be one of the most popular Western ways of representing the "problems of Islam"' (1994: 153). Indignation supposedly relating to the oppression of Muslim women, but deployed primarily to insist on the retrograde, pre-modern characteristics of Islam compared with western progressiveness, is nothing new, despite its recent resurgence. Leila Ahmed recounts how misogynistic men of colonial times justified their suppression of indigenous culture by claiming liberalizing intentions towards their oppressed women: 'The idea that Other men, men in colonized societies or societies beyond the borders of the civilized West, oppressed women was to be used, in the rhetoric of colonialism, to render morally justifiable its project of undermining or eradicating the cultures of colonized peoples' (1992: 151). 'The veil', in itself a generic referent for a range of different styles of Islamic dress for women (from the full-body covering of the Afghan burqa to the simple head-covering of the scarf), serves also to obscure the different attitudes to Muslim women prevailing in different countries and cultures.

The denial of women's rights to education and to free movement in Afghanistan under the rule of the Taliban, and the brutal treatment meted out to any woman caught infringing sacred codes of sexual honour in Saudi Arabia have been presented not as specific instances of oppression but as generic indices of the essential nature of Islam. By contrast, the West has eagerly presented moves away from state-supported suppression of women's rights to at least official claims of egalitarianism as confirmation of its enlightened progress and its commitment to modernism. A sanitized version of western egalitarianism is once again the counterpoint used against the most brutal versions of oppression by 'the Other'.

Even if it took the events of September 11th 2001 to put Afghanistan on the popular media map, discourses of women's lack of rights in 'the Islamic world' had surfaced in several earlier accounts of 'barbarity', such as the sentencing in 1997 of the Scottish nurse Lucille McLauchlan to 500 lashes for her alleged part in assisting in the murder of a fellow nurse in Saudi Arabia. The *Sun*'s headline 'BARBARIC' (24 September 1997) set the tone for much of the coverage, with the Foreign Secretary's comment that the sentence was 'wholly unacceptable in the modern world' being widely used as a primary definer of the Saudi action. The Scottish popular newspaper, the *Daily Record*, re-invoked the controversy that erupted between Britain and Saudi Arabia in 1980 following the screening of *Death of a Princess* on British television (an ITV drama-documentary dealing with the public execution of a Saudi princess who had committed adultery). The *Record*'s Editorial reminded its readers: 'This is a corrupt, backward society which still executes women whose only crime is to fall pregnant out of wedlock. This is a society which beheaded one of their own princesses because she committed adultery' (24 September 1997). The outrage of the verbal text was supported in several newspapers by pictures of Saudi police flogging a prisoner in Riyadh or of an 'Islamic execution', anchored by captions underlining the savagery involved. The subsequent pardoning of both nurses by King Fahd in 1998 received less prominent attention. In 1995, when Jemima Goldsmith (an English society heiress) married Imran Khan, the Pakistani cricketer, the British press were scathing about her 'fate', representing it as a passage into slavery and as instituting subservience to her husband that would require the abandonment of her glamorous lifestyle.

These constructions of a backward, oppressive Islam, where women's rights are quashed, have been generalized to be universally applicable. Yet considerable differences exist in the position and treatment of Muslim women, especially between Islamic states and secular societies, and between autocratic and democratic forms of government. As in other practices within Islam, variations in attitudes to women's rights depend on the political context and on the varying interpretations of the Qur'an and the subsequent interpretations of Muslim law inscribed, by male law-givers, in the *shari'a*. In addition the *hadith*, short narratives reputedly based on the sayings of Muhammad, are used to aid in the interpretation of conduct. Here, women did play a significant role as respected authorities (Leila Ahmed, 1992: 46–7), signalling that Islam's respect for women's contribution was in advance of that of many other religions of the time, including Christianity. In its origins, as Leila Ahmed illustrates (1992), Islam established an ethic of equality, even, in principle, between the sexes, while at the same time aligning itself with misogynistic practices already extant in several of the cultures that embraced it. In common with other religions, the growth of male interpretations of Islamic principles allowed misogyny to dominate. As Nira Yuval-Davis indicates, fundamentalism, in the original sense of the term, impacts on the lives of women especially harshly, because they are 'seen as the "cultural carriers" of the collectivity who transmit it ["proper" behaviour] to the future generation' (1992: 285). While it is important not to elide this from accounts of the exaggeration and universalization of the oppression of Muslim women, it is not a feature unique to Islamic forms of fundamentalism.

The denial of women's rights in countries such as Saudi Arabia attracts justifiable censure, but presenting this as typical is misleading. In most Arab Muslim countries, women have access to education and to job opportunities on a par with their non-Muslim counterparts. Women in many parts of the Muslim world have risen to prominence in politics, in academic life and in the creative arts, and active Muslim feminist movements exist in a number of countries, even if, as in Egypt, they have come under increasing pressure from Islamists eager to ensure the continuance of traditional practices. Even in Taliban-held Afghanistan, the Revolutionary Association of the Women of Afghanistan (RAWA) campaigned, and continues to campaign, for women's rights and for peace, freedom, democracy and an end to fundamentalist rule. Operating underground within Afghanistan, and in refugee camps in Pakistan, its sophistication in running its own website and in exhibiting consummate public relations skills accords ill with the image of Afghan women as universally powerless, downcast victims living in the dark ages and awaiting western enlightenment and rescue. RAWA's success in gaining recognition in the West includes coverage on *Oprah* (11 October 2001) an appearance on CNN's *Larry King Live* (1 October 2001) and an award from *Glamour* magazine (October 2001). Although this flurry of exposure may have been a byproduct of September 11th, RAWA had achieved more limited access to western readers and listeners even before this.

The conventions of veiling provide a symbolic fuse for arguments about the restrictions imposed on Muslim women. To western cultures that have especially equated the liberation of women with a more open attitude to female sexuality (even if that is still defined in predominantly masculine terms), lack of sexual and bodily freedoms for women in Islamic culture becomes symbolic of a widespread oppression of human freedoms. Controversies over the practice of veiling are, however, indicative of the discursive elasticity of customs, which are not even unique to Islam, in acquiring totemic significance. These conventions vary from country to country, involving total face-masking in some but the adoption only of head-covering in others. As Anne Sofie Roald (2001) makes clear, terminological differences throughout the Islamic world impede precise comparisons between injunctions about female dress, but dispute about what Islam requires, even among Muslim women writers, centres on interpretations of the Qur'an, the *hadith*, and the writings of scholars across the generations. Despite their contrasting ideological outlooks, both feminists (such as Mernissi, 1985, and Leila Ahmed, 1992) and non-feminists (such as Roald, 2001) agree that there is no explicit or unmistakable reference to the need for women to veil in the Qur'an itself, although modesty of dress and demeanour (for both men and women) is required in public (Qur'an: 24:30; 24:31). In the *hadith* likewise, although several instructions are given about dress styles, these focus more on men than on women and veiling is not explicitly required (Roald, 2001: 264–7). The custom of veiling pre-dated Islam, as a feature of some of the societies (including Christian societies) that were subject to Islamic conquest (Leila Ahmed, 1992: 5). During the lifetime of Muhammad, only his wives were required to veil. How veiling, as a contested tenet of this particular faith, has become such a pivotal concern for western views of Islam requires explanation.

In a persuasive argument, Leila Ahmed links this phenomenon to western colonialism's desire to denigrate Islam. As the most visible sign, and one particularly at odds with western feminist ideals of female equality, it became the prime target of calumny (1992: 152). If women's liberation could be marked (however inappropriately) by images of a sexualized female body, images of fully veiled women, devoid of individual bodily shape or sexual codification, and dressed in full-length monotonous clothing associated in the West with widow's weeds or Victorian drabness, inspired connotations of repression. This was a form of performing femininity that had no place in the script of experimentation, self-exploration and play with identity, familiar to western conceptualizations of freedom for women. Mernissi (1985) suggests that the repression of female sexuality within Islam depends less on the abnegation of female sexuality and desire that characterizes Christianity, and more on a fear of the challenge an active female sexuality presents to social order and to the central importance attributed by Islam to family and devotional duties. Restrictions, therefore, paradoxically subscribe to a more powerful vision of femininity than the passive westernized model. They are based on an anxiety that self-determining women would re-introduce the ungoverned promiscuity of pre-Islamic societies, as described in Arab literature (Mernissi, 1985: 166), and are now additionally encouraged by antipathy to westernized forms of sexual liberation, often seen by Muslims as a betrayal of Islamic principles (Mernissi, 1985: 167–8).

When imposed by patriarchal and oppressive regimes, the veil does, of course, inevitably connote loss of personal freedoms, but what causes surprise to many western observers is the evidence that Muslim women in many cultures *choose* to adopt the veil. Beyond obeisance to perceived religious principles, the reasons given for this decision are often pragmatic, and include the desire for anonymity, protection from male sexual advances and even the saving of money because fashionable clothing is not required. As one of the women interviewed by Anne Sofie Roald comments, 'in my head-scarf I have freedom. I am not ruled by the needs of men' (2001: 290). Another reflects: 'Sometimes at my work I can reflect that I am the only one with *hijab* and it gives me the feeling that the head-scarf is something majestic and dignified. It gives a woman dignity (*waqqar*) and it reflects that which is inside her. I see the head-scarf as a protection for women, giving them space' (Roald, 2001: 291). In addition, for many the wearing of the veil has become a political decision, based on an antipathy to western secular values and western commercialism. As Leila Ahmed observes, the veil became the symbolic core of a 'resistance narrative' bent on casting aside the edicts of colonial discourse and reinstating 'the dignity and validity of all native customs' (1992: 164). Yet, as she also points out, the symbolic status accorded to the veil in both colonial and anti-colonial discourse became a distraction from crucial arguments about the best means of combating misogyny and promoting women's rights.

In western media representations, the veil has equally become the dominating signifier of Muslim women's oppression. Visually, it epitomizes an alienation of the 'Other' that immediately connotes a gulf of chronology as well as custom. The veiled woman is, in addition, a woman without a voice, drifting anonymously through public spaces where she does not belong. The image of a burqa-clad Afghan mother being executed in a stadium in Kabul in 1999 for allegedly killing her abusive husband, despite the clemency granted by his relatives, became an icon regularly screened and reproduced as justification of western action in waging a 'war on terrorism' in the wake of September 11th. Such brutality towards women at the end of the twentieth century symbolized the ruthless terror of the Taliban regime. Yet, many of the reproductions of this image told only part of the story. In a country that outlawed television and foreign journalists, this footage was shot by a member of RAWA, using a digital video camera concealed behind the very burqa that was the object of so much disquiet. The brave determination to give voice to the unspoken, in a country where discovery would have meant certain death, was totally at odds with the 'victim' image of burqa-wearing women that fitted more comfortably with western discourses. Almost a year after the widespread distribution of these pictures, the British popular paper, the *Mirror* (19 June 2002), devoted extensive space to the story of the woman who was killed, but only a single paragraph to how the images were produced. Instead, the paper's emphasis was on the gruelling account of the fate of 'a woman beneath veils of violence, madness and terrible sadness'.

The veil has, however, been an unstable signifier in representation, possessing a dual history: 'as an overt symbol of the oppression of women under Islam, or a romanticized view . . . as part and parcel of the exotic, sensual Otherness of Oriental traditions' (Watson, 1994: 153). Consistent throughout both has been the denial of voice to the veiled woman. Since speaking rights are rarely given, they are all the more arresting and revealing when they do occur. An award-winning documentary, *Divorce Iranian Style* (Kim Longinotto and Ziba Mir-Hosseini, 1998), shot in Iran by an all-woman team and screened on British television (Channel 4, 23 August 1999), depicts a number of articulate and assertive *hijab*-clad women pleading for divorce in a family court. The skill they exhibit in not merely stating their cases but in manoeuvring around the constraints of an oppressive system, confounds their 'victim' image.

The general equation between 'veil' and 'silence' in western discourses was further broken in an edition of the BBC2 current affairs series, *Correspondent*, devoted to the plight of Afghan refugees in the wake of the 'war on terror' ('The dispossessed', 20 January 2002). The film-maker, Taghi Amirani, travels to a Taliban-controlled refugee camp where he comes upon a young woman, clad from head to (nail-varnished) toe in the familiar blue burqa, confidently berating the surrounding, and increasingly bewildered, Taliban about the conditions in the camp. The assertiveness and articulacy of her unhesitating tirade produces an acute contrast with the visual framing of the lone, helpless veiled woman surrounded by her oppressors (see Figure 7.1). Later in the documentary, following the 'liberation' of Kabul, Amirani rediscovers the same woman in a different camp now controlled by the Northern Alliance. She has cast off her burqa, signalling, to a western consciousness, freedom from constraint. But the image we are now shown (see Figure 7.2)

Figure 7.1  Afghan woman berating Taliban, *Correspondent*, 20 January 2002. By kind permission of BBC News and BBC Worldwide.

Figure 7.2  Burqa-less femininity, *Correspondent*, 20 January 2002. By kind permission of BBC News and BBC Worldwide.

accords with the western norms of a passive and compliant femininity (intensified by the conventions of the ethnographic gaze at women from 'Other' cultures). As a result, this articulate and courageous young woman is ironically co-opted within a conventional discourse of feminine quiescence that her representation in the anonymous protection of the burqa belied. Granting the veiled woman voice confounds the simple associations of docility and victimhood that western representations have forged around the veil, and requires attention to Muslim women's diverse subjectivities, experiences and circumstances. As images of 'silent, shrouded Afghan women' proliferated on the news, journalist Laura Flanders inverted the usual pattern of blame: by treating them as voiceless victims, 'the US media veil Afghan women, too' (Flanders, 2001).

## CONCLUSION

In this chapter's exploration of western media constructions of the 'risk' of Islam, a number of issues have emerged. A discourse of risk has been shown to be reductive: suggesting universal features and oppressive practices where diversity prevails, and blocking receptiveness to Muslims' own divergent range of voices. The 'difference' of Islam has been repeatedly emphasized, serving both to alienate Islamic practices from modernity and from civilization, and to shore up the West's own sense of self-worth, and its liberal and fair-minded credentials. Signifiers of difference can be apparently modest, but insistent in their reiteration. British radio news items making reference to Islam almost without exception feature the 'sound effect' of the Muslim call to prayer (this is included also in many documentaries, as well as films). Underlining alienation by repeatedly drawing attention to difference helps to produce fears and apprehensions.

Yet, another possibility is also hinted at: that constructions of Islam, by being 'exotic', can also become an object of fascination, arousing the 'thrill' of the risky outlined in the Introduction to this section of the book. Irrational anxiety about the 'riskiness' of Islam can lead to an equally irrational and false embrace of that which is feared, with no better motive than the hope of exorcizing the phobia. The controversial columnist Julie Burchill created a storm of protest when she cast 'Islamophilia' as a curse equal in scale to 'Islamophobia' (2001). Portraying Islam as a religion universally intolerant of human rights, she concluded that 'ill-sorted Islamophilia is just as dangerous as mindless, ill-sorted Islamophobia'. Although her opinion was based on scathing generalizations, her mockery of 'media gullibility' that finds Islam 'fun' and 'something essentially "joyous" and "vibrant"; sort of like Afro-Caribbean culture, only with fasting and fatwas' captured the condescension that can also be displayed towards ideologies that challenge hegemonic values. As the British Muslim writer Yasmin Alibhai-Brown insists, idealizing Islam is a patronizing and debilitating response to its challenge. The repressive elements within autocratic and ultra-patriarchal versions of Islam need to be contested and not whitewashed out of the picture (Alibhai-Brown, 2001a; 2001b). In the wake of September 11th, tendencies to condemn and tendencies to eulogize both got in the way of listening attentively to what Muslims themselves were saying.

# Chapter Eight

# SEPTEMBER 11TH: RETHINKING ISLAM?

Pre-existing discourses of Islamophobia received corroboration, but also official denial, in the wake of the attacks on the World Trade Center and the Pentagon in September 2001. In an eerie replication of the narrative of the Hollywood terrorist movies, the source of risk had invaded the symbolic heartland of western capitalism. Yet, memories of over-zealousness in attributing blame to Islamic militants after the Oklahoma City bombing injected wariness into official pronouncements of responsibility, at least initially. In a move familiar from van Dijk's (1992) model of 'the denial of racism' (discussed in Chapter 2), even once Islamic terrorists were pinpointed as the likely suspects, western leaders were assiduous in affirming their distance from any suggestion of hostility to the Muslim publics of their own countries. This chapter explores the aftermath of September 11th in terms of its impact on the discourse of 'risk' around Islam, and considers the role of contests over word and image in managing an official discourse that reasserted western values while denying Islamophobia.

As Chapter 3 has already indicated, the attacks on the World Trade Center in New York and on the Pentagon set a challenge for journalists and picture editors to find forms of representation adequate to convey the magnitude of what was happening. As Bill Nichols points out, capturing magnitude has always been a problem for representational media dominated by a desire to explain and tell stories at the same time: 'Narrative and exposition are always forms of miniaturization that seek to encapsulate a "world" that bears some meaning for us' (1991: 230) whereas, quoting Jameson (1981: 102), '"history is what hurts" … A magnitude of excess remains' (1991: 231). As I have discussed elsewhere (Macdonald, 1998), it is often to the personal dimension that television turns to attempt its embodiment of magnitude. The experiences of witnesses and survivors are deployed to bring the events within the miniaturizing scale that makes them affectively intelligible to viewers. But on September 11th, the liveness of what was unfolding on screens across the globe, and its immediate failure to be contained by conventional expositions and narratives, meant that for once the rawness of history could not be filtered out. Atypically, television had not (yet) been processed into packaged blandness.

The event itself broke new ground in western perceptions of risk. Neither the most prophetic insurance expert, nor the most acutely paranoid defence analyst had foreseen the nature of this attack. As Nik Kowsar's cartoon underlines (Figure 8.1), its 'magnitude of excess' was ironically emphasized by the impotence of the United States' own planned 'son of Star Wars' defence system to prevent such an eventuality. The happenings of this

**Figure 8.1** **Cartoon by Nik Kowsar,** *The Iran News.* **By kind permission of the cartoonist and Cartoonists & Writers Syndicate/CartoonWeb.com.**

day appeared to challenge anyone in the West who argued that perceptions of globalized and latent risk had been overestimated or emanated from the ravings of the apocalyptically minded. In the shock and confusion of live rolling news coverage, the horror of what was being recorded was intensified by the unanswered questions: Who was responsible? Why had the security services not succeeded in protecting American airspace? How many aeroplanes were still unaccounted for? The unfamiliarity of the coverage was accentuated by the unusual disjunction between sound and image, as endlessly repeated footage of the destruction of the twin towers, or of the smoking ruins of part of the Pentagon in Washington, was played across a variety of interviews with aviation specialists, defence analysts, political experts, specialist correspondents and reporters on the spot, most of whom remained out of vision. On the BBC's News 24 coverage, captioned reports that both towers had collapsed appeared over the anchor's claim that one of the towers had fallen. Those involved in the process of events, broadcasting from the spot, struggled to bring analysis and exposition into line with their emotional responses. Only those professionally habituated to offering instant reactions, such as British Prime Minister Tony Blair, offered confident assessment. Speaking briefly at the Trades Union Congress in Brighton (where he had been due that day to give his annual speech), PM Blair declared, 'This mass terrorism is the new evil in our world today. It is perpetrated by fanatics who are utterly indifferent to the sanctity of human life. And we, the democracies of this world, are going to have to come together and eradicate this evil completely from our world.'

This rhetoric immediately reaffirmed the comforting polarity between (western) 'good' and (terrorism) 'evil' that helped to set the perpetrators of these acts beyond the pale of rationality or civilization. 'Evil' in this vision was firmly placed back outside the 'imaginative geography' of the 'democracies of this world'. As commentaries proliferated across the airwaves that day, this pattern was to become entrenched in a variety of discursive oppositions: civilization versus barbarism; (natural) grief and despair versus (pathological) celebration and rejoicing; victim versus assailant. The amorphous face of a barbarity without possibility of containment began to sharpen into specific shape. In the process, reassurance was offered that this risk, too, despite its magnitude, could be managed and reined in. As Beck indicates, much of contemporary 'risk management' requires decision-making *in the absence of* secure knowledge (1999: 78). He identifies science, 'the queen of error', as providing a last bulwark against perceptions that risk eludes control (1999: 53), but the media also have considerable power to quell the spectres of risk they themselves have raised. In the weeks following September 11th, three intertwined discourses served to bring the events of that day into a frame that obviated rethinking of western ideological positions. First, the mainstream media reasserted a strong, and then belligerent, claim to western 'civilization' that nevertheless sought to distance itself from racism; second, they offered reminders of the callousness of the 'Other' from whom the enemy supposedly came; and, third, by identifying the key suspect as charismatic, powerful, but highly elusive, they laid the conditions for an ongoing narrative of risk, but one that could now apparently be particularized.

## CIVILIZATION RAMPANT

The attack on America was presented in the emergent discourses within the West as an assault, first, on American identity and then, by extension, on the 'civilized world'. Risks routinely reported with some complacency when they occurred in other parts of the world, changed complexion on home ground. As the newspapers the following day insistently declared, September 11th produced a seismic change in Americans' perceptions of danger and vulnerability. The *New York Times* (Opinion column, 12 September 2001) was not alone in remarking: 'If four planes can be taken over simultaneously by suicidal hijackers, then we can never be quite sure again that any bad intention can be thwarted, no matter how irrational or loathsome.' In the more popular *USA Today*, the omnipresence of potential risk was expressed as an unravelling of the American dream:

> When the twin towers of the Trade Center crumpled to the ground like so much dust, at a cost of countless lives, something less tangible was lost as well – a uniquely American sense of freedom and security. That is a loss the nation can endure only temporarily, lest it hand the terrorists the victory they seek and diminish the essence of who we are.
>
> (Opinion column, 12 September 2001)

On British television, on the day of the attacks, one commentator, summing up the impact, asked 'If this can happen in America, then are any of us safe?' (Kirsty Lang, on Channel 4 News at 7 pm). Those most immediately at risk, of course, were precisely those airbrushed out of the imagined communities under threat: anyone who looked like an Arab (whether Muslim or otherwise) or, in Britain, anyone of Asian appearance (women in *hijabs*, by being visibly identifiable as Muslims, were particularly vulnerable).

In the developing discourse of this day, the attacks came to be defined as an assault less on civilians than on symbols of American power, and on 'civilization' itself. Mythic constructions of American-ness as synonymous with civilized values were repeatedly reproduced. A number of commentators highlighted how the targets had been shrewdly chosen for their symbolic and instantly recognizable status. The destruction of central icons of the West's economic and military might was represented as a blow against 'freedom', 'democracy' and 'civilization'. Although wholly plausible in a western context, any internationalization of perspective would have opened this conceptualization to immediate contest, especially in parts of the world where American involvement was seen as meddling interference, driven not by a commitment to democracy or freedom but by an imperialist desire to protect the power and self-interest of the USA itself. As the previous chapter indicated, American support for the wholly undemocratic and repressive regime in Saudi Arabia (in return for protection of oil supplies) has been especially provocative to Muslims who regard Saudi Arabia as their holy land. 'Freedom' and 'civilization', like 'terrorism', are terms that cannot escape discursive construction. What they signify depends fundamentally on the position from which one is speaking, and the kinds of interests that are felt to be at stake in the protection that these concepts offer. Making better sense in an interrogative form that exposes their partiality – Whose freedom? Whose civilization? – they appear nevertheless to offer absolutes and certainties that only those inspired by evil intent will fail to recognize. When the news agency, Reuters, decided not to overturn its policy of banning the words 'terrorist' and 'terrorism' (unless they formed part of a quotation) shortly after the events of September 11th, it caused outrage amongst other news organizations. Intended, however naively, to retain impartiality, and also to protect its staff in Arab- or Muslim-dominated parts of the world, this policy was regarded by many of its competitors as a betrayal of civilized values. ABC News also attracted some censure for the allegedly unpatriotic act of banning its journalists from wearing flags in their lapels.

Politicians, rather than journalists, were the first to interpret the events of September 11th as an assault on the concepts of freedom and civilization, even if the media, as the disseminators of these views, quickly appropriated them as their own. James Rubin, former Assistant Secretary of State in the United States, commented: 'An attack on the World Trade Center is an attack on all the civilized countries in the world' (Channel 4 News, 11 September 2001). President Bush was seen across the networks asserting that 'Freedom itself was attacked this morning by a faceless coward and freedom will be defended', while Prime Minister Blair, issuing his second message of the day, declared, 'This is not a battle between the United States and terrorism but between the free and democratic world and terrorism.' The evolving metaphor of a battleground set the scene for declarations of 'war', with the protagonist cast as the proactive 'enemy', allowing any action on America's part to appear as retaliation, and to be couched in terms of 'proportionate response'. This scenario was mapped out on British television only four hours after the first attack. Robert Moore, the diplomatic editor of ITN, commented:

'What has occurred this afternoon is a declaration of war on America. ... This is Manhattan – images that will live along with Pearl Harbor in infamy' (ITV Early Evening News at 6 pm, 11 September 2001).

The analogy to Pearl Harbor resonated through a number of reactions. Moore's 'in infamy' was in itself an echo of President Franklin D. Roosevelt's well-known assertion that 7 December 1941, the day when the US military came under sustained and unexpected assault from the Japanese during the Second World War, would be 'a date which will live in infamy'. Similar references to the 'infamy' of that day appeared in the editorial columns of the *Washington Post* (12 September 2001) and the *Independent* (12 September 2001). The parallels between Pearl Harbor and the attacks of September 11th, in setting a nationalistic paradigm for the construction of the victim, also begged a number of questions since in this case there was no clearly identifiable 'enemy', and certainly none that could be defined by national identity. The enemy, by remaining elusively associated with an antipathy to freedom, democracy and civilization, could be associated transnationally with Islam and with Islamic extremism in particular. The casting of America as the victim of warfare, rather than its initiator, was vital in establishing the moral high ground. Cartoonists, confronted with the difficulty of dealing sensitively with a national disaster, sought refuge in symbolism of attacks on freedom or, more optimistically, of American heroism in the face of onslaught. Several depicted a distressed and bowed Statue of Liberty, while others (see Figure 8.2) replicated the play on the famous Iwo Jima photograph from the Second World War (also deployed in a widely reproduced newsphotograph in several newspapers). American fire-fighters raising the stars and stripes over the scene of devastation symbolized the heroism not merely of the fire-fighters who lost their lives in the World Trade Center, but the United States' invincibility in confronting a ferocious enemy (the original photograph was taken by Joe Rosenthal in 1945 to raise American morale in the battle for the Pacific against the Japanese). The *Washington Post* argued that defence of the United States merited international co-operation, but, failing that, it supported an isolationist response. The USA, it declared, 'must seek to assemble an international alliance to identify and eliminate all sources of support for the terrorist networks that would wage war on the United States. If necessary, it must act alone' (Editorial, 12 September 2001).

Yet, the warmongering rhetoric was accompanied by denials of Islamophobia or of any official enmity towards 'ordinary' Muslims. In a Britain still conscious of the summer riots in northern towns, Tony Blair repeatedly distanced himself from any disparagement of Islam as a religion. Strategically addressing the press in the company of British Muslim leaders, Blair emphasized that the attacks were the work not of Muslim or Islamic terrorists but 'of terrorists pure and simple' (reported in the *Guardian*, 28 September 2001). The *Sun* newspaper, to the surprise of many of its critics, ran an extensive Editorial two days after the attacks under the headline 'Islam is not evil religion'. Whether this was a sign of the paper's responsiveness to the blandishments of the government's spin doctors, following the transfer of its allegiances to New Labour in 1997, or a self-motivated reaction, the terms

**Figure 8.2    Cartoon by Marshall Ramsey, *The Clarion Ledger*. By kind permission of Atlantic Syndication.**

of its distancing from Islamophobia were significant. Based on the presupposition that Islam *might* be thought to be a deleterious force, it avoids political interpretation in favour of moral simplicities. If the principle being opposed is neither Islam, nor even terrorist action, but 'evil', the unification that Thompson (1990) and Eagleton (1991) present as a key characteristic of ideology is easier to achieve. By universalizing the forces of good in the opening paragraph ('the whole world has turned against the murderous fanatics who destroyed the Twin Towers'), it attempted to unite all right-thinking people everywhere on the side of justice. Yet later, in a departure from this inclusivity, the Editorial constructs the newspaper's readers as non-Muslim: 'the Muslims in Britain ARE British. *They may have a different culture to most of us* [my italics] but they love this country and they respect democracy' (*Sun*, 13 September 2001). The claimed distancing from Islamophobia (despite its own slide into constructing the Muslim as 'Other') is reinforced by the inclusion of a number of statements from Muslim leaders in Britain condemning the attacks.

In Europe, only Italy's Silvio Berlusconi overtly broke this consensus. Providing a defiantly Occidentalist account of the situation in remarks made in Berlin on 26 September 2001, he claimed western culture and civilization to be superior to Islam, producing a rush of criticism. The *Sun*'s moralistic discursive construction was more typical of strategies deployed to win and sustain support for America without exploring the political complexities of either the causes for anti-American feeling or the planned 'war on terror'. On the day that attacks were launched against Afghanistan (7 October 2001) President George W. Bush declared the United States of America to be 'the friends of almost a billion worldwide who practise the Islamic faith', but the enemy of 'those barbaric criminals who profane a great religion by committing murder in its name'. His visit to a mosque in the week following the September 11th attacks was also a carefully calculated move to distance him from Islamophobia while retaining his right to launch his self-declared 'war on terror'.

The benign rhetoric was belied by a number of actions, including the detention without trial of a number of American citizens, newly suspected because of their names or origins. According to the Council on American–Islamic Relations almost a thousand Arabs and Muslims had been arrested by the end of October 2001, despite very few of them having any demonstrable links to terrorist attacks. With even civil liberties groups finding information on these cases hard to glean from the authorities, little coverage of these penetrated the mainstream media. When the war in Afghanistan began in October 2001, the role of the now 'friendly' Northern Alliance in rape and killings in Kabul in 1992, which might have questioned their association with a 'civilized' war, was little mentioned. Presented as 'rugged' rather than 'barbaric', they could be reconstituted as allies.

## 'LOATHSOME REACTIONS'

A discourse based around the treachery of 'evil' acts might of itself have been sufficient to win hearts and minds for American retaliation, but it gained sustenance from the controversial, but powerful, images beamed around the West on the day of the attacks, showing Palestinians celebrating in the streets of the Arab section of Jerusalem. The *Sun* Editorial described this behaviour as a 'loathsome reaction', but cautioned at the same time against confusing these ordinary Palestinians with 'the enemy' (13 September 2001). The footage in question later became embroiled in a controversy over its authenticity, indicating the precariousness of reporting on a day when appearance and reality seemed unusually badly aligned, and demonstrating the sensitivities of broadcasters to accusations that they were leaping to conclusions about a Middle-Eastern involvement. These pictures were deployed in a variety of ways across the British networks in the course of the day. The footage, as it was broadcast on British television, consisted of shots showing children and men celebrating by waving Palestinian flags, clapping and making victory signs. Images of a woman, her face framed in close-up, appeared in some versions, and on the BBC's main evening bulletin (10 pm) a shot not included elsewhere of men firing their guns in the air was incorporated. Sounds of horns hooting, and shouts of celebration accentuated the joy being felt. That this was a reaction for the western cameras was foregrounded in the BBC's footage, where people on the street were seen responding to the presence of at least two camera crews. Because of their rarity, as the principal insight offered in the course of this day into the reactions of the non-western world to the events unfolding in America, these pictures acquired powerful symbolic significance. Early claims (later denied) from the Democratic Front for the Liberation of Palestine that they were responsible for the attacks intensified their aura. Although some commentators from Jerusalem referred verbally in their reports to the eruption of these types of impromptu rejoicing, without the accompaniment of related pictures, it was the footage that prompted strong reactions.

Yet, in the anchoring of these images within the bulletins, considerable caution was articulated about the significance that viewers should attach to them. Jon Snow, commenting on their first release on Channel 4, about two and a half hours after the initial US attack, was dismissive: 'Well, frankly, I mean that's the kind of scene you could shoot anywhere at any time in West [sic] Jerusalem. I hardly think it a key indication of exactly what's going on.' With time for more reflection, Gaby Rado, foreign affairs correspondent, later stated in Channel 4's main evening news broadcast: 'Among Palestinians there was a certain amount of celebration at the attacks although it's not clear the full horror of the likely death toll was understood.' On the more popular ITV network, the main news bulletin showed the pictures only after John Irvine had provided the following context:

> Palestinian organizations in general have denounced it [the attacks on the USA] and distanced themselves from it. Of course, we did see scenes of celebration on the Palestinian streets of East Jerusalem and in the West Bank city of Nablus. Many in the western world will find such scenes repugnant. Yassar Arafat has ordered his security services to prevent any repeat of that. But I think those images must be seen in the context of 12 months of fighting and dying here. There is a sense within the Arab community that the Americans have allied themselves strongly with Israel.

Helpful although this contextualization is, it is presented as commentary over hypnotically repeated images of the attack on the twin towers, thereby diminishing its ability to focus the viewer's attention, however fleetingly, on a non-western perspective.

The BBC was least critical in its use of the pictures, although Orla Guerin was careful to remind viewers that these images could not be taken as representative of the Palestinian response. The voice-over commentary on the footage itself offers no reminder of the point of view of the Palestinians, with James Robbins, the diplomatic correspondent, restricting himself at 6 pm to the generalized abstraction that 'It's evidence of how much hatred has already been refuelled by this disaster.' By 10 pm, George Eykyn adopts a more unstintingly Eurocentric version: 'For some, the horror and carnage inflicted on the United States today is a cause of celebration' (with 'celebration' coinciding with images of Palestinian gunmen firing shots in the air). On a day when the western world was stunned by the scale of this unprecedented attack on key symbols of its global power and influence, codes of 'good taste' ensured that scant attention only could be paid to the grievances that might have fuelled such atrocities. Memories of previous reactions to supposedly unpatriotic reporting in times of international crisis were no doubt at the forefront of producers' thinking. In 1986, the BBC had been attacked by the then Conservative government for the commentary on its report of a United States air attack on Libya (in revenge for its support for international terrorism), which suggested less than wholehearted support for the American action (Corner, 1995: 68–74). During the Gulf War, the BBC was similarly dubbed the 'Baghdad Broadcasting Corporation' for critical reports of the bombing of a supposed military command centre in Al-Amariya, a suburb of Baghdad, which turned out to have been used as a shelter by women and children (see MacGregor, 1997, for a detailed account of western television coverage of this event). Although all western broadcasters censored the worst images of charred bodies being removed from that scene, suggestions of Allied guilt in a time of war were interpreted as acts of treachery. In the United States, also, vehement criticism followed ABC anchor Peter Jenning's reporting of this incident (Kellner, 1995: 219).

Despite these fears, isolated insights into other perspectives did occasionally find airtime on 11 September 2001. Jon Snow, questioning James Rubin, former Assistant Secretary of State under President Clinton, asks, 'But ... what about attending to the discomfort and the distress of the people behind whose skirts these terrorists hide?', echoing the insistence from Professor Paul Rogers of Bradford University that understanding the injustices that stimulate such atrocities is not incompatible with condemning the acts themselves. These glimpses were, however, evanescent on a day preoccupied with trying to cope with the scale of the tragedy that was unfolding and the difficulty of bridging the gap of perception between the spectacular, movie-like, quality of the repeated images and the actuality of real death, trauma and loss. As Jon Snow, the anchor of Channel 4 news, put it two and a half hours after the first strike: 'It is something from the most awful of images in movies. I mean it's Spielberg, it's Nagasaki, it's something unimaginable and yet it is New York, and it is New York without the telling twin towers of the World Trade Center . . . '. His halting struggle for a suitable analogy captured the difficulty many viewers must have been experiencing in locating these developments securely in the 'real' world. The astute choice of New York as the prime setting for the attacks allowed disorientation in the responses of people worldwide who had never been there, but were familiar with Manhattan's normally affluent and majestic appearance as a film location. Intertextual echoes of film imagery and narratives bled into the typification of the *Palestinian* rejoicing as representative of the entire Arab world (a typification that was especially misleading since none of the individuals involved in the attacks of September 11th turned out to be of Palestinian origin).

The images of the rejoicing Palestinians became a focal point for controversy when a student at the Universidad Estatal de Campinas-Brasil circulated by e-mail claims that these were 'fake' images, reproduced out of context and taken to celebrate the invasion of Kuwait by Iraq that led to the Persian Gulf War. With a number of media-watchers on alert for possibilities of this kind, these allegations quickly spread and became difficult to arrest even after the originator issued a retraction (which he did as soon as it became clear that supporting evidence promised by his supposed source was not forthcoming). In some ways the issue of fakery became a distraction from the issue of how these images had been used, and why they were so potentially controversial. In a day of outrage and terror caused by attacks on civilian targets, it might not have been so hard for the western media to devote further attention to the reactions of those who felt themselves to be the victims of American (or American-supported) terrorism. However unpalatable this might have been, it was a missing piece in the jigsaw puzzle that seemed otherwise to defy sense. The relative invisibility of this perspective underlines again how discourse often operates more strongly by omission or denial than by what it includes or emphasizes.

## OSAMA THE ELUSIVE ONE

If the enemy remained harder to specify than in Pearl Harbor, the identification of Osama bin Laden as the most likely source of aggression became progressively more assured as reactions to the attacks settled. Initially, despite the wariness about attributing direct blame to Muslim extremists, a strong set of presuppositions was in operation. The reaction of Brian Hanrahan, the BBC's diplomatic editor, was typical. Invited to suggest likely perpetrators, he speculated about the root cause lying in the turmoil in the Middle East, but added, 'that is not to say that this is proof. We've seen before that one can go too quickly on this . . . ' (BBC News 24, around 4.45 pm, 11 September 2001). The pointers used to identify a militant Islamic connection were the suicide nature of the missions, the choice of the targets, and the rough equivalence between the co-ordination behind these attacks and the attacks on US embassies in Africa in 1998. These, together with the bombing of the World Trade Center in 1993, and the assault on the USS *Cole* in 2000, were assumed to be the handiwork of followers of Osama bin Laden, already high on the US security services' wanted list. Despite his increasingly clear identification as 'the arch-enemy', less had been publicized about his past as a Saudi exile and billionaire who had fought with the *mujahidin* against the Soviet Union during their occupation of Afghanistan in the 1980s, receiving at that time strong American backing and support from both the CIA and MI6. Subsequently allying himself with the ultra-conservative Taliban faction in its battle for power in the civil war that followed the withdrawal of the Soviet troops, he gained sufficient influence in Taliban-controlled Afghanistan to use that country as the headquarters of his Al-Qaeda ('the base') network formed to wage war on 'the infidel'. On September 11th, news reporting increasingly assigned bin Laden the prime responsibility, although other names such as Colonel Gaddafi of Libya and Saddam Hussein of Iraq also surfaced tenuously and without being given much credibility.

The ability to demonize bin Laden was intensified, not reduced, by his aloofness and his refusal ever to admit responsibility for any of the terrorist attacks attributed to him. One of the conditions of risk in the global world, as we have seen, is a continuing uncertainty about its source, and ensuing dubiety about whether it can successfully be contained. As Bauman puts it, 'the other of order is the miasma of the indeterminate and unpredictable. The other is the uncertainty, that source and archetype of all fear' (1991: 7). As politicians and the media identified Osama bin Laden as prime suspect, lack of clarification about the evidence on which this was based remained. In addition, the loading on to a single individual of the full weight of outrage, when all the evidence pointed to Al-Qaeda being a highly synchronized and efficient network that crossed geographical boundaries, was a discursive feat, helping to obscure both the unpredictability of the risk and its penetration of 'protected' borders. The pilots who flew the planes that became the means of attack had, after all, been trained in the United States and accepted as residents in that country. They had penetrated boundaries that were supposed to be secure and heavily monitored by the security services. The reduction of bin Laden into a one-dimensional portrait that obscured his complexity was achieved in part by his conventional visualization and in part by his lack of direct voice. However mild his demeanour, images emphasized the steeliness of his eyes and the ever-present Kalashnikov. Dressed in clothes that confirmed his identification by westerners as a warlord from a remote culture, his wealth and education were obscured. Rahimullah Yusufzai, a Pakistani journalist writing about his interviews with Osama bin Laden in the *Guardian*, comments on how the 'softness of his hands … spoke of a wealthy background, of never having done much physical work' (26 September 2001), but this perception was elided in his visual portrayal. In addition, his perceived 'Otherness' and threat were intensified by the absence of direct access to his voice in English, and his reliance on language resonant with the fundamentalist conviction that always conveys a sense of menace to secular ears, whatever its particular religious source.

The simplicity of bin Laden's image belied a number of complexities that emerged as part of the biographical investigation only in quality newspapers' verbal text, or on websites. Despite being closely linked with Afghanistan, bin Laden had no fixed homeland. An exile from his native Saudi Arabia (expelled in 1994 for criticizing the Saudi royal family), and from his brief refuge in Sudan, his re-association with Afghanistan was tactical only. In supporting 'the war on terror', however, a number of media outlets implied a simple equation between Osama bin Laden/Al-Qaeda/Taliban to suggest that the purpose of the war was to 'liberate' the oppressed Afghan people. In this respect, Osama bin Laden's demonization could be brought within the framework familiar from the representation of other 'evil' leaders, from Hitler to Saddam Hussein. The 'rural' image reinforced by the visualization of bin Laden against a tent backdrop (later intensified by the claims that he was hiding out in remote mountain caves) also masked the technological sophistication of the Al-Qaeda operation. According to evidence accumulated from the trials of other Al-Qaeda suspects, the training and recruiting of young fighters was achieved in part through the use of videos showing footage of the savagery inflicted on Muslims in the West Bank, Bosnia, Chechnya and Iraq, and bin Laden's communication strategies clearly included sophisticated use not merely of contemporary technologies such as satellite phones, but of highly honed public relations skills. His appearances on the Al-Jazeera television channel, beamed from Qatar, but thought by many to be emanating from Afghanistan, were indicative of his alertness to the impact of timing and elusiveness in sustaining both his menace to the West and the morale of his own followers. Al-Jazeera, formerly welcomed by American commentators for its willingness to criticize Arab corruption, became an object of attack from both Bush and Blair for supporting the 'wrong' side in the 'war against terrorism', especially when it began broadcasting alternative accounts of the war in Afghanistan (Ali, 2002).

Previously associated with barbarism and fervour, the sophistication of the co-ordination behind the attacks in America took several commentators by surprise. If cold-blooded barbarity was fearsome, its alignment with meticulous organizational skills and an evident ability to detect and exploit weaknesses in western intelligence and security systems (constructed in discourse as themselves highly sophisticated surveillance weapons) increased phenomenally the perceived level and potential sources of risk. The image of global risk was, however, contained within a familiar figure: male, bearded, driven by Islamic conviction, committed and visionary. Connotations of Islam's medieval barbarism and pre-modern fanaticism were confirmed in his presentation.

## ISLAMOPHOBIA POST-SEPTEMBER 11TH

Those most at risk from media discourses that relentlessly repeat the association of 'Islam' with 'terrorism' are Muslims themselves. Following each major attack on civilians (whether directly targeted, as on September 11th, or as accidental victims in a brutal conflict, as in the Middle East), those who suffer most from 'revenge' attacks are ordinary people who become identified as 'the enemy' through a crude and unthinking failure to distinguish between 'all' and 'some'. Evidence that a minority of Muslims believe that the prosecution of their faith depends on extirpating those who, in their view, follow false idols, and work to desecrate their holy places and their deepest beliefs, is assumed to mean that all do. The Osama bin Laden image of fanatical, joyless preachers wanting to exert their will on everyone throughout the world rebounds particularly harshly on those who can be identified as Muslim by their dress or, much more precariously, by their appearance. In the wake of the September 11th attacks, several victims of assault were mistakenly assumed to be Muslims.

Despite the token attempts by politicians and newspaper editorials to distance themselves from Islamophobia, the more general attention to an Islamic 'Other' with fanatical intent did little to prevent the antipathy experienced by ordinary Muslims. Given widest coverage in the Muslim press, verbal or physical assaults on Muslims were sporadically reported also in the broadsheet papers, both in Britain and the United States. Significantly, the most active critics of this phenomenon were Muslim commentators, including (in Britain) Faisal Bodi (former news editor of Q News, a Muslim magazine) and Yasmin Alibhai-Brown (British Muslim commentator and frequent participant on television programmes relating to Islam). These writers had been warning long before September 11th of the exposure of Muslims to immediate suspicion as soon as evidence arose of any malevolence attributable (on however weak a hunch) to Islam.

Media discourse had widely acknowledged the existence of Islamophobia on the publication of the Runnymede Trust's report of that title in 1997 (Conway, 1997), but this was easier to recognize abstractly than in its repercussions for ordinary Muslims. As

Yasmin Alibhai-Brown commented in the wake of the September 11th attacks, 'Living in the West we will be seen as the enemy within by both sides': traitor-Muslims within Britain, and infidel westerners by devout fellow Muslims. Women in particular, easily identifiable as Muslims by their *hijab*, reportedly felt most at risk. Alibhai-Brown explained that many Muslim women had stopped wearing it for fear of reprisals, and her own mother 'has told me not to wear *shalwar khameez* but saris over the next few weeks' (2001c). In the United States also, threats against Arab-Americans and South Asians increased dramatically, and led to some apparent cases of indiscriminate murder of individuals thought to resemble the terrorists responsible for the attacks; one, a Sikh killed in Phoenix, Arizona, demonstrated how wide of the mark public anger could be (Sikhs were also mistakenly attacked in Britain). Attacks on mosques (including arson) rose substantially, and several Asian owners of cornershops in English towns found their custom evaporated virtually overnight. These incidents also revealed the tenacity of the assumption that Muslims can be identified from their appearance, without any need to ponder varying relationships between ethnicity, national identity and religious faith.

Although the media (especially in their more informational forms) did give some space to these attacks, there was less attention to the climate of fear into which Muslims in many western countries were plunged. In an atmosphere reminiscent of previous crises (such as the Rushdie *fatwa*, the Gulf War and the Oklahoma bombing), Muslims bore the brunt of the majority public's distress and anger. The media's occasional pleas for respect for ordinary practitioners of the faith of Islam appeared to make little impact, revealing again how shifts in discourse may be relatively powerless to shift engrained ideological positions, especially if these are simultaneously bolstered by competing discourses. In Britain, support for Islamophobia could be garnered from those Muslim clerics who vehemently refused to condemn the attacks, preferring instead to indict American imperialist foreign policies and pro-Israeli bias in the most strident of terms. As Yasmin Alibhai-Brown put it, 'wretchedly for the rest of us, the media loves these men with their wild eyes and hot words' (2001d). The British media regularly focused on Sheikh Abu Hamza, *imam* at a North London mosque, who was accused of inciting young British Muslims to fight for the Taliban in Afghanistan. His rugged physical appearance (a hook replaces one of his hands and he has only one eye) conjured up more mythically gruesome associations than even Osama bin Laden. As Andrew Marr put it, well before September 11th, 'Was there ever a better bogeyman than Sheikh Abu Hamza, the viper of Finsbury Park, with his steel claw-hands, his bitter tirades, his rolling squint and his sinister "training camp"?' (Marr, 1999).

The risk to ordinary Muslims was not a prominent part of the media's construction of 'risk' around the events of September 11th. Indeed, despite the official distinctions being made between ordinary Muslims and terrorists, the media continually fretted about the lack of support for the British involvement in the United States' declared 'war on terrorism' being offered by the Muslim community. An early instance of the alarm raised by any Muslim who publicly dared to question British alignment with the United States was provided by the BBC's *Question Time* programme, broadcast live in the immediate aftermath of the attacks (BBC1, 13 September 2001). This attracted controversy because of the anti-American tone adopted by a number of the audience, and the grilling of the US Ambassador, Philip Lader, who was one of the panel members. The United States was accused by some of bringing the tragedy upon itself because of its imperialist and uncaring foreign policy. With more than 600 viewers ringing the corporation to complain, and a volley of criticism in the newspaper press, the BBC's director-general, Greg Dyke, quickly issued an apology for the programme's tone and for any offence caused to the ambassador and to viewers. The question that raised especial hackles, relating to the possible connection between the attacks and the hatred of the USA's international dealings, was asked by Fareena Alam, the news editor of London-based *Q News*, Europe's biggest Muslim magazine. Described in the *Sun* and *Daily Mail* as 'Arab' or 'Middle Eastern', her identity as a British South Asian was distorted and the impression of her danger accentuated. The threat of Muslim disloyalty was a recurring theme, especially in the more right-wing press, but it extended even beyond this.

An ICM opinion poll of Muslim views, conducted by telephone for the BBC in November 2001, using the snowballing method of asking initial contacts to recommend others, found a large majority (80 per cent) of Muslims were against the military action taken by the United States and Britain against Afghanistan, while opinion polls in Britain and the United States as a whole were showing a clear majority in favour. This poll, together with other even less scientific ones, was used to support a wider discourse questioning British Muslims' loyalty to their home country. Claims of hundreds of young British Muslims being recruited to fight with the Taliban were frequently reported in October 2001, although they were often unsubstantiated and exaggerated the available evidence. The issue of Muslim loyalty, especially on the part of young Asian Muslim men, resurfaced repeatedly in media reports, and was linked to the anxieties about male Asian youth raised during the previous summer's disturbances in northern British towns and cities. The BBC news website reported accurately that three-quarters of the Muslims polled by ICM had not been in favour of British Muslims going to fight for the Taliban, but managed to present this in threatening terms: 'While a majority of those polled for the BBC disapproved of British Muslims going to fight for the Taleban, nearly 25 percent said they were in favour of it' (news.bbc.co.uk/low/english/uk/newsid_1655000/1655288.stm, 14 November 2001, accessed 4 January 2002). While this was given prominent location in the website report, information about the degree of threat felt by the Muslim population itself was left until the end, with almost a third of those polled declaring that 'they had encountered hostility or abuse since the terror strikes on New York and Washington'.

Little attention was paid by most of the mainstream media to an extensive MORI poll of British Asian attitudes conducted by *Eastern Eye*, a weekly newspaper that describes itself as 'the voice of Asian Britain'. The poll, published on 23 November 2001, on findings taken before and after the fall of the Afghan capital, Kabul, found that 87 per cent of the Muslims questioned said that they were loyal British citizens, although 64 per cent of them opposed the military action in Afghanistan; 62 per cent, however, also thought that British Muslims were wrong to fight for the Taliban. At the same time, *Eastern Eye* discovered growing unease about race relations in Britain following the events of September 11th, with 57 per cent of Muslims declaring that race relations had deteriorated in the intervening period, and 46 per cent endorsing the view that the events and their consequences had 'created divisions within the Asian communities of Britain'. The paper's editorial was concerned both to debunk accusations of British Muslims' lack of loyalty to Britain, but also to recognize the 'tremors of fears across the community' produced by non-Asian reactions to the attacks on New York and Washington. The discourse of risk emerging here differed substantially from the mainstream media in foregrounding the damage being done to Muslims and other Asian groups. The BBC's Radio 4, which had given prominent attention to the ICM poll in its news programmes, relegated the findings of this MORI poll to its early-morning *Sunday* programme (25 November 2001), which provides the most regular coverage of religious issues on BBC radio.

In the wake of September 11th, hypothetical risks of further terrorist strikes against the United States or against Britain absorbed media attention to a much greater extent than the real risks being encountered by innocent Muslims in both countries. Within a fortnight of the attacks, British popular and middle-market newspapers were devoting pages of speculation to the risk of biological terrorism. When that risk looked likely to be moving from 'potential' to 'actual' status, as anthrax made sporadic and apparently random appearances in the US postal system, the media could revive their flagging evocation of the risks facing dominant social groups (many of the affected packages were being found in official buildings). The initial assumption (later questioned) that the most probable source lay in Iraq, associated with biological terrorism since the Gulf War, marked a further stage in perpetuating links with Islam.

The events of September 11th certainly stimulated British media attention to Islam, in a series of articles and programmes that often gave much away about the degree of ignorance assumed in the audience. Even the *Sun*, scarcely distinguished by its foreign news coverage, provided an extensive account of Middle-Eastern and Arab countries' position in relation to the West, under the heading 'Why do they hate the West?' (13 September 2001). Muslim journalists suddenly acquired a high profile, as newspapers and broadcast media competed for their insights. But this increased explanatory attention struggled to widen the discursive range against a predominant ideology of Eurocentrism, as the western media attempted first to do justice to the suffering of those bereaved in the tragedy and, then, to demonstrate a patriotic hegemony in their approach to the declared 'war'. While this allowed sporadic space for voices to emerge that were not usually heard in the western media, it was often in the electronic versions of the most liberal newspapers that access to these was most readily available. Website links to overseas sources, such as newspapers of countries accused of protecting Muslim interests, widened the ability of readers with access to the Internet to set opposing discourses against each other, but this diversity of perspective was absent elsewhere.

## CONCLUSION

In this and the previous three chapters' consideration of three distinctive sources of turn-of-the-century anxiety, a discourse of 'risk' has emerged as a common discursive frame. This masks the very different claims for power being played out within these varying phenomena, but also ensures their continuing ability to absorb audiences' and readers' attention. Discourses of risk demonstrate qualities that link them in to the definitions of the shifting discourses within the media discussed in the second part of this book. The seriousness of the risks being identified locates them firmly within a public sphere, 'out there' in the 'real world'. Yet, at the same time, in their metaphorical construction, they are repeatedly portrayed as *invading* territories that were once thought of as 'safe', or at least 'protected'. It is this dislocation of boundaries, more than any escalation in quantifiable terms, that produces the pleasurable *frisson* of anxiety that grips our imagination and draws us into participant engagement. A discourse of risk, in its very instability, offers its own excitements.

In each case, however, the abstract quality of risk, its very uncertainty of provenance and management, acquires, within media discourse, a human face. Despite conjuring up a problem that exceeds human capacity for control and containment, risk for the media demands the closure of an identifiable form of human culpability. In this respect, the Foucauldian promise of the concept, its capacity for destabilizing existing certainties and opening up clarity of vision about the contested and provisional nature of naturalized frameworks of thinking, is eroded. It is in this process that discourses of risk become especially ideological, freezing the complexity of competing ways of thinking that should be opening up debate, by turning them into freshly morphed, but still simplistic, versions of old demons. Instead of thinking in a contested way about the difficulties of managing children's ability to grow, experiment and learn within the kinds of environment adults provide for them, it becomes easier, but also more cowardly, to replay versions of bogeymen risk that offload responsibility on to those least likely to obtain an attentive public ear. Challenges of responding to the contradictory claims of protecting the ecosystem, managing biodiversity, contesting the power of multinational organizations and feeding the planet, are more simply reduced to domestic concerns about the safety of food in the supermarket, and the attribution of blame to bad governance and unreliable science. Confronting the threat of international terrorism, it is less uncomfortable to look for alien enemies than to inspect the West's own role in fostering movements hostile to human rights and modern freedoms.

Discourses of risk have the power to take us on challenging imaginary journeys, but these have their own diversions. As Lawrence Wright, the scriptwriter of *The Siege*, puts it, 'Terror really is theatre and the idea is to shock people out of their normal sensibilities and cause them to focus on the terrorists and what their grievances are. That's why terror is always waiting for the cameras' (in *Panorama*, 'A warning from Hollywood', BBC1, 24 March 2002). In media discourses, the spectacle of the theatrical and its reductive designation of the sources of risk can also become so involving that this opportunity for re-orientating perspectives passes by unnoticed.

# BIBLIOGRAPHY

Adam, B. 2000: The media timescapes of BSE news. In S. Allan, B. Adam and C. Carter (eds), *Environmental Risks and the Media*. London: Routledge, 117–29.

Adcock, C. 2002: *When Women make Newspapers: bylines, sidelines and gender(ed) story lines*. Unpublished DPhil thesis, University of Sussex.

Ahmed, Akbar S. 1992: *Postmodernism and Islam: predicament and promise*. London: Routledge.

Ahmed, Akbar S. 1993: *Living Islam: from Samarkand to Stornoway*. London: BBC Books.

Ahmed, Leila 1992: *Women and Gender in Islam*. New Haven: Yale University Press.

Al-Azmeh, A. 1989: The Satanic flame, *New Statesman and Society*, 20 January, 16–17.

Ali, T. 2002: Letter to a young Muslim, *Guardian Weekend*, 13 April.

Alibhai-Brown, Y. 2001a: Please don't make us out to be angels, *Independent*, 20 August.

Alibhai-Brown, Y. 2001b: The truth about Islam and women, *Independent*, 1 October.

Alibhai-Brown, Y. 2001c: This fireball of fear and loathing, *Independent*, 14 September.

Alibhai-Brown, Y. 2001d: Who are these self-appointed clerics that so mislead our young Muslims?, *Independent*, 22 October.

Allan, S. 1998: (En)gendering the truth politics of news discourse. In C. Carter, G. Branston & S. Allan (eds), *News, Gender and Power*. London: Routledge, 121–37.

Allan, S., Adam, B., and Carter, C. (eds) 2000: *Environmental Risks and the Media*. London: Routledge.

Anderson, A. 1997: *Media, Culture and the Environment*. London: UCL Press.

Ang, I. 1985: *Watching 'Dallas': soap opera and the melodramatic imagination*. London: Methuen.

Ashcroft, J. 2001: Text of press conference on the child pornography case, *New York Times* on the web, www.nytimes.com/2001/08/08/national (accessed 9 August 2001).

Association of Medical Microbiologists 1995: The facts about salmonella, www.amm.co.uk/pubs/fa_salmonella.htm (accessed 8 September 2001).

Bakhtin, M. 1984: *Problems of Dostoevsky's Poetics* (translated by C. Emerson). Manchester: Manchester University Press.

Barker, M. 1997: The Newson Report: a case study in 'common sense'. In M. Barker and J. Petley (eds), *Ill Effects: the media/violence debate*. London: Routledge, 12–31.

Barker, M. and Petley, J. (eds) 1997: *Ill Effects: the media/violence debate*. London: Routledge.

Barnett, S. and Seymour, E. 2000: You cannot be serious, *Guardian*, 10 July.

Barnett, S., Seymour, E. and Gaber, I. 2000: *From Callaghan to Kosovo: changing trends in British television news 1975–1999*. London: ITC/BBC.

Barthes, R. 1973: Myth today. In R. Barthes, *Mythologies*. London: Paladin (first published in French, 1957), 117–74.

Bauman, Z. 1991: *Modernity and Ambivalence*. Cambridge: Polity Press.

BBC News/UK website 1998: BSE Timeline, 23 November, news.bbc.co.uk/hi/english/uk/newsid_218000/218676.stm (accessed 15 September 2001).

Beck, U. 1992: *Risk Society: towards a new modernity*. London: Sage.

Beck, U. 1999: *World Risk Society*. Cambridge: Polity Press.

Bell, A. and Garrett, P. (eds) 1998: *Approaches to Media Discourse*. Oxford: Blackwell.

Benhabib, S. 1992: *Situating the Self: gender, community and postmodernism in contemporary ethics*. Cambridge: Polity Press.

Bennett, T., Boyd-Bowman, S., Mercer, C. and Woollacott, J. (eds) 1981: *Popular Television and Film*. London: BFI/Open University.

Bird, S.E. 1997: What a story! Understanding the audience for scandal. In J. Lull and S. Hinerman (eds), *Media Scandals*. Cambridge: Polity Press, 99–121.

Bird, S.E. 2000: Audience demands in a murderous market. In C. Sparks and J. Tulloch (eds), *Tabloid Tales*. Boulder, Colorado: Rowman & Littlefield, 213–28.

Birkett, D. 1997: Monsters with human faces, *Guardian*, 27 September.

Birkett, D. 1998: To unmask the devil, *Guardian*, 19 January.

Birkett, D. 1999: Strangers can be kind, *Guardian*, 25 May.

Birkett, D. 2000: If it's daddy, we don't care, *Guardian*, 20 July.

Blumler, J. 1999: Political communication systems all change: a response to Kees Brants, *European Journal of Communication* **14**(2), 241–9.

Bondebjerg, I. 1996: Public discourse/private fascination: hybridization in 'true-life-story' genres, *Media, Culture and Society* **18**(1), 27–45.

Bourdieu, P. 1998: *On Television and Journalism*. London: Pluto Press (translated from French by P. Parkhurst Ferguson).

Brants, K. 1998: Who's afraid of infotainment?, *European Journal of Communication* **13**(3), 315–35.

Brants, K. 1999: A rejoinder to Jay G. Blumler, *European Journal of Communication* **14**(3), 411–15.

Bridges, G. and Brunt, R. 1981: *Silver Linings: new strategies for the eighties*. London: Lawrence & Wishart.

Brookes, R. 1999: Newspapers and national identity: the BSE/CJD crisis and the British press, *Media, Culture and Society* **21**(2), 247–63.

Brookes, R. 2000: Tabloidization, media panics, and mad cow disease. In C. Sparks and J. Tulloch (eds), *Tabloid Tales*. Boulder, Colorado: Rowman & Littlefield, 195–209.

Brookes, R. and Holbrook, B. 1998: Mad cows and Englishmen. In C. Carter, G. Branston and S. Allan (eds), *News, Gender and Power*. London: Routledge, 174–85.

Brunsdon, C. 1986: *Films for Women*. London: BFI.

Brunsdon, C. 1989: Text and audience. In E. Seiter, H. Borchers, G. Kreutzner, and E.-M. Warth (eds), *Remote Control: television, audiences and cultural power*. London: Routledge, 116–29.

Bruzzi, S. 2000: *New Documentary: a critical introduction*. London: Routledge.

Buckingham, D. (ed.) 1993: *Reading Audiences: young people and the media*. Manchester: Manchester University Press.

Buckingham, D. 1996: *Moving Images: understanding children's emotional responses to television*. Manchester: Manchester University Press.

Bulte, A., de Coninck, D., van Heeswyck, M.-J. 1999: *Les Dossiers X*. Brussels: Editions EPO.

Burchill, J. 2001: Some people will believe anything, *Guardian*, 18 August.

Burkeman, O. and Beaumont, P. 2002: CNN chief accuses Israel of terror, *Guardian*, 18 June.

Butler, J. 1990: *Gender Trouble: feminism and the subversion of identity*. London: Routledge.

Cameron, D. 1994: 'Words, words, words': the power of language. In S. Dunant (ed.), *The War of the Words: the political correctness debate*. London: Virago, 15–34.

Carrington, B. 2001–2: Fear of a black athlete: masculinity, politics and the body, *New Formations* **45**, 91–110.

Carter, C., Branston, G. and Allan, S. (eds) 1998: *News, Gender and Power*. London: Routledge.

Carvel, J. 2000: Survey reveals widespread child abuse, *Guardian*, 20 November.

Cleto, F. (ed.) 1999: *Camp: queer aesthetics and the performing subject*. Edinburgh: Edinburgh University Press.

Cohen, S. 1972: *Folk Devils and Moral Panics: the creation of mods and rockers*. London: MacGibbon & Kee.

Cohen, S. and Young, J. (eds) 1973: *The Manufacture of News: social problems, deviance and the mass media*. London: Constable.

Conway, G. 1997: *Islamophobia: a challenge for us all*. London: Runnymede Trust.

Corner, J. 1991: Meaning, genre and context: the problematics of 'public knowledge' in the new audience studies. In J. Curran, and M. Gurevitch (eds), *Mass Media and Society*. London: Edward Arnold, 267–84.

Corner, J. 1995: *Television Form and Public Address*. London: Edward Arnold.

Corner, J. 1996: *The Art of Record: a critical introduction to documentary*. Manchester: Manchester University Press.

Crisell, A. 1997: *An Introductory History of British Broadcasting*. London: Routledge.

Cumberbatch, G. 1998: Media effects: the continuing controversy. In A. Briggs and P. Cobley (eds), *The Media: an introduction*. London: Longman, 262–74.

Curran, J. and Sparks, C. 1991: Press and popular culture, *Media, Culture and Society* **13**(2), 215–37.

Dahlgren, P. 1995: *Television and the Public Sphere*. London: Sage.

Davies, M.M. 1989: *Television is Good for Your Kids*. London: Hilary Shipman.

Dovey, J. 2000: *Freakshow: first person media and factual television*. London: Pluto Press.

Dyer, R. 1997: *White*. London: Routledge.

Eagleton, T. 1991: *Ideology: an introduction*. London: Verso.

Evans, D.T. 1993: Embryonic sexual citizenship: children as sexual objects and subjects. In D.T. Evans, *Sexual Citizenship: the material construction of sexualities*. London: Routledge, 209–39.

Fairclough, N. 1994: Discussion: 'Mainly Muslim': discourse and barbarism in Bosnia, *Discourse and Society*, **5**(3), 431–2.

Fairclough, N. 1995: *Media Discourse*. London: Edward Arnold.

Faludi, S. 1992: *Backlash: the undeclared war against women*. London: Vintage.

Fisk, R. 1998: US media mirror distorts Middle East, *Independent*, 10 June.

Fiske, J. 1987: *Television Culture*. London: Routledge.

Fiske, J. 1992: Popularity and the politics of information. In P. Dahlgren and C. Sparks (eds), *Journalism and Popular Culture*. London: Sage, 45–63.

Fiske, J. 1996: *Media Matters: race and gender in US politics*. Minneapolis: University of Minnesota Press.

Fiske, J. and Hartley, J. 1978: *Reading Television*. London: Methuen.

Flanders, L. 2001: Afghan women speak from behind the media veil, 4 October 2001, rawa.false.net/alternet.htm (accessed 2 July 2002).

Foucault, M. 1972: *The Archaeology of Knowledge*. London: Tavistock (translated by A.M. Sheridan Smith, originally published in French as *L'archéologie du savoir* in 1969).

Foucault, M. 1979: *Discipline and Punish: the birth of the prison*. Harmondsworth: Penguin (translated by A. Sheridan, originally published in French as *Surveiller et punir* in 1975).

Foucault, M. 1981: *The History of Sexuality, Volume One: an introduction*. Harmondsworth: Pelican (translated by Robert Hurley, originally published in French as *La volonté de savoir* in 1976).

Fowler, R. 1991: *Language in the News: discourse and ideology in the press*. London: Routledge.

Fox, N. 1999: Postmodern reflections on 'risk', 'hazards' and life choices. In D. Lupton (ed.), *Risk and Sociocultural Theory: new directions and perspectives*. Cambridge: Cambridge University Press, 12–33.

Franklin, B. 1997: *Newszak and News Media*. London: Arnold.

Franklin, B. and Parton, N. (eds) 1991: *Social Work, the Media and Public Relations*. London: Routledge.

Fraser, N. 1992: Rethinking the public sphere: a contribution to the critique of actually existing democracy. In C. Calhoun (ed.), *Habermas and the Public Sphere*. Cambridge, Massachusetts: MIT Press, 109–42.

Giddens, A. 1998: Risk society: the context of British politics. In J. Franklin (ed.), *The Politics of Risk Society*. Cambridge: Polity Press, 23–34.

Gittins, D. 1998: *The Child in Question*. London: Macmillan.

Gledhill, C. 1988: Pleasurable negotiations. In E.D. Pribram (ed.), *Female Spectators: looking at film and television*. London: Verso, 64–89.

Glynn, K. 2000: *Tabloid Culture*. Durham: Duke University Press.

Goffman, E. 1972: *Interaction Ritual: essays on face-to-face behaviour*. London: Allen Lane.

Gordon, C. (ed.) 1980: *Michel Foucault: Power/Knowledge: selected interviews and other writings 1972–1977*. Hemel Hempstead: Harvester Wheatsheaf.

Greenberg, S. 1998: Root of the matter, *Guardian*, 25 November.

Greer, G. 2001: Review of Lara Marks' *Sexual Chemistry: a history of the contraceptive pill*. (Yale University Press, 2001), *Sunday Times*, 20 May.

Grindstaff, L. 1997: Producing trash, class, and the money shot: a behind-the-scenes account of daytime TV talk shows. In J. Lull and S. Hinerman (eds), *Media Scandals*. Cambridge: Polity Press, 164–202.

Habermas, J. 1987: *The Theory of Communicative Action, 2, Lifeworld and System: a critique of functionalist reason* (translated by T. McCarthy). Boston, Massachusetts: Beacon Press.

Habermas, J. 1989: *The Structural Transformation of the Public Sphere: an inquiry into a category of bourgeois society* (translated by T. Burger with the assistance of F. Lawrence). Cambridge: Polity Press, and Cambridge, Massachusetts: MIT Press (first published in German in 1962 as *Strukturwandel der Öffentlichkeit*).

Habermas, J. 1992: Further reflections on the public sphere. In C. Calhoun (ed.), *Habermas and the Public Sphere*. Cambridge, Massachusetts: MIT Press, 421–61.

Hall, S. 1973: The determinations of newsphotographs. In S. Cohen and J. Young (eds), *The Manufacture of News*. London: Constable, 176–90.

Hall, S. 1980: Encoding/decoding. In S. Hall, D. Hobson, A. Lowe and P. Willis (eds), *Culture, Media, Language*. London: Hutchinson, 128–38.

Hall, S. 1981: The whites of their eyes: racist ideologies and the media. In G. Bridges and R. Brunt (eds), *Silver Linings: some strategies for the eighties*. London: Lawrence & Wishart, 28–52.

Hall, S. 1992: The West and the Rest: discourse and power. In S. Hall and B. Gieben (eds), *Formations of Modernity*. Cambridge: Polity Press/Open University, 275–320.

Hall, S. 1996: New ethnicities. In H.A. Baker, M. Diawara, and R.H. Lindeborg (eds), *Black British Cultural Studies: a reader*. Chicago: University of Chicago Press, 163–72 (first published in 1987).

Hall, S., Critcher, C., Jefferson, T., Clarke, J. and Roberts, B. 1978: *Policing the Crisis: mugging, the state and law and order*. London: Macmillan.

Hall, S. 2002: Parents who kill 'often go free' *Guardian*, 24 January.

Hansen, A. 1993: *The Mass Media and Environmental Issues*. Leicester: Leicester University Press.

Hansen, M. 1991: Pleasure, ambivalence, identification: Valentino and female spectatorship. In C. Gledhill (ed.), *Stardom: industry of desire*. London: Routledge, 259–82.

Hartley, J. 1982: *Understanding News*. London: Methuen.

Hartmann, P. and Husband, C. 1974: *Racism and the Mass Media: a study of the role of the mass media in the formation of white beliefs and attitudes in Britain*. London: Davis-Poynter.

Hinerman, S. 1997: (Don't) leave me alone: tabloid narrative and the Michael Jackson child-abuse scandal. In J. Lull and S. Hinerman (eds), *Media Scandals*. Cambridge: Polity Press, 143–63.

Hobsbawm, J. 1995: Rough sea of publicity, *Guardian*, 26 June.

Holland, P. 1987: When a woman reads the news. In H. Baehr and G. Dyer (eds), *Boxed In: women and television*. London: Pandora, 133–50.

Holland, P. 1992: *What is a Child? Popular images of childhood*. London: Virago.

Holland, P. 1997a: *The Television Handbook*. London: Routledge.

Holland, P. 1997b: Living for libido: or, *Child's Play IV*: the imagery of childhood and the call for censorship. In M. Barker and J. Petley (eds), *Ill Effects: the media/violence debate*. London: Routledge, 48–56.

Holland, P. 1998: The politics of the smile: 'soft news' and the sexualisation of the popular press. In C. Carter, G. Branston and S. Allan (eds), *News, Gender and Power*. London: Routledge, 17–32.

Hollingsworth, M. 1986: *The Press and Political Dissent*. London: Pluto Press.

hooks, b. 1984: *Feminist Theory: from margin to center*. Boston, Massachusetts: South End Press.

Humphrys, J. 2000: *Devil's Advocate*. London: Arrow Books.

Jackson, S. and Scott, S. 1999: Risk anxiety and the social construction of childhood. In D. Lupton (ed.), *Risk and Sociocultural Theory*. Cambridge: Cambridge University Press, 86–107.

Jameson, F. 1981: *The Political Unconscious: narrative as a socially symbolic act*. London: Methuen.

Karim, K.H. 1997: The historical resilience of primary stereotypes: core images of the Muslim other. In S.H. Riggins (ed.), *The Language and Politics of Exclusion*. London: Sage, 153–82.

Keighron, P. 1993: Video diaries: what's up doc?, *Sight and Sound* 3(10), 24–5.

Kellner, D. 1995: *Media Culture: cultural studies, identity and politics between the modern and the postmodern*. London: Routledge.

Kitzinger, J. 1998: The gender-politics of news production: silenced voices and false memories. In C. Carter, G. Branston and S. Allan (eds), *News, Gender and Power*. London: Routledge, 186–203.

Kitzinger, J. and Reilly, J. 1997: The rise and fall of risk reporting, *European Journal of Communication* **12**(3), 319–50.

Klein, N. 2001: *No Logo*. London: Flamingo.

Kress, G. and van Leeuwen, T. 2001: *Multimodal Discourse: the modes and media of contemporary communication*. London: Arnold.

Kress, G., Leite-García, R., and van Leeuwen, T. 1997: Discourse semiotics. In T.A. van Dijk (ed.), *Discourse as Structure and Process*. London: Sage, 257–91.

Kuhn, A. 1995: *Family Secrets: acts of memory and imagination*. London: Verso.

Langer, J. 1998: *Tabloid Television: popular journalism and the 'other news'*. London: Routledge.

Lees, S. 1997: *Carnal Knowledge: rape on trial*. Harmondsworth: Penguin.

Lewis, J. 1991: The power of popular television: the case of *Cosby*. In J. Lewis, *The Ideological Octopus*. London: Routledge, 159–202.

Livingstone, S. and Lunt, P. 1994: *Talk on Television: audience participation and public debate*. London: Routledge.

Lorde, A. 1984: *Sister Outsider*. Trumansburg, New York: Crossing Press.

Lukács, G. 1972: *Studies in European Realism*. London: Merlin Press.

Lull, J. 1990: *Inside Family Viewing: ethnographic research on television's audiences*. London: Routledge.

Lupton, D. (ed.) 1999a: *Risk and Sociocultural Theory: new directions and perspectives*. Cambridge: Cambridge University Press.

Lupton, D. 1999b: *Risk*. London: Routledge.

Lury, K. 1995/6: Television performance: being, acting and 'corpsing', *New Formations* **27**, 114–27.

Macdonald, M. 1995: *Representing Women: myths of femininity in the popular media*. London: Edward Arnold.

Macdonald, M. 1998: Politicizing the personal: women's voices in British television documentaries. In C. Carter, G. Branston and S. Allan (eds), *News, Gender and Power*. London: Routledge, 105–20.

Macdonald, M. 2000: Rethinking personalization in current affairs journalism. In C. Sparks and J. Tulloch (eds), *Tabloid Tales*. Boulder, Colorado: Rowman & Littlefield, 251–66.

MacGregor, B. 1997: International television coverage of the bombing of the Baghdad 'bunker'. In B. MacGregor, *Live, Direct and Biased? Making television news in the satellite age*. London: Arnold, 147–73.

Marr, A. 1999: Forget about Hamza the horrible, we can all live with Islam but can Islam live with itself?, *Observer*, 31 January, www.guardian.co.uk/Archive/Article/0,4273,3816020,00.html (accessed 4 January 2002).

Marty, M. and Appleby, R.S. 1991: *Fundamentalisms Observed*. Chicago, Illinois: University of Chicago Press.

McLachlan, S. and Golding, P. 2000: Tabloidization in the British press: a quantitative investigation into changes in British newspapers, 1952–1997. In C. Sparks and J. Tulloch (eds), *Tabloid Tales*. Boulder, Colorado: Rowman & Littlefield, 75–89.

McLaughlin, L. 1993: Feminism, the public sphere, media and democracy, *Media, Culture and Society* **15**(4), 599–620.

McLaughlin, L. 1998: Gender, privacy and publicity in 'media event space'. In C. Carter, G. Branston and S. Allan (eds), *News, Gender and Power*. London: Routledge, 71–90.

McNair, B. 1998: New technologies and the media. In A. Briggs and P. Cobley (eds), *The Media: an introduction*. London: Longman, 173–85.

McRobbie, A. 1996: *More!*: new sexualities in girls' and women's magazines. In J. Curran, D. Morley and V. Walkerdine (eds), *Cultural Studies and Communications*. London: Arnold, 172–94.

McRobbie, A. and Thornton, S. 1995: Rethinking 'moral panic' for multi-mediated social worlds, *British Journal of Sociology* **46**(4), 559–74.

Mercer, K. 1988: Imaging the black man's sex. In R. Chapman and J. Rutherford (eds), *Male Order: unwrapping masculinity*. London: Lawrence & Wishart, 141–53.

Mernissi, F. 1985: *Beyond the Veil: male–female dynamics in Muslim society* (revised edition). London: Al Saqi Books (first published 1975).

Miles, R. 1989: *Racism.* London: Routledge.

Mills, S. 1997: *Discourse.* London: Routledge.

Modleski, T. (ed.) 1982: *Loving with a Vengeance.* London: Methuen.

Modood, T. 1992: British Asian Muslims and the Rushdie affair. In J. Donald and A. Rattansi (eds), *'Race', Culture and Difference.* London: Sage/Open University Press, 260–77.

Moore, S. 1995: Sea changes in political talk, *Guardian,* 22 June.

Moores, S. 1993: *Interpreting Audiences: the ethnography of media consumption.* London: Sage.

Morley, D. 1980: *The 'Nationwide' Audience.* London: BFI.

Morley, D. 1986: *Family Television: cultural power and domestic leisure.* London: Comedia.

Nahra, C. 2001: British and American television documentaries. In M. Bromley (ed.), *No News is Bad News.* Harlow: Pearson Education, 109–23.

Nichols, B. 1991: *Representing Reality.* Bloomington and Indianapolis: Indiana University Press.

NSPCC 2001: Summary of child protection register statistics 2001, www.nspcc.org.uk/inform/Statistics/Protect2001.asp (accessed 1 June 2002).

O'Brien, M. 1997: She who sups with the media …, *Times Higher Education Supplement,* 14 February.

Palmer, P. 1986: *The Lively Audience: a study of children around the TV set.* Sydney: Allen & Unwin.

Peer, L. 2000: Women, talk radio, and the public sphere(s) in the United States. In A. Sreberny and L. van Zoonen (eds), *Gender, Politics and Communication.* Cresskill, New Jersey: Hampton Press, 299–327.

Persaud, R. 2000: Car-crash television, *Guardian,* 17 July.

Pew Internet and American Life Project 2001: Fear of online crime, April 2, www.pewinternet.org/reports (accessed 1 June 2002).

Pew Research Center for the People & the Press 1998a: Internet news takes off, people-press.org/reports/display.php3? Page ID = 564 (accessed 8 January 2001).

Pew Research Center for the People & the Press 1998b: Internet news takes off, people-press.org/reports/display.php3? Page ID = 565 (accessed 8 January 2001).

Pew Research Center for the People & the Press 2000: Rising price of gas draws most public interest in 2000, people-press.org/reports/display.php 3? Report ID = 19, (accessed 8 January 2001).

Phillips (2000): *BSE Inquiry Report*. London: HMSO.

Philo, G. 2002: Missing in action, *Guardian*, 16 April.

Pilger, J. 2002: If you got your news only from the television . . ., *New Statesman*, 27 June, http://pilger.carlton.com/print/109424 (accessed 30 June 2002).

Plummer, K. 1995: *Telling Sexual Stories: power, change and social worlds*. London: Routledge.

Pollock, G. 1977: What's wrong with images of women?, *Screen Education* **24**, 25–33.

Poster, M. (ed.) 1988: *Jean Baudrillard: selected writings*. Cambridge: Polity Press.

Postman, N. 1983: *The Disappearance of Childhood*. London: W.H. Allen.

Potter, J. and Wetherell, M. 1987: *Discourse and Social Psychology*. London: Sage.

Pribram, E.D. 1993: Seduction, control, and the search for authenticity: Madonna's *Truth or Dare*. In C. Schwichtenberg (ed.), *The Madonna Collection*. Boulder, Colorado: Westview Press, 189–212.

Priest, P. 1995: *Public Intimacies: talk show participants and tell-all TV*. Cresskill, New Jersey: Hampton Press.

Probyn, E. 1993: *Sexing the Self: gendered positions in cultural studies*. London: Routledge.

Radway, J. 1987: *Reading the Romance: women, patriarchy and popular literature*. London: Verso.

Rapping, E. 2000: US talk shows, feminism, and the discourse of addiction. In A. Sreberny and L. van Zoonen (eds), *Gender, Politics and Communication*. Cresskill, New Jersey: Hampton Press, 223–50.

Reeves, R. 1999: Relax, you're a good mum, *Observer*, 10 October.

Rich, A. 1979: *On Lies, Secrets and Silence*. New York: W.W. Norton & Co.

Roald, A.S. 2001: *Women in Islam: the western experience*. London: Routledge.

Said, E. 1991: *Orientalism: western conceptions of the Orient*. Harmondsworth: Penguin Books (first published 1978).

Said, E. 1997: *Covering Islam: how the media and the experts determine how we see the rest of the world* (2nd edn). London: Vintage (first published 1981).

Scannell, P. (ed.) 1991: *Broadcast Talk*. London: Sage.

Scannell, P. 1996: *Radio, Television and Modern Life*. Oxford: Blackwell.

Scarman, Lord 1981: *The Brixton Disorders, 10–12 April (1981)*. London: HMSO.

Schlesinger, P. 1990: Rethinking the sociology of journalism: source strategies and the limits of media-centrism. In M. Ferguson, (ed.), *Public Communication: the new imperatives*. London: Sage, 61–83.

Shaheen, J. 2001: *Reel Bad Arabs: how Hollywood vilifies a people*. New York: Olive Branch Press.

Shattuc, J. 1997: *The Talking Cure*. London: Routledge.

Shohat, E. and Stam, R. 1994: *Unthinking Eurocentrism: multiculturalism and the media*. London: Routledge.

Silverstone, R. 1999: *Why Study the Media?* London: Sage.

Simmel, G. 1950: *The Sociology of Georg Simmel*. Glencoe, Illinois: Free Press of Glencoe.

Skidmore, P. 1998: Gender and the agenda: news reporting of child sexual abuse. In C. Carter, G. Branston and S. Allan (eds), *News, Gender and Power*. London: Routledge, 204–18.

Smith, A.C.H., Immirzi, E. and Blackwell, T. 1975: *Paper Voices: the popular press and social change 1935–1965*. London: Chatto & Windus.

Smith, J. 2000: Man offers to resign for not having sex, *Guardian*, 11 August.

Soothill, K. and Walby, S. 1991: *Sex Crime in the News*. London: Routledge.

Southwood, R. 1989: *Report of the Working Party on Bovine Spongiform Encephalopathy*. London: HMSO.

Sparks, C. 1988: The popular press and political democracy, *Media, Culture and Society* **10**(2), 209–23.

Sparks, C. 1998: Introduction (to special issue on tabloidisation and the media), *Javnost/The Public* **V**(3), 5–10.

Sparks, C. and Tulloch, J. (eds) 2000: *Tabloid Tales: global debates over media standards*. Boulder, Colorado: Rowman & Littlefield.

Squire, C. 1997: Empowering women? The *Oprah Winfrey show*. In C. Brunsdon, J. D'Acci and L. Spigel (eds), *Feminist Television Criticism*. Oxford: Clarendon Press, 98–113.

Steedman, C. 1986: *Landscape for a Good Woman*. London: Virago.

*The Stephen Lawrence Inquiry: report of an inquiry by Sir William Macpherson of Cluny*, February 1999. London: HMSO.

Stokes, J. 1999: Use it or lose it: sex, sexuality and sexual health in magazines for girls. In J. Stokes and A. Reading (eds), *The Media in Britain: current debates and developments*. London: Macmillan, 209–18.

Tester, K. 2001: *Compassion, Morality and the Media.* Buckingham: Open University Press.

Thompson, J.B. 1990: *Ideology and Modern Culture: critical social theory in the era of mass communication.* Cambridge: Polity Press.

Thompson, J.B. 1997: Scandal and social theory. In J. Lull and S. Hinerman (eds), *Media Scandals.* Cambridge: Polity Press, 34–64.

Thompson, J.B. 2000: *Political Scandal: power and visibility in the media age.* Cambridge: Polity.

Travis, A. 1999: Children experience pros and cons of modern life, *Guardian,* 14 January.

Trinh, T.M. 1991: *When the Moon Waxes Red: representation, gender and cultural politics.* London: Routledge.

Turner, G. 2001: Sold out: recent shifts in television news and current affairs in Australia. In M. Bromley (ed.), *No News is Bad News.* Harlow: Pearson Education, 46–58.

van Dijk, T.A. 1988: *News as Discourse.* Hillsdale, New Jersey: Lawrence Erlbaum.

van Dijk, T.A. 1991: *Racism and the Press.* London: Routledge.

van Dijk, T.A. 1992: Discourse and the denial of racism. In *Discourse and Society* 3(1), 87–118.

van Dijk, T.A. (ed.) 1997: *Discourse as Structure and Process.* London: Sage.

van Dijk, T.A. 1998: *Ideology: a multidisciplinary approach.* London: Sage.

van Leeuwen, T. 1996: The representation of social actors. In C.R. Caldas-Coulthard and M. Coulthard (eds), *Texts and Practices.* London: Routledge, 32–70.

van Zoonen, L. 1991: A tyranny of intimacy? Women, femininity and television news. In P. Dahlgren and C. Sparks (eds), *Communication and Citizenship.* London: Routledge, 217–35.

van Zoonen, L. 1998: One of the girls? The changing gender of journalism. In C. Carter, G. Branston and S. Allan (eds), *News, Gender and Power.* London: Routledge, 33–46.

Walker, A. 1984: *In Search of our Mothers' Gardens.* London: Women's Press.

Walkerdine, V. 1986: Video replay: families, films and fantasy. In V. Burgin, J. Donald, and C. Kaplan (eds), *Formations of Fantasy.* London: Methuen, 167–99.

Warner, M. 1994: *Managing Monsters: six myths of our time. The 1994 Reith lectures.* London: Vintage.

Watney, S. 1987: *Policing Desire: pornography, AIDS and the media.* London: Comedia/Methuen.

Watson, H. 1994: Women and the veil: personal responses to global process. In A.S. Ahmed and H. Donnan (eds), *Islam, Globalization and Postmodernity*. London: Routledge, 141–59.

Williams, F. 1958: *Dangerous Estate*. London: Readers Union.

Williams, F. 1969: *The Right to Know: the rise of the world press*. London: Longman.

Wilson, K. 2000: Communicating climate change through the media: predictions, politics and perceptions of risk. In S. Allan, B. Adam and C. Carter (eds), *Environmental Risks and the Media*. London: Routledge, 201–17.

Winn, M. 1985: *The Plug-in Drug*. London: Penguin (first published 1977).

Wykes, M. 1998: A family affair: the British press, sex and the Wests. In C. Carter, G. Branston and S. Allan (eds), *News, Gender and Power*. London: Routledge, 233–47.

Young, L. 1996: *Fear of the Dark: 'race', gender and sexuality in the cinema*. London: Routledge.

Yuval-Davis, N. 1992: Fundamentalism, multiculturalism and women in Britain. In J. Donald and A. Rattansi (eds), *'Race', Culture and Difference*. London: Sage/Open University Press, 278–91.

# INDEX